THOREAU'S FABLE OF INSCRIBING

THOREAU'S
FABLE OF INSCRIBING

FREDERICK GARBER

PRINCETON UNIVERSITY PRESS

PRINCETON, NEW JERSEY

Library of Congress Cataloging-in-Publication Data
Garber, Frederick.
Thoreau's fable of inscribing / Frederick Garber.
    p. cm.
Includes bibliographical references and index.
ISBN 0-691-06873-9 (acid free paper)
1. Thoreau, Henry David, 1817–1862.—Criticism and
interpretation. 2. Thoreau, Henry David, 1817–1862.
Week on the Concord and Merrimack Rivers. I. Title.

PS3054.G29   1991   818'.309—dc20   90-44497   CIP

This book has been composed in Linotron Baskerville

Princeton University Press books are printed
on acid-free paper and meet the guidelines for
permanence and durability of the Committee on
Production Guidelines for Book Longevity
of the Council on Library Resources

Printed in the United States of America by
Princeton University Press,
Princeton, New Jersey

10 9 8 7 6 5 4 3 2 1

FOR MY WIFE,

Marjorie Ann Terret Garber

I well remember the time this year when I first heard the dream of the toads. I was laying out house-lots on Little River in Haverhill. We had had some raw, cold and wet weather. But this day was remarkably warm and pleasant, and I had thrown off my outside coat. I was going home to dinner, past a shallow pool, which was green with springing grass, and where a new house was about being erected, when it occurred to me that I heard the dream of the toad. It rang through and filled all the air, though I had not heard it once. And I turned my companion's attention to it, but he did not appear to perceive it as a new sound in the air. Loud and prevailing as it is, most men do not notice it at all. It is to them, perchance, a sort of simmering or seething of all nature. That afternoon the dream of the toads rang through the elms by Little River and affected the thoughts of men, though they were not conscious that they heard it.

—THOREAU, *Journal*, October 26, 1853

CONTENTS

ACKNOWLEDGMENTS

I HAVE ALREADY expressed part of my debt to some of the major readings of Thoreau. That expression continues throughout this study as I touch on the work of other critics, partly in order to lay out a series of relevant issues, partly also to lay out my own position in relation to them. Though this book differs considerably from my earlier book on Thoreau, the ideas that it develops fit coherently with the material developed in the previous study. They stem in large part from what I have since come to see about Thoreau and his ways of being in the world. In the Introduction to the earlier book, I spoke of the possibility of putting Thoreau into the framework of an encompassing reading of Romanticism. This is still not that study of Thoreau's ultimate setting, a study which may yet find its way, but it is a preliminary to what such a setting would have to include.

I am particularly indebted to those who have invited me to lecture and write on Thoreau, as well as to the students in my seminars on his work.

Permission has been given to reprint the following previously published materials: "A Space for Saddleback. Thoreau's *A Week on the Concord and Merrimack Rivers*," *Centennial Review* 24 (1980): 322–37; "Thoreau's Ladder of Alertness," *Thoreau Quarterly* 14 (1982): 111–24; and "Henry David Thoreau," in *The Columbia History of American Literature*, 399–412 (New York: Columbia University Press, 1987).

ABBREVIATIONS

AW   *A Week on the Concord and Merrimack Rivers*, ed. Carl F. Hovde, William L. Howarth, and Elizabeth Hall Witherell (Princeton: Princeton University Press, 1980).

CC   *Cape Cod and Miscellanies*, vol. 4 of *The Writings of Henry David Thoreau* (New York: AMS Press, 1968).

EMM   *Early Essays and Miscellanies*, ed. Joseph J. Moldenhauer and Edwin Moser (Princeton: Princeton University Press, 1975).

Excursions   *Excursions* (New York: Corinth Books, 1962).

J   *The Journal of Henry D. Thoreau*, ed. Bradford Torrey and Francis H. Allen, 14 vols. (New York: Dover Publications, 1962).

*J   *Journal, Volume 1: 1837–1844*, ed. Elizabeth Hall Witherell, William L. Howarth, Robert Sattelmeyer, and Thomas Blanding (Princeton: Princeton University Press, 1981); *Journal, Volume 2: 1842–1848*, ed. Robert Sattelmeyer (Princeton: Princeton University Press, 1984).

MW   *The Maine Woods*, ed. Joseph J. Moldenhauer (Princeton: Princeton University Press, 1972).

RP   *Reform Papers*, ed. Wendell Glick (Princeton: Princeton University Press, 1973).

W   *Walden*, ed. J. Lyndon Shanley (Princeton: Princeton University Press, 1973).

THOREAU'S FABLE OF INSCRIBING

INTRODUCTION

IN A *JOURNAL* entry written sometime after July 27, 1840, Thoreau speaks to the question of our at-homeness in the world:

> In vain the sun challenges man to equal greatness in his career— We look in vain over earth for a Roman greatness to answer the eternal provocation.
>
> We look up to the gilded battlements of the eternal city, and are contented to be suburban dwellers outside the walls. (*J, 1:159)

It seems that we settle into at–homeness only after acknowledging failure, our inadequacy in the face of the grandest possible challenge. We are dared to work out a "career" comparable to the sun's diurnal stint, the play on "career" as "course" and as "lifelong occupation" potent enough to show our way of working in the world to be a radically mobile one. The passage, then, has to do with actions in the world that are a species of "answering," in this case responding to a challenge. In what, precisely, does the challenge consist? It demands that we show we can be in the world in a way comparable in grandeur to the most exalted position we can imagine, the position of the chief occupant in the Eternal City of the Sun. Of course we cannot match up. Our settling-in is a second best to what we can envision but cannot possibly do.

What Thoreau's readers can envision is something else again, the lay of the land within which these frustrated acts occur. The focal point of that landscape is, naturally, the place where we settle in. That act of self-locating has profound cartographical consequence, for we settle in outside the walls, establishing thereby a sense of within and without. That starts an elaborate mapping, because the looking up to the sun and the looking over the earth combine with our point of settlement to produce a rich and specific geography, an up and down, a there and here, in which we find a (second-best) place. It is clear that these are not indifferent, neutral places but components of a geography that is as much moral as physical; much of their importance ensues from what we do when we occupy them. In this case the importance comes from a series of visual gestures, multiple acts of looking. The acts of looking *up* have a counterpart in the looking *over* that reveals what the earth can never grant to us. What we have in this passage, then, is the outline of a narrative that defines modes of vision and turns them into modes of quest, the search for a

"Roman greatness," that is, a potent mode of being in this really quite intricate landscape.

Putting the point another way, we have the outline of a fable, one so profoundly imagined that it has its spaces all worked out, a geography of the spirit that we might also choose to think of as the geography within the spirit. It is a fable about a quest for a way of being in the world that is also a preferred way for being at home in the world. That these multiple ways are related to the question of our ultimate acceptance within the walls of the Eternal City comes through clearly in the concluding sentence. Our fable, thus, has finally to do with desire, the energy that derives the narrative coming in part from our passion to answer the eternal provocation and pursue magnificent careers, in part from our simultaneous passion to be urban dwellers within the eternal walls. That those passions are ultimately related and perhaps even the same seems a very good guess. The single, manifold passion revealed by that guess is one of the subjects of this book.

This narrative/landscape/fable can be found throughout Thoreau's work and never essentially changes. Quite early in his career, he glimpsed the center of an obsession, the problem of getting to be at home in the world, and he sought from the beginning to find ways of figuring it, giving it verbal substance—here through the act of camping outside the Eternal City of the Sun, elsewhere through acts as different as shouting to a lost friend in the Maine woods or digging the cellar of a house in land borrowed from another friend. That obsession, so active and profound that it resounds through most of what he does, has to do, in one of its aspects, with the relations of being and doing. Readings of those relations appear in several studies of Thoreau that I have found particularly useful; for example, those of Stanley Cavell and Sherman Paul. The following study offers another such reading, focusing on that obsession, that determinant of actions large and small, daylong and lifelong, what is figured in the snippet of fable as parking oneself outside the walls of the sun's Eternal City. This parking, the snippet says, was what we finally had to do and not what we really wanted to do (settling, as we did, for this second-best settling-in). We ought, then, to think of the relations of being and doing not only in terms of how we shape a self, or how we are able to speak what we most need to say, but also how we learn what we cannot be or do in terms of getting ourselves to be at home in the world. The snippet of fable records a partial failure, and so too does this book; yet this book also shows not only that successes do come but how hard they are to come by, what Thoreau had to struggle against in order to achieve his quite magnificent moments of success. Once he glimpsed that central obsession, he had to learn how difficult it was to bring it to fruition, to find a way of being everything that he wanted to be and *also* find a way of being at home in the world. He had to ponder whether those desires could ever be made compatible and, if so, how that meeting could ever be brought about. The following study ponders precisely the same questions, worrying the "if so" and the "how" through all manner of manifestations.

Part of the "how," as we have seen, has to do with figuration, the modes we have for speaking these most basic forms of desire. Our passage tells the fabulous openly and with joy, though the passage itself defines a species of disappointment. That joy has little to do with the not–quite–convincing "contented." It comes, most of all, from the overt pleasure in finding a way of speaking the fabulous that, even at this early stage, puts his current condition credibly, persuasively, in the form of an ancient mode of speech. (The Eternal City of the Sun has counterparts all over history, many of which Thoreau obviously knew well.) Yet if he is joyful, that is ultimately because he knows that home making in the world may well be the central business of living, and that living and writing, in fact, the whole business of inscribing, may be not only cooperative/corroborative acts but perhaps even the same act, when viewed in the proper perspective. That means that an act of success in figuring, such as he shows in the *Journal* snippet, is an act of success in living. We ought not to mistake this for an inchoate aestheticism, because it is much more solemn and dangerous, a recognition of the complicity between writing and being in the world. Thoreau speaks several times of writing in terms of the sharp edge of a blade, which shows how well he knows how much is at stake in such endeavors.

He began to explore these matters in his first important essays: "The Natural History of Massachusetts," solicited by Emerson for the Dial in 1842; "A Walk to Wachusett," published elsewhere later in the same year; and "A Winter Walk" and "The Landlord," both published in 1843. Together these essays play out early versions of those intricate relations among ourselves, our places, and texts that were to follow in his finest work. The Nature of "The Natural History of Massachusetts" is a place of elemental joy, the qualities of which, he argues at one point, must determine the radical qualities of being: "surely joy," he wrote, "is the condition of life" (*Excursions*, 40). But Thoreau was too lucid and canny, too hard-nosed and perceptive, to continue such sentimentality for long; even in this early essay he set about making the requisite adjustments. The things of Nature typify, suggest, and represent and, thereby, turn Nature into a text to be read. If other ideas of typifying were put to momentous contemporary use in Emerson's *Nature* in 1836, Thoreau turned into intricate textures his own special sense of the way the things of this world speak to each other, bringing the world into elaborate converse by imitating each other in a gesture he always called "answering": "Every tree, shrub, and spire of grass, that could raise its head above the snow, was covered with a dense ice–foliage, answering, as it were, leaf for leaf to its summer dress" (66). But, as the fabulous snippet shows, there are kinds and kinds of converse, more levels and hierarchies than Emerson broached in his essay, all manner of modes of awareness that have their own sort of elocution. If Thoreau compares the written to the preached word, he can also say, in a clumsy early poem to Walden Pond, that "our converse a stranger is to speech" (*J 1:47; June 3, 1838). To be at home in the world is to know *all* its modes of converse, not only its various ways of "answering" but the questions to which "answering" is one sort of response.

Put that way, the point is ominous. If to be fully at home means knowing all the modes, then we cannot be so at home if we do not know them all. That is also true if the modes of converse we know do not answer all the questions or do not answer them wholly. One of the problems we shall be facing is whether the ways he chose to answer the radical questions put to him (his chief occupations, writing and surveying, were prominent among those ways) were themselves insufficient. If we gathered a sense of lack in the tale from outside the walls, we may be gathering a counterpart sense in these questions about questions and answers. Once again, we are getting to see the sort of struggle Thoreau had to make.

Certainly the questioning never ceased, which means that answering was demanded of him at every step of the way—sometimes even in the nightlife of the mind. At the beginning of *Walden*'s chapter on "The Pond in Winter," Thoreau tells how he "awoke with the impression that some question had been put to me, which I have been endeavoring in vain to answer in my sleep, as what-how-when-where?" (282). That question, it turns out, had not been put by Nature, which, when he awoke, looked in at his window "with serene and satisfied face, and no question on *her* lips." In fact the passage implies that Nature itself has an answer, because he "awoke to an answered question, to Nature and daylight," the apposition suggesting identity, though the text never openly makes that claim. Reacting to apposition as we normally do, *we* are the ones who make that claim, while the "innocent" text watches us stumble into perplexity and then toward a new awareness. The perplexity comes from what follows, where we are told not only that "Nature puts no question" but also that it "answers none which we mortals ask." Perhaps we ought to say that Nature does not give the answer but is itself, the answer, a tidy possibility that does not solve all the problems. We ought to take this puzzle as a warning to go slowly. If a quick reading of the passage leaves us with the impression that every issue has been cleared up, then that impression is mistaken. Who or what was it that put the question to Thoreau? Who or what gave him the answer? Aside from the negative point that it could not have been Nature in either case, the passage proffers no answer. If it was some aspect of Thoreau himself, that means he was so troubled about the basic nature of things that he put to himself basic questions, a point that leads us to wonder just how satisfied he was by the answer he received. Was that answer the response to the question that was put? It is easy to say yes, in fact, much too easy, because what he wakes up to was *an* answered question, which may not be the one that responds to the question he was asked. One may even want to argue that Nature was given as an answer to forestall any further questions, or, what comes to the same thing, that she was given as the only answer now available to such questions. A quite plausible case can be made for either of these paired alternatives. Still, however we take all this, the passage offers one certainty: these lines are an object lesson in just how much attention Thoreau's words demand, what I shall later (following Cavell) be speaking of as the need to give the fullest attention to *all* that Thoreau's words say. What they say here is, at once, less and more than a casual reading will claim: less because we do not have an assured answer; more because the passage leaves some questions so open that we may well be spinning out a potentially endless series of questions and answers, questions that grow out of answers.

This is the third mode of answering we have so far seen. The first had to do with the challenge of the sun, the second with the world's elaborate converse. If the first failed in its answer and the second seemed gloriously complete, the third leaves us uncertain about the relations among members of a dialogue, uncertain, in fact, about not only who the members are but whether it is a dialogue at all. The puzzles go even further, for there are no assured answers, not only to the questions within the passage ("what–how–when–where") but to those the passage generates, the quandaries we have uncovered. We are left with an open-endedness that cannot seem to resolve, at least given the answers we seem able to make now. Versions of such open-endedness turn up all through Thoreau's writings; we shall be focusing on them specifically in the last chapter of this study. For now, though, there is cause for a more elemental questioning. Could it be that our language is not an adequate instrument to ask what we want to know? Or, if we have a better sense of the questions than the answers, is our language so insufficient that we cannot use its words to formulate the fullest answers?

That issue of adequacy dogged Thoreau so naggingly that this study will have to give it the most particular attention. In fact, the issue will get our major questioning going. To see one reason why, consider what I said about the need to take our words in their absolute entirety. Thoreau wants us to mean, in and by means of our lives, all that our best words can say. Our lives should take that saying and make out of it the fullest sort of living the words can disclose—a fullness that comes, we learn in *Walden* and other texts, from stripping down to a pure simplicity. Thoreau's paradoxes tend to make crucial demands on us, and the demands of this one are particularly critical: how do we reconcile the manifold need for fullness, which is finally a moral need, with the equal need to be sharp, to have our speech so acutely honed that our case for simplicity will be subject to no mistake? Full words, after all, press hard on their contours, making it difficult for us to make those pushed-out contours incisive. Such demands were, for Thoreau, an ongoing problem, as witness the second paragraph of *Walden*. He had been asked all sorts of questions about what he did at the pond and why he did it, and was shrewd enough to see not only that the questions were pertinent but that the answers, though he knew them well, would be very difficult to make. That the questions could be asked at all shows not only that *Walden* had to be written but that its language had to be both packed and precise, both full and finely edged. That Thoreau did learn to take his language to its utmost capacity shows that he was more than one kind of hero. That he could do so given what may well be the radical insufficiency of language shows, once again, the difficulties he experienced in relating being and doing.

Thoreau went about solving these difficulties of relation in all sorts of ways. One set of examples will do not only to prepare us for some of those issues as they appear in the following study but to prepare us with some sense of the center of their import. The "Economy" chapter of *Walden* is an elaborate leg-pull that plays with the terminology of the bookkeeper's ledger—the business of America as business—in order to subvert the context in which the terminology moves: "My purpose in going to Walden Pond was not to live cheaply nor to live dearly there, but to transact some private business with the fewest obstacles" (W, 19–20). He did not go there to live by some calculated plan of expense but to take care of some private affairs with the least possible hindrance. Those affairs occupied him chiefly, and he says nothing directly about making exemplary gestures designed to instruct others. Yet his way of turning the words back upon themselves ("I determined to go into business at once" [19]), his implication of language by language, shows that in his telling of his actions he is practicing exemplary subversion. Put into the proper context, shown for what they portend for *all* our economies, his private actions could subvert the town's established ways. His words became that proper context. By telling of his affairs in language that mimics the town's language, he turns his personal affairs into profit for the spirit of the town as well as his own. But he is in no indisputable sense being disobedient or uncivil. After all, as he makes clear, he is privately preoccupied, and when he turns to speak to us it is in words that we all use regularly. Yet those words have a curious capacity to mirror what we do, showing what the language we use says about our usage, not only of our words but of ourselves. *Walden's* chapter on "Economy" is a grammar of such usage and, therefore, a profound pondering of our relations of being and doing. His turning of language upon itself is part of his telling of what he intended when he went to the woods to live in the world.

More accurately, it is a single telling, one among several. The next chapter elaborates on his purpose and, in a summary section, echoes its partner in "Economy" and counterpart passages in "Civil Disobedience": "I did not wish to live what was not life, living is so dear" (*W*, 90). He cannot resist twitting the bookkeepers even here, and he does so in a passage beginning with so many negatives (the first two sentences contain five *nots* and a *nor*) that it becomes clear how much his activities force him to say no until he can finally say yes. Similar negations appear in "Civil Disobedience": "It is not a man's duty, as a matter of course, to devote himself to the eradication of any, even the most enormous wrong" (*RP*, 71); "I came into this world, not chiefly to make this a good place to live in, but to live in it, be it good or bad" (74). Of course this is as subversive as the language in "Economy" and in precisely the same way, by his insistence that he is only going about his private business. In this rhetoric of negatives, affirmations are made by going through negations. That is why he has to reword his purpose again and again, seeking to make clear through his language that all the unmaking is for the sake of the purest making.

The passage continues with another kind of rewording, this time with a Shelleyan heaping up of images, each coming at the point from a different angle to see what it looks like when we put it *that* way. He digs for the sake of nourishment ("I wanted to live deep and suck out all the marrow of life"); imitates the sparest sort of heroism ("to live so sturdily and Spartan-like as to put to rout all that was not life"); clears a path to the edge of the truth ("to cut a broad swath and shave close"); seeks to trap his quarry and then to ponder its essence ("to drive life into a corner, and reduce it to its lowest terms") (91). That essence, he guesses, may well turn out to be mean, but he is ready to accept what he finds at these various terminuses, at the marrow, at the edge of the swath, in the corner. All his negatives may lead him to conclude that life is the work of the Great Negator (most men, he says, have hastily concluded otherwise); but if that is the result, he can tolerate it too. Whatever the result, his purpose is to find out what *is*. He will then publish that essence, whatever it turns out to be. If it is mean, then he will show "the whole and genuine meanness of it," sparing nothing to get at all of the truth his swath has led him to. Getting at the whole will require words of extraordinary fullness (thus does that point recur), words meaning all they can say so that we can mean in our living all that they say. Publishing its genuine wholeness is part of what he intends, that publishing the finishing of the part of his quest which can be handled by our words, but first and very much foremost, he has to make life out. Making it out was his main concern when he wrote these words in the *Journal* on his second full day of living at Walden Pond, July 6, 1845:

> I wish to meet the facts of life—the vital facts, which where [sic] the phenomena or actuality the Gods meant to show us—face to face, And so I came down here. Life! who knows what it is—what it does? If I am not quite right here, I am less wrong than before—and now let us see what they will have. (*J 1:156)

He had not yet thought about publishing meanness or anything else. That was to come later, when he would have a clearer sense of the totality of his activity and what was needed at various points within it. Publishing was part of that activity. Living, and to a purpose, was all of it.

Yet all that we have seen of the problematizing of the relations of being and doing—the relations of language and living are part of those larger relations—shows that, when he thinks of publishing meanness or anything else, the exuberant confidence of these early days at the pond may well give way to questions for which no stable (closed–off, sufficient) answer is now available. The fullness he can imagine may well be no more than imaginable. It may be that our best available words are still not full enough, so that part of what we imagine are words that *are* so full.

That such imagining has finally to do with our acts of home making in the world was apparent to Thoreau at every point in his work. Sometimes that awareness came on him unexpectedly and with warm surprise. On a pleasant day in the spring of 1853, he was on his way home to dinner, walking past a shallow pool, "green with springing grass," where a new house was just going up (*J* 5:453). Right at that point, where a neighbor was asserting his own at-homeness in the world, Thoreau paused, and for good reason: "it occurred to me that I heard the dream of the toad." At one time he had not heard it, but now it rang through the air. Most men, he says, do not notice it at all, thinking of it as no more than "a sort of simmering and seething of all nature"; yet it affects their thoughts, however unconsciously they hear it. The fable is Thoreau's version of the dream of the toad. The largely subliminal speech of the nightlife of his mind affects our thoughts of Thoreau in the same way that most people are affected by the dream of the toad, those ringing sounds they are not quite conscious of hearing. That Thoreau puts this hearing in the context of an act of home making in the world phrases the emphasis fittingly for the study that follows. Part of the study's intent is to bring to our awareness the shape and content of this toad's pervasive dreams and the relation of those dreams to his sense of at-homeness in the world.

Chapter One

WORDS, INSTITUTIONS, HIERARCHIES

T HAT THOREAU is centrally and crucially a writer has rarely needed argument, and certainly needs none now, after the studies in recent years by Sharon Cameron, Stanley Cavell, John Hildebidle, and William Howarth.[1] *The Senses of* Walden, for example, makes an eloquent case for Thoreau as a man of words. Cavell shows that *Walden* is, at every level, obsessively self-reflexive, concerned with its ways of describing and with its status as a prophetic text ("*Walden* is itself about a book, about its own writing and reading,"[2] and he goes on to show how the making of such texts has a great deal to say about our own quite necessary remaking. For Cavell's Thoreau understands that America has failed in its initial promise but that the words of our writing can show us how to redeem both ourselves and that promise—can show us, that is, if we are willing to do with those words all that the words permit. We may well not be so willing. Cavell argues repeatedly that, as Thoreau sees the situation, the insufficiency is in us. Words have what we seek, and we must somehow live out that seeking and learn to live up to their extraordinary potential. No new ways of working are needed, only a return to old ones from which we have fallen away, "a rededication to the inescapable and utterly specific syllables upon which we are already disposed." We must learn once again to turn them into Scripture, and, however difficult that learning, we can work at it with the confidence that words will come through with what we ask of them. As Cavell puts it at the end of the chapter on "Words," "If we learn how to entrust our meaning to a word, the weight it carries through all its computations will yet prove to be just the weight we will find we wish to give it." Thus, we have to seek "a literary redemption of language" that "simultaneously requires a redemption of the lives we live by [our words], religiously or politically conceived, inner and outer." The book seems to argue—indeed, it leaves the most vivid impression that it argues—that the lives we live by our literary words are the best among our lives, certainly the most significant ones, because words take so large a role in our ultimate self-redemption. In Cavell's reading of *Walden* the book takes upon itself the full dimensions of that burden: "The quest of this book is for the recovery of the self, as from an illness."[3] Much of the argument of *The Senses of* Walden is

that *Walden* takes up that task through language because we have ne-
glected to do so, allowing our words to fall away from the best that is
in ourselves.

Yet there are prior questions to be asked about the nature of
words, and none of them is asked in Cavell's eloquent, seminal study.
Thoreau considered those questions quite often, coming back to
them repeatedly in every one of his works. We too need to consider
them so as to put assertions like those in *The Senses of* Walden in their
most accurate perspective. For we must take into account not only
what we have done with words, what Cavell has argued to be the slippage in our relationship with them; we also must consider what
words are in themselves, especially the slippage within words that
may well be nearly inevitable and has to make the making of words,
especially the redemptive sort, a very difficult process indeed. Thoreau certainly takes their potential slippage seriously into account,
and we ought to take his concern into our own accounts of his words.[4]

Sharon Cameron, in *Writing Nature*, appears to share Cavell's reading of Thoreau as confident about words and what they can do, but
she offers a number of requisite corrections of Cavell's overall emphases. Where Cavell's *Walden* is centripetal and intensely self-reflexive, the *Walden* Cameron presents is only theatrically so and actually
makes "elaborate provisions for an audience."[5] But if she sees *Walden*'s indifference to the reader's presence as finally only figurative,
that attitude is literal in her understanding of the *Journal*. Indeed,
what Cavell sees as *Walden*'s obsession with its own making is turned
by Cameron into the *Journal*'s concern with metaphors that show no
human significance but, instead, reveal nature's own infinite self-
referentiality. Thus, to make the *Journal* into *Walden* Thoreau had to
lessen "the distance between the natural and the human," and he did
so in the most direct way, through manipulating conventions of writing such as "beginnings and endings and representative symbols."
But, Cameron argues, these emblems of accepted order—imposed by
the human on the world, needed by Thoreau to communicate with
his Concord contemporaries—have nothing to do with the nature
emergent in the *Journal*. To handle the reading of nature in the *Journal* (a reading that would be, implicitly, the most accurate one) Thoreau had to subvert the whole process of analogy on which Transcendentalism built so much of its literary making, and he ended with a
genre of writing whose strangeness had no parallel, a genre at which
he was a master. Analogy implies relation and maybe a certain kind
of equality, yet Cameron makes the point that Thoreau can get
through to the overwhelming presence of nature only by turning
himself into nature (and not the expected reverse), a process both

difficult and unlikely. Or, in another way, her Thoreau seeks to turn himself into "sheer medium, 'absent' from his speech." Not until then can he discern nature's lack of determination, its concern only with "contrasts, dissociated from story, progression, from anything at all."[6] Cameron is eminently convincing on what Thoreau sought to do in the *Journal*. The distinctions she makes between the modes of the *Journal* and *Walden* put *Walden* into a far more complex perspective, truer to its place in Thoreau's writings, than the one Cavell offers. She is particularly useful in correcting that centrality of the human which stems, inevitably, from the approach Cavell takes. Yet there emerges from Cameron's book the sense that the writing of words (though in her study *slightly* problematized) is Thoreau's ultimate practice, his fullest gesture. She shares that sense with Cavell, whatever her demurrals about his reading of *Walden* as a text.

Part of the problem with such readings is that we are led too easily astray about Thoreau and the question of writing by focusing on a single text, as Cavell does with *Walden*, or by convenient compartmentalization, as Cameron does with her binary distinction between the mode of writing in *Walden* and the mode at work in the *Journal*. (For one, and just one thing in this very complex business, we ought to be more aware of Thoreau's uneasiness with binary structures, his conviction of their capacity to mislead.) But the problems are far larger than the choice of texts to study. The Thoreau I read does not share the unquestioning confidence in words and writing of the Thoreau read by Cavell and Cameron, as well as by Hildebidle and Howarth. If Thoreau's role as a writer is indeed so central and crucial, there is a mass of evidence in his work that his attitude toward writing, and toward attendant issues such as language and figuration and the relations of ourselves and our texts, is never unequivocal, even within a single work. The argument of Cavell and others that the word is the ground upon which writer and reader will meet assumes a steadiness to that ground which Thoreau himself does not assume.[7] It is not that writer and reader do not meet on that ground but that it is hardly so secure as to inspire so much confidence. Further, there are several sorts of acts that share significant features with what we traditionally call writing, acts that Thoreau thinks of in a class I shall call "inscribing," a class that includes traditional writing but much more as well. This means that we ought to take careful cognizance of the multiple ways in which inscribing can incur, and the fact that traditional writing is one member of that class ought to affect our ideas on Thoreau as a writer of words, whether as Cavellian writer of Scripture or Cameronian writer of Nature. Finally (putting a temporary close to this rapid inspection of problems), we cannot fully understand Thoreau's attitude toward writing and himself as a writer unless we also understand the role of writing in what may well be our most basic act, getting to be at home in the world. If writing is seen only in the context of Thoreau as a man of words (Cavell's formulation) or even of Thoreau in encounter with a nature that demands to be written by the fiction of an obliterated self (Cameron's formulation), then his writing is not seen as fully as it ought to be, or as Thoreau makes it to be. In Cavell's and Cameron's studies, a requisite sense of the context of the work as a whole is missing, a context that includes its elemental, endemic issues and how those issues fit together (or have trouble fitting together) with Thoreau's business as a writer. Cavell properly shows Thoreau as a kind of hero of words, but we ought also to see the full dimensions of that heroism. That Thoreau could write all those extraordinary books (not just *Walden* or the *Journal* alone), given his elaborate, pervasive concerns with questions of language and writing, adds to the contours of his heroism in a way that we ought to understand better. We should start, then, with a look at several features of the question of writing, beginning with some of the ways Thoreau talks about words, in order to establish the basis of the issues and to see where they lead.

• I •

In a passage entered into the *Journal* after July 27, 1840, Thoreau talks about language with a kind of awe over what words are able to do:

> A word is wiser than any man—than any series of words. In its present received sense it may be false, but in its inner sense by descent and analogy it approves itself. Language is the most perfect work of art in the world. The chisel of a thousand years retouches it. (*J 1:160)

The second sentence may echo theories of the nature and origin of language that had some influence on Thoreau from fairly early in his career.[8] There is, he argues, a logic and truth within the inner life of the word, a history of itself that it carries within itself, and that logic manages to hold even if it conflicts with what we think the word means now, "its present received sense." The statement is actually quite daring, implying, as it does, that the centripetal aspects of language take precedence over their opposites, those that support referentiality. The word's self–approval has to do, clearly, with the truth to itself established by the shape of its inner history; and that approval, in its turn, begins with the analogy from which the word developed, and may well continue with further analogies that grew up as part of its history and enriched its inner life.[9]

Whatever fun Thoreau had in playing out the implications of this statement, he was cautious enough to leave it behind when he drew on this passage at the end of the "Saturday" chapter of *A Week*. There he describes the animal sounds of the night, especially the variations in the voices of dogs, then leads into a generalization which picks up part of the text that had gone into the *Journal*:

> All these sounds, the crowing of cocks, the baying of dogs, and the hum of insects at noon, are the evidence of nature's health or *sound* state. Such is the never failing beauty and accuracy of language, the most perfect work of art in the world; the chisel of a thousand years retouches it. (41–42)

There is a good deal more at work here than old saws about nature's language, saws Thoreau played on regularly, and that makes the last sentence take on a rather different import than it had in the *Journal*. Shifting from man to animal required leaving out the first sentence from the *Journal* entry, with its exclusive reference to man. Most important, though, is what happens to referentiality, for in omitting the second sentence, with its stress on the word's inner life, Thoreau made it possible for what was left of the original statement to take on very different implications. Where the *Journal* version stresses the internal logic of the word, the version in *A Week* refers to the refining of nature's expressiveness and also, with particular emphasis, to what all these sounds point to, "nature's health or *sound* state." The later version is largely centrifugal, concerned mainly with what the words tell us about their referent, nature's current condition. But the earlier version, as we have seen, is largely centripetal, concerned mainly with what we can learn about the word's essential health (though it is also ready to acknowledge the need for at least some skepticism about the word's received sense). Still, whatever the differing thrusts of these passages, they agree on supporting the soundness of language itself. Yet we ought not to gloss over the implications in the *Journal* entry about the difficulties words might have in telling the truth about something more than themselves and their relationships with other words. We are beginning to see some problems in pinning Thoreau down, even on so basic a matter as the reliability of words.

That difficulty extends also to the relations of nature and language when it is *his* language that is in question, and not that of dogs and cocks. The latter have no problem expressing nature's sound state because they are not only the makers of sounds but, metonymically, part of the soundness they express. Their acts of expression not only point to nature's health but *are* that health. One could ask for no fuller perfection in the correspondence of expression and deed, the reflection in each other of the import of the expression and the expresser of it.

There are times when Thoreau sees a related correspondence between human words and natural affairs, an equally easy fit which does not, however, assume that we are speaking about nature from the inside out, as dogs and cocks do, but that we are, as it were, parallel with nature and delighted to work along with it. When Thoreau speaks that way he is at his most Emersonian:

> He is the richest who has most use for nature as raw material of tropes and symbols with which to describe his life. If these gates of golden willows affect me, they correspond to the beauty and promise of some experience on which I am entering. If I am overflowing with life, am rich in experience for which I lack expression, then nature will be my language full of poetry,—all nature will *fable*, and every natural phenomenon be a myth. (*J* 5:135)

This passage is much like one in the "Bean-Field" chapter of *Walden*, and a number of comparable comments appear elsewhere in Thoreau's work (see, e.g., *J* 5:359). The stance taken in the passage assumes the smoothest of relations, a well-oiled system of reaction and correspondence between a pair of good-humored partners, just as it is in Emerson's *Nature*. If he is touched by the beauty of the willows, that means they match up with the beauty in what he is about to do. And if the life within himself is more than he can contain, then nature can become his language, his means of expression, that is, his fable and myth. Of course fables and myths come to us in human language, so that at some point nature will have to be turned into consciousness and consciousness into correspondent human language. If Thoreau, in his Emersonian phase, cannot speak from within nature, that is, in the perfect balance of forces he intuits in the sounds of dogs and cocks, he can find a correspondence between nature and himself that does what seems to be much the same thing.

Other potential relations among nature, language, and man show how words can be especially effective when performed by active men like Walter Raleigh. "A perfectly healthy sentence," Thoreau argues in *A Week*, "is extremely rare," though surely less rare in Raleigh's time than our own (103). Raleigh's distinguished contemporaries "possess a greater vigor and naturalness than the more modern," because with the earlier writers "you have constantly the warrant of life and experience in what you read" (104). He supports and amplifies this claim by images of a green world whose boughs and grass figure the fresh life within. But the vigor and fecundity he finds in healthy sentences are not just those of nature but of those who made the sentences out of their own strength and naturalness. The paragraph ends with a peroration on words and deeds, summing up not only Raleigh but the status of words in the world:

> The word which is best said came nearest to not being spoken at all, for it is cousin to a deed which the speaker could have better done. Nay, almost it must have taken the place of a deed by some urgent necessity, even by some misfortune, so that the truest writer will be some captive knight, after all. And perhaps the fates had such a design, when having stored Raleigh so richly with the substance of life and experience, they made him a fast prisoner, and compelled him to make his words his deeds, and transfer to his expression the emphasis and sincerity of his action. (105)

It seems that the best words are almost not words at all. As Thoreau put it in a variation in a *Journal* passage written some time after January 8, 1844, "writing may be either the record of a deed or a deed. It is nobler when it is a deed" (*J 1:495). Given the various modes of performance by which one can live a life, words take on an inescapable secondariness, that condition defined in part by their being an alternate avenue, one taken out of necessity by that exuberance of self which would rather emerge in deeds. Writing, after all, generally takes place behind walls, whether of a prison or a study. For Thoreau in this passage, writing is not a deed but the record of a deed and, therefore, some steps away from the immediacy of a deed. The secondariness of language thus becomes apparent in still another way, through the relative distance of language from contact with the immediate. Secondariness means, for Thoreau, "second-best" and "second in line." We could also, in this context, speak of "secondhand."

Still, we must be careful to get at Thoreau's precise distinctions, for this passage is the site of a subtle but intense struggle to get the points exactly right. It is, after all, no small thing to make the finest of words, such as those vigorous, natural ones that create a green world. Nor is the reach of such words small, for, as Thoreau points out just before the quoted passage, they take in a large sum of living: "A man's whole life is taxed for the least thing well done. It is its net result. Every sentence is the result of a long probabion" (105). We saw such an awe over words in the passage from the *Journal* about their descent and inner life, a passage which began by stating that "a word is wiser than any man." We shall see similar awe in other of his comments about the business of writing. Those bouts of awe *and* the recognition of secondariness obviously exist simultaneously in Thoreau's understanding of words. His reading of the nature of language has therefore to be described as decidedly oxymoronic. It is a reading that places language into a context larger than itself.

We are now beginning to discover some basic sense of the place words have in Thoreau's world. It is a complex in which words play a central role (a role confirmed by the critics I cited at the beginning of this chapter) but in which there are other roles—all of them, it seems, playable by the same person, whom Thoreau here calls Sir Walter Raleigh but whom he might have been able to call Henry David Thoreau. We could speak of a web of roles, one of which handles words and shows them to be extraordinary, one of which handles deeds, possibly of the extraordinary sort Raleigh performed. But this image does not quite work, for we are also compelled to recognize the secondariness of words, set out explicitly in this passage, as well as in others we shall read. There is, clearly, a hierarchy involved, and webs, however vertical, are not hierarchical.

This ladder of deeds and words is one of several we shall find in Thoreau. As for that way of splitting our lives neatly into deeds and words, the failure of this binary structure to take in the true contours of the question shows the capacity of such structures both to soothe and to mislead. Their charm is in their symmetry and comfort, and such symmetries and comforts are rare events in Thoreau's way of being in the world.

As an indication of their rarity, take this early passage from the *Journal*, which can be matched with many others from other times:

> For our aspirations there is no expression as yet, but if we obey steadily, by another year, we shall have learned the language of last year's aspirations. (*J 1:244)

Our language ought to be right there beside us, our active and partisan contemporary that speaks what needs to be spoken about where we would like to go, but it is not. We ought to be able to use our language to fix with precision and delicacy what it is we now envision, but we cannot. We are looking for a fusion between our immediate conditions and a language just as immediate, but this passage from the *Journal* says it is always otherwise. (That "always" is, of course, Thoreauvian extravagance, as his more sanguine, Emersonian moods make clear. The only thing that is "always" is his ambivalence about the whole business.) Between what we want our language to do and what we are able to make it do there is, this passage claims, a shortfall, an insufficiency. Our language cannot catch up to the reach of our incessant longing. To put it another way, our language is out of synch. There is a continual slippage between our words and what we seek to lock them into, and within that space of slippage is the place where we stand, seeking to make the elements cohere. To shift the image slightly, we live in a place of gap or lacuna between ways of putting our feelings. Our condition is curiously spatial, or spatiotemporal: wherever it is that we stand, our language is always in back of us, our aspirations always ahead, and ourselves somewhere in the middle, reaching backward and forward at once. As the passage from the *Journal* shows, we seek, through that reaching, steadily to obey. But the passage does not make clear what it is that we obey. If it is language to which we attend, only irony can result. If it is our aspirations, there can be only frustration.[10]

All of this could mean that somewhere ahead of us there is a way of expressing desires that is perfectly coincident with them. And we can be certain the new way of putting would be involved with geographies like those in the passage on aspirations; we are, after all, using terms like "ahead." In fact, such spatializing turns up frequently in Thoreau. It is one of his favored ways of giving form and dimension to his reading of his status, of how he *is* in his world. In effect, he makes a location within which to place himself. The geography laid out in the example we inspected results from a spatializing of time, as it often does in the canon. Similar versions of that practice come out in other of his comments on language, confirming how the curious business of verbal delay and slippage happens in temporal space. Some of those comments also confirm our guess that there will be words and sentences ahead which will pull it all together in a single place or time—neither of which, it is clear, he is in a position to occupy now.

In *A Week*, for example, Thoreau wonders at one point about how one says farewell to a friend about to embark on a journey. What language will suffice, what "palaver," "message," "statement"? (273). We have, it seems, no words at hand that can encompass this sort of finality:

> Have you any *last* words? Alas, it is only the word of words, which you have so long sought and found not; *you have not a first* word yet. (273)

"*Last*" and "*first*" sketch out the temporal geography rapidly, sufficiently. "*You*" establishes him precisely within that geography. The rest sketches out much more, beginning with what the *Journal* passage on words and aspirations had implied, that there is a narrative whose participants are words and the wielders of words, a narrative that looks like an old-fashioned quest. This quest seeks "the word of words," the one that will take in all possible words and thus be sufficient to express every farewell—and, of course, every aspiration. And yet, ironically, paradoxically, that ultimate word is itself one of the objects of our aspiration, what we need in order to say what most needs to be said. Given that complex of needs, the spatialization within this passage takes on intricacies that did not appear in the one we just inspected. Note, for example, what happens with *"first."* If *"you* have not a *first* word yet," that means you have not yet even begun, have not yet arrived at the condition and place of origin. You have begun the quest, but you have not even arrived at the first successful words, not to speak of the last, the word of words that will be able to speak all words. If in the beginning there is a word, there is one at the end as well.

The following is another version of that vision of ultimate language, this time from March 15, 1842:

> I should like to meet the great and serene sentence—which does not reveal itself—only that it is great.—which I may never with my utmost intelligence pierce through and beyond—(more than the earth itself)—which no intelligence can understand—There should be a kind of life and palpitation to it—under its rind a kind of blood should circulate forever—communicating freshness to its countenance. (*J 1:375)

That great and serene sentence is clearly made from the word of words, yet were he to find the sentence, he might not be able to decipher it. With our utmost intelligence we cannot pierce beyond the earth, and we can no more pierce that sentence, which we are aware of only in its greatness. But we are not completely at a loss. Although the serene sentence will not reveal itself to us, we are able to know of it because we can envision its basic component, the word of words. Further, whatever its inaccessibility, we can know enough of the sentence to know that it is not cold or aloof, however serenely it speaks. Under the tough rind there is a palpitating life that keeps the sentence forever fresh and, thus, forever capable.

Still, this little that we know ought not to trick us into thinking that we have it all at hand:

> As I am going to the woods I think to take some small book in my pocket whose author has been there already—whose pages will be as good as my thoughts—and will eke them out—or show me human life still gleaming in the horizon—when the woods have shut out the town. But I can find none—none will sail as far forward into the bay of nature as my thought—they stay at home—I would go home. When I get to the wood their thin leaves rustle in my fingers. They are bare and obvious and there is no halo or haze about them. Nature lies far and fair behind them all. (*J 1:375)

Once again it is a question of desire and capacity, this time on several levels. There is the desire of the speaker to be *given* words so capacious that they can take in what he thinks of, but he is given no such words. And there is also, more implicitly, the desire of wielders of words, this speaker and all others, to *find* words that will encompass what they envision, and they find no such words. Though the authors of the books he would carry have already been to the woods, they have not been able to put the woods into their words. Their language has fallen short. Again we are standing in the spaces between words and what we can envision or experience, in this case not only what we have managed to see but how far we have managed to go, deep into nature's bay.

But this time Thoreau seems more confident about what he is able to do, so much so, in fact, that in order to explain the conditions he is describing in this passage, he turns to twitting the written, turning one of its most cherished recent analogies back upon itself. Much of the literature of the preceding half century had played with the relation of natural and bookish leaves. Shelley's "Ode to the West Wind" can stand as a sufficient instance, one that leaps upon the analogy as a way of extending ourselves into nature and beyond the temporal term that nature has set for us. Shelley uses the analogy, and his usage is typical: it is salutary, salvational. Thoreau, thoroughly canny, does not overtly reject this well-known assertion of likeness but appears, instead, to accept it without question. Intention and result, though, are sardonic and subversive. When he gets to the place of natural leaves it is then that the thin leaves of books, bare and unsubtle and no longer vital, rustle in his fingers—unlike their viable counterparts, which he can see in this place and at the other end of the analogy. In pointing that out he manages to sound like no one so much as Heine. Though apparently acquiescing to this cherished analogy, he succeeds in turning the analogy sour, denying the validity of its main assertion, the likeness of natural and bookish leaves, at the same time as he plays out the assertion, maliciously giving it room to show itself fully. (Clearly it is not only the written that is twitted in this bit of business but the Emersonian as well, that which argues for the easy transportability of one pole of a metaphor to the place of the other, of nature's permanent usefulness as a source of perfect analogy.) In fact, the ironies are manifold, their multiplicity telling much about the complexities of his reading of language. In denying the efficacy of this popular analogy, and denying at the same time that words can go as far as his thoughts, he yet offers an instance of the wonderful capacity of language to subvert what it claims to support. He turns the smug language of likeness back upon itself, using other, more lucid language, words far more self–aware, to expose the comfortable (and comforting) assumption that runs through so much of the writing of his time. Thoreau takes away and gives, both in the same gesture, undoing and then redoing (but in another way) the status of words in our lives. We shall see the same sort of subversion, managed the same way, turned on the town of Concord and some of the languages it wields.

There is more to be observed in this passage. A curious spatialization, much like the others we have seen, turns up in the middle of the paragraph. The words in the books he knows cannot accompany him as far into the bay of nature as he would like them to go but, instead, they "stay at home," a figure we can understand. What is more difficult to understand is his statement, "I would go home." The home to which he would go is not the one where the words have stayed but one toward which he alone aspires. This brings us back to the passage about language and aspiration, for the words now available to him are obviously not sufficient to take him where he would go. Because "home" is that place, it must also be the locale of the word of words and the great, serene sentence. Thus, this passage helps us to see that the quest for the ultimate word and the sentence that can say it all is finally a quest for home, a home that has "a kind of life and palpitation to it." The full meaning of this business will not become apparent until we look at much more of Thoreau. We can, however, wonder whether the home referred to here is that of Odysseus or that of Aeneas, that is, is it an old home to which one returns after long journeys or a new one to which one arrives after journeys equally long? We see the possibility that the quest might well be circular, like that of Odysseus, but perhaps there is a way of conceiving the attainment of home that makes both journey and home like those of Aeneas *as well*, however impossible that may sound. Given Thoreau's passion for contrariety as well as his unease with binary choices, we should not be surprised were it to turn out just that way.

• II •

Thoreau is most apt to fall into the comforts of binary classifications when he works with clichés. Yet even in those situations there are very often hints that lead well beyond such comforts, complications that take the passage out of the condition of either/or. Take, for example, a related pair of paragraphs entered into the *Journal* on August 5, 1838 (*J* 1:50). The first, entitled "Sphere Music," talks about two kinds of sounds, one earthbound, seeming "to reverberate along the plain, and then settle to earth again like dust," while the other, the true sphere music, springs heavenward (and has, Thoreau points out, no sound of a wail within it). The true sort, he says, he can "catch from steeples and hill tops in their upward course." Thus there are two directions involved, each sound seeking instinctively the direction proper to itself. The first reverberates enough to get itself off the ground, then sinks again. The second goes straight up after performing reverberations off the steeples and hilltops. The geographies emergent in some of the comments on language appear also in this one on sounds, and there is, clearly, a hierarchy in this version, since going in one direction is "better" than going in the other.

Given these geographies of sound, we should not be surprised to see words as the subject of the second passage, where the sounds are more clearly defined as language:

DIVINE SERVICE IN THE ACADEMY-HALL

In dark places and dungeons these words might perhaps strike root and grow—but utter them in the day light and their dusky hues are apparent. From this window I can compare the written with the preached word—within is weeping, and wailing, and gnashing of teeth—without, grain fields and grasshoppers, which give those the lie direct.

The impulse to make pure distinctions of the sort seen in the first paragraph is now beginning to fade. Though the first did little more than say there is "this" and then "this," the second complicates the issue considerably. For one thing, there is no simple contrast of the sterile and the fertile, as there would have been had he followed the earlier, easier impulse. Instead there are two kinds of fertility, each of which has a place where it can do very well what it is designed to do. If the dusky kind fails or is seen as inferior, that occurs only when it is removed from its proper place. To utter (speak, sound) that kind of word in the daylight is not only to show it as a stranger to the light but also, less dramatically, as perfectly adapted to the duskiness from which we took it. Thoreau refuses to accept neatly squared-off confrontations. In doing so he also acknowledges that our acts of valorization may well (in fact, may always) precede what we see, that there may be no innocent seeing. Of course that also means that it will always be very difficult to find innocent language as well (or, conversely, language that is purely negative). As this paragraph shows, each of the various modes of language seems to have its own home place, and within those places there is a perfect congruence between the locale and the language it speaks (a prefigurative version of the congruence for which we seek when we track down the word of words). In this second paragraph of the entry, Thoreau is obviously looking back and commenting on the rawer simplicities of the first.

In fact, the second is a very good example of Thoreau's rhetoric of self–correction, a canny gesture designed to show him thinking out his utterances, the thinking, in this case, acted out in the rhetoric. Part of the purpose of the rhetoric is to have us go through the correction with him and thus learn in ourselves not only what he has done but the fuller import of the doing.

Yet there is much more at play in this entry, and that takes us into some of Thoreau's more intricate concerns with words and how they work. If the argument about the proper home of words is an attempt to offset the push of a priori judgments, that push makes itself felt in other aspects of the text, even in the way the text is designed to make its point. Outside there is nature—open, bright, arguing that "weeping, and wailing, and gnashing of teeth" are actually lies about the world. What is inside, however, is not something other than nature but another version of nature—closed, dark, secretive. Inside is the Academy-Hall, the place of the divine service, not literally a place of nature, yet the metaphor Thoreau uses turns it into such. Though the words of the divine service have their own mode of discourse, it is not allowed to have its play, to say these things in its own way and with its own appropriate comparisons. Instead, the tenor of the world within is attached to a vehicle that is drawn from the world without. The procedure is hardly fair—how could that tenor be given its due when it is tied to an alien vehicle drawn from the discourse of its antagonist?—but then, as we have seen, there is an a priori judgment driving the entire business, and fairness cannot be expected. Where in the first paragraph of the entry the sounds went off in two different directions, terrestrial and transcendental, the words in this paragraph go in exactly the same direction, whatever the difference in their inclinations. As we now can see, the source of the a priori judgment has its own mode of discourse, a discourse of such power that it can push its way into a place where it does not belong and undermine the very expressions in which its antagonists are discussed.

There is still a good deal more to this matter of discourse and power. The words of the divine service, of the preaching within the hall, are obviously both spoken and written. Yet this paragraph openly contrasts written and preached words (the latter implicitly and illogically identified with the oral, the "natural" opposite of the written). It puts forth a false distinction, that the written goes on inside and the preaching goes on outside. The purpose of much of this play seems clear enough; Thoreau obviously argues that the *true* preaching goes on outside, in the grainfields with their grasshoppers. Yet what goes on inside is not, in fact, all written, nor is the written that is inside to be divorced from preaching. What we see at work here is something quite unexpected, not the inside/outside business on which much of the paragraph is based or even the artifice/nature business built into the arrogant, pushy discourse we have been inspecting. What comes into the picture in this curious distinction of the written and the preached is another set of assumptions, the set we have already seen that places the written in a state of secondariness. That is, the poles of another pairing, elements from a different dialect of what is surely the same discourse, push through into the text and exert their peculiar power. What they seek is further territory they can take over and colonize, and they do exactly that when they place the written inside the Academy-Hall and the preached/oral outside in the fields of the natural world. Things do not quite mesh, the result being somewhat open-ended, but it really does not matter. Two related dialects shoulder each other for a place at center stage. In watching that shouldering we come close to some central issues in Thoreau's understanding of discourse. One way of handling words may be inferior to another—or at least, "secondary" in some of the senses we have worked out—but all of the discourses in which words find a place appear to have considerable power. Yet the odd situation of the tenor with an antagonistic vehicle, as well as the invasion of the text by another set of assertions, show that some modes of discourse, and some dialects within discourse, have more power than others. We are therefore entitled to suspect that, though all discourses are equal, some are more equal than others. What Thoreau is revealing to us is part of the tyrannies that moved his times.

Thirteen years later he was making the same point and making it in a way that shows how much it was reinforced by his growing obsession with the *Journal,* especiallly its status as a repository of the reports of his encounters with nature. Authoritative statements of fact, he says on November 1, 1851, have to be made simply and cleanly, but before that, they have to be seen with the same sort of clarity and precision (*J* 3:85–86). Standing nearly midway in the line of succession that runs from Blake to Stevens, Thoreau argues that "first of all a man must see, before he can say." Later in the passage he shifts the emphasis slightly: "as you *see,* so at length will you *say.*" Implicit in this argument is a set of priorities in which those acts through which we establish ourselves in the world are given privilege and responsibility: the way we are in the world has to precede the way we see, and the latter precedes our capacity to make significant words. As everywhere in the line that goes from Blake to Stevens, how we are in the world and how we make our words are gestures that ensnare each other.

That the simplest, most adequate seeing is both uncommon and capacious appears in several images in the passage; Thoreau derides, in those images, common speaking and superficial (shallow) seeing. But the images involve much more. The nature of seeing and saying may well be the same as our own nature. At the very least we know that these natures have a homologous relation, that each demands capaciousness not only for itself but also for its partner.

> But I would have [facts] expressed as more deeply seen, with deeper references; so that the hearer or reader cannot recognize them or apprehend their significance from the platform of common life, but it will be necessary that he be in a sense translated in order to undertand them: when the truth respecting his things shall naturally exhale from a man like the odor of the muskrat from the coat of the trapper. At first blush a man is not capable of reporting truth; he must be drenched and saturated with it.

Thoreau's insistence on theses homologies appears once again but in another, more complex form. In this form he argues for the kinship of being and saying, the implication of each in the other. (This is another way of defining the ideology of the Blake-Stevens line.) To phrase in different terms the matter of our capacities to take in and put forth (and Thoreau phrases it several ways in this long and intricate paragraph, flitting among figures to find other ways of making the point), we have to be able to take the fact up within ourselves, to give in to the hunger we ought to have for ingesting the world in order to make the fact fertile. In a wonderfully sardonic parody of the imagery seen in poems like Shelley's "Ode to the West Wind"—where the poet wants his thoughts to become leaves that will engender new thoughts—Thoreau turns the Shelleyan desire mildly scatological, realizing it differently while keeping the tenor precisely the same. Speaking of how difficult it is "to digest some experience cleanly," he goes on to note how difficult it also is "to conceive and suffer the truth to pass through us living and intact, even as a waterfowl an eel, as it flies over the meadows, thus stocking new waters." As he puts it less blatantly later, "taste the world and digest it."[11]

These powers to see and say, ingest and put back out, are pitted against powers like those we saw in an earlier passage, those that dwell within discourse. "Statements," he says, "are made but partially. Things are said with reference to certain conventions or existing institutions, not absolutely." And again later in the passage: "When facts are seen superficially, they are seen as they lie in relation to certain institutions, perchance," the pun on "lie" subtle and potent. (For a more extended and angrier version of similar comments, see *J* 5:131.) What we see in this passage that we did not see in the other is the awareness Thoreau came to of the source of the power that resides within discourse. Discourse comes out of and speaks for institutions. It is one of the primary ways in which an institution perpetuates itself and strengthens its hold upon our lives. We find it difficult to utter simple and adequate words because the language afforded us is, as we guessed earlier, never innocent. One of the reasons for its lack of innocence is its relation to the institution that harbors the words and uses them in order to further its own case. (This is part of what Thoreau means when he argued that our current understanding of the meaning of a word may well be a lie [see p. 15, above] and that we have to go to its history to find it speaking truly.) The extraordinary power of certain discourses surely can be explained not only by the power of the institution for which the discourse is speaking but by the energy the institution puts forth in order to keep its words within its purview. We have seen how that energy can cause a discourse to push its way into passages that support the words of other institutions, so greedy is its own institution for new images to digest in order to stock new waters. There are not only some discourses but also some institutions that are more equal than others.

Among the problems involved in dealing with such equalities are the difficulties Thoreau sees about words: their unshakable secondariness; their correspondence with the natural but also their occasional penchant for putting the natural aside; their current status as searchers for a sentence that finally says it all, though they have yet to find ways in which to word the beginning; their capacity for slippage but also for subversion of other words; their odd ways of occupying space; their sense of their own home places. Only the latter leads directly into the matter of discourse and institutions, and even such a lead ignores the fact that discourse itself often ignores: institutions are human phenomena and discourses are therefore bundles of human words. They are replete with human powers that seek to affect not only the human but everything we use to create habitable human worlds. Thoreau knows so well the complications this engenders that it is impossible to fix on a single attitude that will sum up all he sees about words and their possible contexts. Sometimes it seems that the only coherence available is the one afforded by ambivalence. Yet there are times when Thoreau would argue that there is indeed a potentially discernible pattern in our relations with words. It is a difficult pattern to work out, and we manage to do so only if we seek no immediate answer to every nagging question. For the rest of this chapter we shall inspect two passages, one that puts forth the potential for ambivalence, another that puts forth the potential for a coherent pattern of relations.

The first is from *A Week*:

The sight of this tree reminded us that we had reached a strange land to us. As we sailed under this canopy of leaves we saw the sky through its chinks, and, as it were, the meaning and idea of the tree stamped in a thousand hieroglyphics on the heavens. The universe is so aptly fitted to our organization that the eye wanders and reposes at the same time. On every side there is something to soothe and refresh this sense. Look up at the tree-tops and see how finely Nature finishes off her work there. See how the pines spire without end higher and higher, and make a graceful fringe to the earth. And who shall count the finer cobwebs that soar and float away from their utmost tops, and the myriad insects that dodge between them. Leaves are of more various forms than the alphabets of all languages put together; of the oaks alone there are hardly two alike, and each expresses its own character. (159–60)

The serenity of mood is endemic, and so are the paradoxes. The travelers are strangers within this place, yet their serenity seems unruffled. One aspect of the scene that surely contributes to the serenity is the fact that they are capable readers of what they see, however strange the place. The tree to which they refer was named in the previous paragraph as "the bass, *tilia Americana*, also called the lime or linden, which was a new tree to us" (158). The land is strange, as the strange tree reminds them, and yet they have words to put that tree precisely in its proper category. Any discourse that can so quickly find a place for the new and strange must be exceedingly powerful. The strong words we bring to the strange succeed in domesticating the strange, or, if that is too strongly put, they succeed in making a place for it in which there are several comforting areas to which we have given coherence. We do so by giving the areas human meaning, that is, by placing them in human discourse. There is nothing here of the personal selflessness Thoreau calls for elsewhere ("express it without expressing yourself") or of the way that discourse gets its institutional structure between us and what we see.

And yet, however comforting, this is not the only mode of discourse that busies itself in this scene. As they sail under the canopy of the tree, they see the sky through the tree's spaces, that is, the tree against the sky. Such seeing against such a background is one of Thoreau's favorite devices for conceiving the place of the earthly in a larger scheme of things. As he puts it in this passage, they saw "the meaning and idea of the tree stamped in a thousand hieroglyphics on the heavens." The discourse at work at this point we can call, for convenience, Transcendental, though the business of hieroglyphics interested others besides Thoreau and his circle.[12] Seeing the tree in such a place, and under such conditions, gives the tree a meaning, that is, a definable status within a body of public discourse. The tree achieves a relation to other elements within that discourse, a relation that the discourse clearly sees as "true" (the passage questions the current meanings of words, what he calls elsewhere their possible falsity). Of course there are ineffable mysteries involved—there are, after all, "a thousand hieroglyphics on the heavens"—yet mysteries of that sort have an accepted part in such discourse. Thus, Thoreau captures the tree and the situation in which it stands through two modes of discourse, one scientific, the other Transcendental. He does not question such a pairing, as he sometimes does elsewhere.

One comment in the passage points to a major reason for the passage's serenity: "the universe is so aptly fitted to our organization that the eye wanders and reposes at the same time." The sentence quite likely echoes the well-known lines from the preface to Wordsworth's *Excursion*:

How exquisitely the individual Mind
(And the progressive powers perhaps no less
Of the whole species) to the external World
Is fitted:—& how exquisitely, too—
Theme this but little heard of among Men—
The external world is fitted to the Mind.

(What Thoreau could not have known, though he sometimes shared the feeling of it, was Blake's response to these lines: "You shall not bring me down to believe such fitting & fitted I know better & Please your Lordship.")[13] In the passages from Wordsworth and Thoreau, there is perfect compatibility of ourselves and our contexts and, therefore, a fluent interrelationship of being, place, and discourse. That appears to be so whatever the kind of discourse in which nature is captured. We are, in fact, *so* fitted that it seems any discourse will do, whatever its components and assertions. That is why Thoreau can treat us to two so different modes.

Yet as the passage goes on, it starts to turn itself around, and it finishes by stating entirely the opposite point. As he continues to admire the treetops and the spiring height of the pines, he focuses more closely on some of the finer components of the scene, the uncountable cobwebs that soar just as the treetops had soared and the "myriad insects that dodge between" the webs that seek to entrap them. The pines' unending spiring and the uncountability of cobwebs lead him to see the awesome multiplicity, the multiple *individualities*, that compose every stratum of nature: "Leaves are of more various forms than the alphabets of all languages put together; of the oaks alone there are hardly two alike, and each expresses its own character." Each therefore takes much of its meaning from its ability to be itself and no other thing, that is, from its capacity to escape categorization. The words that point to multiplicity pile up in their own multiplicity: "without end"; "who shall count"; "myriad"; "more various forms"; "hardly two alike." Putting multiplicity together with the equally intense uniqueness takes cobwebs and insects and leaves out of the range of the likening impulse that had placed the bass tree so neatly within two different bundles of language. The things that he sees are so many and so different that they cannot be contained (consumed?) within any system of language that seeks to find a place for them. What, then, has happened to those confident discourses that, a few lines before, were able to capture nature, scientifically or transcendentally? What has happened to the fitting and fitted that made Thoreau so serene? Though seemingly no less serene, he sounds now like the Blake who scorned fitting and fitted and revered what outline could do in defining individualities. Yet there is nothing comparable to outline which can do that for Thoreau. Language certainly cannot. Instead of that interlocking which leaves no interim spaces, there is an ineradicable gap between the capacities of our languages (the alphabets are synecdoches for the languages as a whole) and nature's various leaves. And yet earlier in the passage a tree was the model instance of the way he uses discourse to bring nature within our purview.

Somewhere between the single tree at the beginning and the myriad leaves at the end there has been a startling slippage—and what slips is not only the capacities of language but our fullest confidence in them. Human language is as secondary here as it is in the comments on words and deeds, as low in the hierarchy as he saw it then. And it is also as oddly spaced as we saw it in several other passages. We are back, then, to that question of the spaces language inhabits, and we are also back to observing language occupying the space between seeing and rendering, what we spoke of earlier as seeing and saying. The curve we observe in this passage takes the passage quite around to end by facing the opposite way. It is *not*, however, that Thoreau denies what he says at the beginning. Rather, both of these positions, whatever their contradictoriness and incompatibility, are at home in the passage and find comfortable places within it. Each possibility takes part in the passage's overall rhythm. One way we can understand this is to go back to what we saw of the way an alternative discourse may seek to take over and colonize the images of another discourse. Something very much like that has happened in this passage, but the result is clearly a standoff. Pulled in opposite directions by forces of equal power, the passage can end only in ambivalence, only in an oxymoronic encounter.

The second of our concluding study passages is the first paragraph of the chapter on "Sounds" in *Walden*:

> But while we are confined to books, though the most select and classic, and read only particular written languages, which are themselves but dialects and provincial, we are in danger of forgetting the language which all things and events speak without metaphor, which alone is copious and standard. Much is published, but little printed. The rays which stream through the shutter will be no longer remembered when the shutter is wholly removed. No method nor discipline can supersede the necessity of being forever on the alert. What is a course of history, or philosophy, or poetry, no matter how well selected, or the best society, or the most admirable routine of life, compared with the discipline of looking always at what is to be seen? Will you be a reader, a student merely, or a seer? Read your fate, see what is before you, and walk on into futurity. (111)

Part of the purpose of this introductory paragraph is to instruct us how to read the chapter we have just completed, the one on "Reading." That chapter had made, among other distinctions, the following: "there is a memorable interval between the spoken and the written language, the language heard and the language read" (101). The spoken is transient and limited ("a dialect merely"), a speech "almost brutish" that we learn "unconsciously, like the brutes, of our mothers." It is, by nature, "our mother tongue." The written, "our father tongue," is reserved and select. It requires a re-origination of ourselves that is the higher, more exalted counterpart of the originating our mothers gave us. The one is part of that experience in which we are made, the other, part of that in which we make ourselves. The one is associated with instinct and our natural being, the other with the higher faculties and those aspects of ourselves for which the *Iliad* is made. With slight adjustments they become the languages of, respectively, Schiller's naive and sentimental poets. Taken in a mode that both makes and mocks pastoral, they become the speech of Blake's Innocence and Experience. Our relations to those languages speak with telling effect of the qualities of our selves. Our relation to reading is a readout of our selves, as witness the Canadian woodchopper: Therien is far closer to his first origin than to his second, a Caliban charmed by hearing Homer but not enough to build himself anew. These are distinctions of immense significance to Thoreau.

This means that we must take the words of the introductory paragraph of "Sounds" in all the fullness and precision with which they come to us. That paragraph is as much a statement of purpose as any of the many such statements Thoreau wrote. And it takes as its way of talking about purpose a commentary on the hierarchy of language he had broached a few pages earlier. The words take as their starting point a version of the rhetoric of self–correction we have already seen at work, a ploy that permits Thoreau to go in whatever direction seems appropriate at the time and then adjust where he has arrived with where he ultimately wants to go. We can hear the adjustments occurring in this paragraph through a number of crucial words such as "confined"; in our engagement with the words on a page we inhabit a limited and closed space, with ourselves at one end and the book at the other, with the small amount of air between us taking up the rest of the space. Those tiny enclosures are separated from the rest of the world by their self–containedness and autonomy, characteristics admirable in themselves but necessarily exclusive. It is hardly too fanciful to think of this confinement as a kind of willed jailing, a fancy well within Thoreau's modes and experience. We are confined further because our written languages are themselves "but dialects and provincial," necessarily the language of a place, however large, and therefore necessarily limited. This is not to denigrate written language—Thoreau does not take back nearly that much—but to show that, however exalted a state of consciousness it represents, it is essentially restricted, encompassed, bounded. Further, because it is written, it is mediated; and because it is so often metaphorical, it is to that degree even more indirect, less immediate.[14] Thoreau worried the matter of immediacy incessantly, bringing it out in a variety of contexts so that it takes its specific content and application from where it sits. This, for example, is from the chapter on "Spring": "The earth is not a mere fragment of dead history, stratum upon stratum like the leaves of a book, to be studied by geologists and antiquaries chiefly, but living poetry like the leaves of a tree, which precede flowers and fruit" (309). As the leaves of a tree precede flowers and fruit so do they precede—and so does the tree become—the leaves of a book. The latter are between us and the tree. Again, this is not to denigrate written language but to narrow our inspection of what it is and can do. What it cannot do, Thoreau tells us, is get down to the marrow or even—continuing the digging but not so deeply—get to that wonderful meat near the bone:

> if you are restricted in your range by poverty, if you cannot buy books and newspapers, for instance, you are but confined to the most significant and vital experiences; you are compelled to deal with the material which yields the most sugar and the most starch. It is life near the bone where it is sweetest. (W, 329)

Of course this is not to say that only the poor can get near such sweetness or that if you are poor you necessarily can. John Field is restricted in this way and others, not only because he is poor but because he probably cannot read; even if he could, it is doubtful whether he would arrive at those qualities of consciousness that could know of such sweetness. Therien appears to have come nearer, mainly because of his instinct for joy, but he did not know what to do with the amount of reading he could handle. We are now coming to see that the introductory paragraph of "Sounds" is not only about language but about the relations of language to kinds and qualities of awareness.

The language that gets us to the sweet meat of this world is not just the language of nature, what the trees speak. It is closer to the language that would be spoken by what Emerson defines as "NATURE": "the NOT ME, that is, both nature and art, all other men and my own body.[15] Thoreau's version of the language is that which "all things and events speak," a simpler expression of Emerson's inclusiveness. It means particularly all to which we can respond, partly in their qualities as things, partly in their qualities as things to which relation is possible. In that meaning, as well as in its inclusiveness, Thoreau is closest to the Wordsworth of "Tintern Abbey," who puts the issue in terms of "a motion and a spirit, that impels / All thinking things, all objects of all thought, / And rolls through all things." For Thoreau the language of such things is open and everywhere. It will therefore include the language of books (books are both things and events, Wordsworthian objects of thought), yet the language imprinted on book leaves is only a small part of it: "Much is published but little printed." Unlike the language of book leaves, it is not a dialect but standard speech. To the degree that we know it, can hear it, and understand all that comes out of the fullness of its components, to that degree can we be at home in the fullness of the world. Ideally we could become the best sort of traveler in this world, for "the secret of successful sauntering"—so Thoreau puts it in "Walking"—involves "having no particular home, but [being] equally at home everywhere" (*Excursions*, 162). It is the language of makers of excursions. We should not, therefore, be surprised that the paragraph which begins "Sounds" ends with an exhortation to walk.

That exhortation completes the sweep of a subsidiary movement that begins in the middle of the paragraph, picking up and developing the implications of the explorations of language in the first half. The language of things and events is necessarily various, as various and encompassing as that which speaks it. Our capacity to take in all that this language is saying has therefore to be as manifold as the elements of the language itself. What the language is like determines what we have to be like in order to take it in; we make much of what we are in the world on the basis of what we have to listen to. As the paragraph goes on to assert, there is a demand made upon us if we want to be more than confined and provincial, a demand that we face up to the necessity of an interface between ourselves and this privileged speech. To do less is to be less. Being and doing imply and implicate each other. Put another way, Thoreau's Transcendentalist argument for the centrality of the individual means that he should be able to do what he has to do wherever he happens to be: "Wherever I sat, there I might live, and the landscape radiated from me accordingly" (*W*, 81). But to be able to sit anywhere, to *live* anywhere ("I did not wish to live what was not life, living is so dear" [*W*, 901]), meant that he had to be able to hear all that was spoken wherever he was. The language of things and events is copious, reflecting the principle of plenitude in the earthly, natural aspects of the Great Chain of Being. A great many channels of response will therefore have to be open in us, a plethora to respond to the plenitude. There is far more asked of us here than in any discipline we read in or even in the best ways we have put together of going about our lives: "What is a course of history, or philosophy, or poetry, no matter how well selected, or the best society, or the most admirable routine of life, compared with the discipline of looking always at what is to be seen?" The extent of the demand is more than our previous affairs had led us to imagine. We must somehow come up to imagining all that such language makes imaginable, all that it has itself imagined in its (previously unimaginable) fullness. To do so we must reimagine our own contours. Since we are literally surrounded, wherever we go, by that to which we must be alive, consciousness has to be fashioned as a sphere. And since that language is always being directed at us, seeking our complicity, the surface of the sphere has to be such as to make possible our full and permanent attentiveness. What Wordsworth called in "Expostulation and Reply" "this mighty sum / Of things for ever speaking" calls for a correspondent perpetuity in our readiness to receive that speech. Wordsworth's description of perpetuity is echoed in Thoreau's comment that "no method nor discipline can supersede the necessity of being forever on the alert."

There is so much at work in this initial paragraph from "Sounds" that we shall need to look at it again as a model for other issues. But its primary purpose is clearly to put some major questions about language into reasonable coherence, not only to readjust the statements that had seemed appropriate in "Reading" but also to settle some difficult issues—the nagging matter of hierarchies, for one—that seem never to go away. What the paragraph does, it does very well, but it does not do nearly enough; and from the samplings we have taken of Thoreau's puzzlings over language, it is certain that no paragraph could encompass them all. This one omits more than it includes, and what it omits is many of the matters that make Thoreau most uneasy, a number of the messier questions, such as the business of language and power or the occasional impulse of language to put the natural aside and seek for other sources of support—these and many more, much of which we have seen, none of which finds a place in this intensely compact package.

Thoreau knew that in fashioning the package he was leaving a good deal out, but he kept any sense of omission from making an overt appearance in "Sounds." We can gather his awareness of omission from an early sketch of the paragraph, which tests some critical insights that were to show only obliquely in the final state of the material. This is from August 23, 1845:

> In all the dissertations—on language—men forget the language that is— that is really universal—the inexpressible meaning that is in all things & every where with which the morning & evening teem. As if language were especially of the tongue. Of course with a more copious hearing or understanding—of what is published the present *languages* will be forgotten. (*J 2:178–79)

Until the end there are no surprises, though the crack about the dissertations on language gives these tentative speculations a self-reflexive quality that did not appear in the final version. At the end, though, there is an assertion, quite startling in retrospect, that, had it appeared in the final version, would have unsettled it severely. However broad the scope of the language now spoken by all things and events, an even more copious language, a language of the future that will succeed all present languages, can clearly be envisioned. Along with that forthcoming language will come an extended capacity for being in the world, the doors of perception so cleansed that we shall have to expand our abilities to meet what they will bring. (Precisely the same point is made toward the end of *A Week*, and in a significantly related context: "Our present senses are but the rudiments of what they are destined to become" [382].) Thus, the language that is to come will be the counterpart in copiousness of a new hearing and understanding, the breadth of which will take in unimaginably much more than our present capacities can handle. We and our language will, as now, explore and explain each other, work in the full knowledge that each will have to keep up with the other in order to realize what is given. But to stay in such intricate alignment we shall have to leave behind all the previous conjunctions of ourselves and our language that had worked in other conditions but are not sufficiently copious for those that are envisioned. Thoreau must have left these speculations out of the paragraph in "Sounds" because, in moving toward greater copiousness, he would have had to leave behind even that universal language that he wanted to make the star of the passage in "Sounds." In exploring the contours of that language in his tentative early statement, he made clear what would have to happen: "of what is published the present *languages* will be forgotten." That emphasized plural noun points to the shock of recognition that his thoughts had brought him to face. What is made public in the final version includes not only written language but every kind known to us now, every one of the dialects, but also that overriding universal language that takes in everything else, absorbs all that is wholly provincial. *All* of our current public languages will concede to their broader successors, will be put by and forgotten as the later, more comprehensive modes seek to keep up with the greedy copiousness that is always walking ahead. It is only this point in the shelved speculations, the sense of the way ahead, that gets broached in the final version, but with a hint that is sufficiently broad. The version in "Sounds" suggests that forward thrust in its final sentence: "Read your fate, see what is before you, and walk on into futurity." This sense of a narrative with a goal fits in with what we saw earlier of what seems to be a pattern of quest. We are getting to see more and more of what may be a radical fable that drives Thoreau's work.

Chapter Two

WRITING, SUBTEXT, SCENE

FABLES are made out of words, spoken or written; and if, as we just concluded, we seem to be seeing more and more of a fable that grounds Thoreau's work, we can be certain that his fable will have something to do with words. More precisely, we can be certain that words will themselves be a subject of the fable in at least two ways: a question of how fables can be made at all, given the problems Thoreau sees with words; and a question of how words and their making take part in the themes and events of the fable's narrative. Such a blending of subject and substance (words and the acts that use them becoming the object of their own concern) promises an elaborately self-reflexive union of form and content. Yet since Thoreau is so often elusive on the matter of words, refusing to say that they are one thing and one thing only—since he himself is acting as words so often act, evading our urge to pin him down—we then have to conclude that words, as he understands them, cannot tell all that we want them to tell. We have already noticed Thoreau acknowledging their centrifugal pull, that requisite (if not always welcome) partner to their self-reflexiveness. The pull is one of the reasons why words have trouble going with us into nature's deeper enclosures and why they are able to tell us little about their most exalted versions, the ultimate word and the serenely encompassing sentence. Self-reflexive, yes; helping to prophesy, yes; but certainly not always sufficient. Stanley Cavell told us much when he spoke of *Walden*'s self-reflexiveness, and we clearly can use such insights in other aspects of the canon, as Sharon Cameron and others have shown. But to be fully satisfied with self-mirroring is to take more satisfaction in the process than Thoreau himself took, or that a broader sampling of his comments, postures, and practices will permit us to take.

By an easy and requisite extension, the same will go for writing, the term taken in both of the aspects I shall intend, as act and as product. But writing will, or course, add even more to these issues. For one thing, it has to take place somewhere, so that the scene of writing, indeed its geography, may come to be of concern. For another, Thoreau's pervasive interest in the person who made the text means that writing has not only a *where* but a *by whom* (which is not to say that "whom" is always complete or settled in). Place and text maker—

whatever their difficulties in getting established and their subsequent problems in getting together in what is sometimes mutual indifference, sometimes mutual respect—can never really be taken in perfectly exclusive contexts. For still another thing, writing never happens alone but along with other acts and products, and it effects, and is affected by, its companions. This comes to mean that other acts and products can be shown to share, in a profound way, some of writing's characteristics. That, in turn, will lead us to see more about writing's role in our ways of being in places and conducting our affairs. Place and text, writing and the world we make out of what the world affords us, cannot be conceived apart from each other. This is not, of course, to say that they never come apart (that they very often do so is part of Thoreau's understanding of the world) but, rather, that we must keep the other always in mind whenever we speak of each. Indeed, the question of their apartness is itself part of the fable, one of the questions that drive its narrative.

• I •

The collective that is *A Week* has, as we would expect, much to say about such matters, and by dint of saying much it says all sorts of contrary things. As a repository of some of Thoreau's earlier experiments in thought and mode, as well as his smoothest work up to that point, it holds a good deal of the conventional, like the two major essays on poetry and books. The first essay appears fairly early in the text, the second quite near the end, as though taking part in a summation. There are few surprises in both, though such anomalies as there are need not only the intensest scrutiny but an ear that can hear the incongruous. The first begins by discussing poetry, then moves into questions of books. The part on poetry strides with obvious pleasure through one commonplace after another, putting most of its effort into an exaltation of poetry as, "though the last and finest result," still "a natural fruit" (91). It continues with comments similar to those in Keats's letters: "As naturally as the oak bears an acorn, and the vine a gourd, a man bears a poem, either spoken or done."[1] What we are hearing at this point is a dialect of the discourse we heard in Shelley's "Ode to the West Wind," the one that links natural and bookish leaves. Still, though we saw Thoreau playing parodically with the analogy and its unquestioning acceptance, there is no such holding back in these remarks on poems as natural objects. Thoreau's long-standing distrust of institutions and their discourses did not carry so far as to these comments on poetry, which have their source in earlier institutions whose discourses (as these pages in *A Week* show) still held on to much of their power. He went along with it for several reasons, most of all because these pages held probings of a vocation that had to be treated solemnly, but also, surely, because there was so much comfort in this feeding on the familiar. As the comments continue, they come close to the dialect that was used to describe figures like Schiller's naive poet: the poet "performs his functions, and is so well that he needs such stimulus to sing only as plants to put forth leaves and blossoms" (91). That passage shifts the analogy with nature from the poem to the poet and, incidentally, shows how these different dialects can hook on to each other.[2] Unsurprisingly, the passage moves, with much enthusiasm, into the near bathos of the identification of Homer and nature, a venerable holdover from the theories of the century before. It goes along in that vein to end the section with comments on poetry's universal truth and—a claim we shall have to ponder carefully—its independence of personal experience, of "any particular biography" (95).

By this point, however, Thoreau had had enough of such institutional mutterings. What he goes on to say reveals a twitching surely prompted by other, subtextual pressures. Not everything printed is a book, whatever its pretensions, but much turns out to be "not Books or Bibles at all" (97). To play that point with precision he picks up a move from the previous game, where poetry is identified with natural objects, and turns these unbookish writings into artifacts that had sought to parade themselves as books: "many a pure scholar and genius who has learned to read is for a moment deceived by, and finds himself reading a horse-rake, or spinning jenny, or wooden nutmeg, or oak-leaf cigar, or steam-power press, or kitchen range, perchance, when he was seeking serene and biblical truths" (97). The play on old business turns into flagrant parody: "Instead of cultivating the earth for wheat and potatoes, they cultivate literature, and fill a place in the Republic of Letters" (97). And that takes the argument into several odd, unforeseeable turns. Books "must not yield wheat and potatoes, but must themselves be the unconstrained and natural harvest of their author's lives" (98), a point that patently contradicts his earlier remark that poetry rises above "any particular biography." Following this newfound impetus, he goes off into extravagance, carrying the point so far that it ends in some new and unusual issues: "We do not learn much from learned books, but from true, sincere, human books, from frank and honest biographies. The life of a good man will hardly improve us more than the life of a freebooter, for the inevitable laws appear as plainly in the infringement as in the observance" (98). Part of what is at stake in this play with book and person will ultimately take Thoreau into some deeply considered ponderings of our relations to our texts. What is especially at stake is the place of writing in living. The passage contains the potential to undo with sardonic thoroughness most of what Thoreau had just said about poetry. It took him as far as he could see (or dare) at this point in his pondering of writing as act and product.

By the end of the book, in the second essay on poetry and the poet, he saw or (dared) much more. As he often does when he must make large points, Thoreau prefigures the content of the essay with some comments toward the end of the previous chapter. Late in the "Thursday" chapter, while he is contemplating history and "true account[s] of the actual" (325), he makes several comments on Goethe, whom he sees as a master at such accounts. Having said, just before this, that Goethe "lacks the unconsciousness of the poet" (327), he makes clear that exact description is not itself sufficient to make the finest writing. Thoreau then turns to distinguishing the Man of Genius from the Artist or Artisan, the former inspired and demonic, the latter his follower. This elaborate fine-tuning turns to rhapsodies on original genius and, more originally, the dangerous talent of composition. Then, like the ending of many other chapters in *A Week*, the diurnal narrative comes around to bedtime and bunking in, this time beside the river.

What happens next turns several tables. Thoreau describes the closing of the day, the travelers' supper and conversation, their writing in their journals. He then offers a not-quite-passing comment (its significance shown in part by its being framed in its own paragraph) that quietly, slyly qualifies all that had just been said. Indeed, it stretches the effects of its undoing not only to the previous comments but back to the early essay on writing:

> Unfortunately many things have been omitted which should have been recorded in our journal, for though we made it a rule to set down all our experiences therein, yet such a resolution is very hard to keep, for the important experience rarely allows us to remember such obligations, and so indifferent things get recorded, while that is frequently neglected. It is not easy to write in a journal what interests us at any time, because to write it is not what interests us. (322)

Journals, it seems, are secondary in several senses. Journals are made out of words, as fables and narratives are, and so they are subject to the secondariness of words, their capacities for being second in line, second-best, perhaps even secondhand. For one thing, journals tend to get the second best, the leavings of the day's business, since what was most important rarely gets into the journal's words. Further, their words are second in line because writing a journal has to tag along behind more important things, Thoreau's doings of the day. But there is much more at stake here, more areas prey to undoing. In the earlier passage on writing, we saw the favoring of biography, the fusing of a text and a life. At work in this passage is an undoing of that fusion, the beginning of a prying apart of the life and the writing, those elements separating out into a relation that is patently hierarchical and not to the favor of journal writing. The main doings of a day not only take primacy over recording but tend to escape the capture of recording. The secondary mode of working can capture only its cousin, the secondary mode of experience. Thoreau is once again uneasy with the status of writing as act compared to others one can perform—here, the important acts of a day. (In a few pages we shall see a different version of the position, one that corrects the extravagance but supports its essential point.) The force of this passage comes not only from its rhetorical play but because of what it does to what had just been said, Thoreau's comments about writing with the fullest sort of reach and the fullest awareness of danger.

The giving and taking away that end the "Thursday" chapter of *A Week* bear very close relations to Thoreau's rhetoric of self-correction, that maneuver which seems to permit him to have it all ways at once. Is it that he wants himself to be forever just beyond our grasp, shifty and slippery and sardonic, arguing that all those fixities we so eagerly (Transcendentally) seek are beset by a dark Other that keeps pulling them away? Or is he so passionate about fine-tuning that he carries it much too far, tuning beyond the edge of harmony into greater and greater dissonance? The Thoreau I have been offering tends to combine such binary distinctions, arguing that only in such contrary pairings do we get at what it means to successfully be in the world. If these gestures tell a little about the substance of Thoreau's fable, they tell a great deal more about the fable's tonality, what it feels like to live it to its fullest.

The second essay on poetry has a structure so like the first that they need to be taken as intended pairs. The later essay is also in two sections: the first section, like its counterpart in the earlier essay, it on poets and poems; where the second section of the earlier essay had taken up Homer, that of the later takes up Ossian.[3] The main points in the later essay are as institutional in content as their counterparts in the earlier, but the points are, if anything, even more miscellaneous now, moving, at the beginning, from the analogy of thoughts and river currents to the poet's requisite toughness to his generation's lack of knowledge of what he is about. Then there intervenes a curious paragraph, part commonplace, part something else. It is about libraries as dust-holes, and it begins with an odd comment:

> When I stand in a library where is all the recorded wit of the world, but none of the recording, a mere accumulated, and not truly cumulative treasure, where immortal works stand side by side with anthologies which did not survive their month, and cobweb and mildew have already spread from these to the binding of those; and happily I am reminded of what poetry is, I perceive that Shakespeare and Milton did not foresee into what company they were to fall. Alas! that so soon the work of a true poet should be swept into such a dust-hole! (341)

What is odd is the statement that the library contains "none of the recording." Libraries, it seems, are places of writing as product rather than act, places where there can no longer be a sense of the poet's touch but only of the touched upon, the paper and not the flesh. Thoreau's language is precise, pitting "recorded" against "recording," past participle against gerund. His main points in the paragraph are that junk and Shakespeare occupy the same location and that the junk overwhelms the rest. In a wonderful distinction that supports his point precisely, he contrasts "accumulated" and "cumulative," the dust-hole unfortunately containing only the former. A more judicious selection would be to make the library hold only the latter. But even so fine a splitting of points cannot take in all the implications of "recorded" and "recording." To see them better we shall have to detour briefly.

It should be clear by this point that subtexts are essential elements in Thoreau's writing and thinking. He promotes not only emphatic gestures that keep the surfaces active but also subterranean moves that seek to keep the surfaces honest. Near the beginning of this chapter, I argued that we have to read Thoreau with an ear for the incongruous. We must be prepared for propositions that cannot jibe comfortably with the surface thrust of statements, that set up radical patterns which tend to complicate that thrust. Sometimes they contradict it, sometimes they urge the surface thrust to slow down and consider *these* factors too. If the prevalence of the subtext offers instructions for reading Thoreau, that prevalence also shows us something of the place writing has in defining our condition in the world. Thoreau knows that no single impulse or comment, no separate thrust of statement that goes its unqualified way, can say all that has to be said about dust-holes or libraries or the images that pull them together. That is one major reason why he takes so often to subtexts, why they do so much to achieve a more accurate vision of things than an unqualified surface text can. Only an order of that sort can describe what it means to live out his fable about being in this world. And yet it may well be questionable whether any sort of packaging, even one replete with subtexts, can say all that has to be said. We are seeing one more reason why Thoreau was so eager to get to the place of the word of words and the great, serene sentence: if all that has to be said could be said anywhere at all, that would be the place and those would be the tools to tell the fable at its fullest.

The subtext of the paragraph on libraries does its business remarkably well. It tonalities nearly subliminal, it picks up some of the suggestions made earlier in *A Week*, especially those that seek to distinguish the book from the person. With the subtext it becomes a question not of Shakespeare or junk but of writing as act and product, what the play with "recording" and "recorded" emphasizes. What we saw at the end of the "Thursday" chapter as the beginning of a prying apart of life and text continues here in a far more complex vein. Once more there is valorization, a hierarchy of modes. Once more there is the question of the relation of text maker and text, this time with a complication that qualifies much of what we have seen.

It now comes clear that the comments we have been inspecting make up a *line* of quirky assertions, not just sporadic and disparate grumblings that turn up on odd occasions. It is, in fact, a developing line whose components seem incongruous in terms of the other concerns of the essay. That line is, of course, the subtext. Its pitch grows higher and sharper, bolder and more urgent, as the related essays develop. We ought, then, to expect that it will emerge at a critical point with a brash and open statement. Subtexts are, at once, brazen and circumspect, passionate and canny; and when they take on subjects so tense and crucial as the one this subtext is developing—the meaning of writing as act and product in the shape and substance of our lives—we can expect the brashness and canniness to reach an extraordinary pitch of intensity in a passage of unmistakable import. In this case, the pitch of intensity turns out to be one of clarity as well:

> The true poem is not that which the public read. There is always a poem not printed on paper, coincident with the production of this, stereotyped in the poet's life. It is *what he has become through his work*. Not how is the idea expressed in stone, or on canvass or paper, is the question, but how far it has obtained form and expression in the life of the artist. His true work will not stand in any prince's gallery.
>
> My life has been the poem I would have writ.
> But I could not both live and utter it.
>
> (343)

In that developing dialogue which gives the intensest life to *A Week*'s essays on writing, this is the subtext's boldest, most open riposte. Its points are perspicuous, its urgency equally so. The lines of poetry that end this passage leave no room for the chance that some of our best acts may get into the text: living one's life and uttering it are now seen to be incompatible. An earlier comment had argued that biography is best because it offers the sense of the writer at work, but the truest of all poems is the life that becomes what it is on the basis of the work. That, we now can see, is what the subtext was driving at, what it was whispering and muttering as the line moved through the essays. Now it says its piece right out, in an open and obvious challenge to the main tenets of the essays. Text and life are now fully pried apart, all of the squeaking and groaning that were the sound of the prying at work now gone as this open statement shows the prying to be completed. All that had been implicit in the earlier appearances of the subtext comes forth with a purity of contour that even an institutional discourse could not possibly misunderstand. The hierarchy, in particular, is patent and potently put, and relates to other hierarchies we looked at in the previous chapter, such as the one in the passage on Raleigh that plays off deeds against words and—far more subtle and with even richer implications—the one that turns up in the first paragraph of *Walden*'s chapter on "Sounds."

There is no question of either side winning the war of text and subtext that energizes these essays on writing. This is, in fact, still another instance of discourses fighting for turf, and, as in others we saw, they end by sharing the turf between them. After this sharply phrased outburst, the first part of the essay ends and the second part sets out on a commonplace reading of Ossian. But this does not mean that the institutional triumphs, for the ear we have to keep cocked to Thoreauvian incongruities cannot block them out of its memory: their mutterings were far too urgent, their final remark too incisive, to be put aside and forgotten as awkward deviations. To read Thoreau and put the mutterings aside is to sentimentalize the sardonic, to simplify for our own comfort what for Thoreau was a difficult business that would never be taken simply if we were attentive to all that was there. Thoreau lived always with his alertness to the complexities and puzzles of writing. Few subjects dogged him more. It is not only a question of how texts touch lives but also one of how texts touch us *as compared to* how lives touch us. For the rest of this chapter we shall look at a number of his probings of touch and watch as they extend into matters of nature and history and various modes of inscribing.

• II •

The sort of probing at play in "recording" and "recorded" turns up at other points in *A Week*. Thoreau likes to remind the reader of the nature of the journey by coming out of a meditation and referring to the voyagers' places in the boat or in their camp beside the stream. His thoughts are permitted to wander wherever they wish. Compared to the bodies on the boat, their potential seems quite limitless. But in most of the essays and meditations, those wanderings of consciousness are followed by a return of the text to a place on or near the river. In so doing, they reaffirm that the wanderers did have bodies and that those bodies were located in that particular place, going about their business in a closer-to-immediate time than the one in the meditation. Sometimes the time is fully immediate: in those cases, Thoreau does not say that during the meditation they *had been* floating down the stream, but that they *have been* doing so and are *continuing* to do so now. This is the gerundive voice at work, the sounds of continuing action in the touchable present rather than those of action completed in the (varyingly distant) past. Most possible temporal modes appear in *A Week*, and their complexities have much to do with questions of presence and absence, the scene and nature of writing, the scene and nature of reading. They take us back not only to issues like those of words and deeds but also to the obsessive business about biography; and they finally take us ahead, as all such questions do, to the intricate relations among ourselves, our places, and texts, relations that now appear to involve temporal issues as well.

A sampling of such situations shows much more variety among them than they seem at first to contain. A set in the "Tuesday" chapter has a complex life of its own and therefore offers a sufficient instance. (This will be our first use of one of the most significant scenes in all of Thoreau's writings.) It begins with a thicker-than-usual version of the mist or fog found so often at these chapter beginnings and then slips, subtly but tellingly, into an interplay of temporal stages and, therefore, of varying degrees of presence. He moves from a standard evocation of continuing past action ("That which seemed to us to invest the world, was only a narrow and shallow wreath of vapor" [180]) to a past definite that appears to refer to an event even further back ("I once saw the day break from the top of Saddle-back Mountain in Massachusetts" [180]) and then shifts into the present as a prelude to the telling of a tale ("As we cannot distinguish objects through this dense fog, let me tell this story more at length" [180]). The voice that speaks from the text shifts its relation to us, shrewdly and quietly fashioning a series of changes in temporal position. In so doing, it shifts its seat (that is, its position vis-á-vis ourselves) until, in its turn to the present tense, it claims to be sitting right there beside us, its sounds as immediate as any in our present circle. No one knows better than Thoreau that such shiftings are a figment. They are also, at the same time, a dense and elaborate statement about the various kinds of relation referred to in the interplay of "recording" and "recorded." When he speaks of the continuing past, we are hearing a common written voice, the kind we expect out of histories like those quoted in *A Week* and of which *A Week* is, in many parts, itself a sufficient example. When the voice shifts to the past definite, it offers even more of the same, the kind of speaking we hear in many historical narratives. But when it shifts to that agreeable intimacy, the speech of a chatty friend seeking to pass a few present moments, the scene of writing becomes, in effect, a scene of telling; or, to put it in another combination, it becomes a scene of immediate writing that, because he is right there writing, is also a scene of telling. (That would mean that the scene of reading, our always immediate scene, becomes in this case a scene of reading/listening, with us as a variously active audience.)

The more we ponder this passage, the less possible it becomes to fix this scene precisely, to say exactly where it is. Telling and writing and listening and reading shift about so rapidly, the claims of each condition seeking to speak so much louder than the others, that the stance of the passage—its location in the narrative flow and therefore in the text's relation to us—slips away from us continually. It is as impossible to hold on to as that flow of the river current which *A Week* uses so often to image the narrative flow. The analogous flows of stream and narrative are among the easier realizations of the text's figurative potential, but the potential is more fully realized when the *slipperiness* of the stream implicates an equivalent slipperiness in the way the narrative works. These lines should also be seen as a set of instructions for reading the chapter that follows, for it is itself very slippery about matters of temporal placement. Further, and most encompassing, the passage makes plain that Thoreau cannot always accede to accepted, ancient wisdom on still another subject, the question of where to locate the various kinds of scenes that make up narrative relations, those of telling and writing and hearing and reading. He sees the distinctions among them as elusive conditions that, when we seek to lock them in, forever evade our grasp. What does all this do to Thoreau's insistence that the best texts are biographies, reeking of the sense of the subject as person? At the least it makes such texts harder to achieve, the person a far more complex issue than simple biographism would make it. Once again we are watching Thoreau catching himself up, qualifying his insistence on one point or another, in what seems a perpetual rhythm in the acts of Thoreauvian thought.

As I indicated earlier, this passage is one of a set, a group whose purpose, we now can guess, is to keep reminding us of what the chapter's beginning sets out. After Thoreau tells the story of his climb up Saddleback, he returns the text not only to a present indicative active but also to an exhortation for the immediate future ("but now we must make haste" [190]). That gesture recapitulates the play of presentness and exhortation ("as we cannot . . . let me tell" [180]), which had led into the tale of the ascent. Thus, we enter the tale and come out of it with precisely equivalent structures. And as though everything were as consistent as this comforting repetition of patterns, he starts the story of their voyage again, going back to the mood of the ongoing past: "We passed a canal boat before sunrise, groping its way to the seaboard" (190). These moves are really quite shrewd. The shift toward the voice of a teller who is at our side, the shift that occurred just before the telling of the tale of ascent, seems now to have become permanent, to have settled in so comfortably that its presence is unquestioned. We accept that the voice now speaks beside us in person-to-person encounter and that it is going on to tell what the travelers had done in that ongoing past. This is a traditional teller's stance, the sort attributed to Homer and Ossian, who are subjects of special emphasis in the two main essays on writing. In fact, the passage repeatedly echoes the content of those essays and, not quite incidentally, picks up for the speaker a reflected stature by virtue of those reverberations. But the comfort of that echo cannot hold on for long. It quickly becomes apparent that what he is telling about, the occurrences of the ongoing past, are precisely those occurrences he says he is *currently* going through ("but now we must make haste back before the fog disperses to the blithe Merrimack water" [190]) in what purports to be the present, the scene and time of telling; of course, once that is seen, the whole pretense collapses. So much not only for a Coleridgean willing suspension of disbelief but for any consistency or coherence of stance, whether that of an agreed-upon figment or some less obvious kind. We have been toyed with mainly to remind us that we ought not to be such dupes, that all of this business about telling and writing and hearing and reading is exceedingly difficult to pin down. Our soothing, unpondered beliefs about presence and absence and the various positions of bard and audience had better be looked at more carefully.

Thoreau, it is clear, did a great deal of such looking. That after so much speculation he still managed to become a man of so many extraordinary words has to be seen by now as a remarkable feat. It is not that Thoreau was uncertain about the central points he was making as a maker of prophecy for his times. He knew very well what they involved. Rather, he was aware that he had to struggle to get words to work sufficiently so that all of the slipperiness attendant upon writing could be kept in adequate control. Then there is the attendant point that all of this (itself sometimes slippery) play with degrees of presence and the relations of bard and audience has a great deal to do with the way we relate to our texts, particularly the nature of the "we" who do that relating. All these issues have ultimately to do with ways of being in a world like the one such questions inhabit. To find out what such being *means*, we must look more carefully at how that being *happens* to a place, how it finds itself *in* a place, because happening and meaning can never be considered as separate. The telling of a tale is one of the conditions in which we can best observe the relations of those two. So many positions are possible, so many degrees of relation—each involving a special connection of teller to audience, time, and place—that the act of telling covers an exceptional number of conditions in which being can happen in a place and in the times of that place. The writing of prophetic texts permits us not only to prophesy but to investigate other issues—some of the profoundest we shall ever encounter—to which writing is inevitably tied. Writing has to be seen as part of a context so rich and intricate that it is difficult to speak about writing, or indeed to perform the act, without having to go off and explore the greater contours of that context.

As for the fable that runs through the canon, we now have further confirmation that a difficulty of fixity turns up often in the tale and that the difficulty now extends to our stance in relation to others (as well as to that within us which seeks to take such a stance). What appears to be most surprising is not the extension of these problems of fixity to questions of presence and absence but that Thoreau seems to take them with a certain equanimity. Indeed, he treats them with such cool skill that he seems to have known them for a long time. He must make certain that they become part of the matter of the fable which is his reading of the world; but since he is a prophet, he also has to make certain that they become part of our reading as well.

We need to see such gestures as a kind of cartography, a mapping of the territory in which telling takes place. We clearly need such a map, considering the difficulty of establishing what part of the landscape we are in. Thoreau seeks to make demarcations among the possibilities of the teller's stance, just as in his surveying he sought to distinguish the boundaries that separated one field from another. From the regularity of his employment as a surveyor, we have to assume that he was more successful in mapping the fields around Concord than he was in demarcating these far more uncertain contours of narrative stance.

It was not only the narrator's stances that Thoreau explored but those stances of the reader/hearer as well. Writing in Thoreau is never done for its own sake, and therefore the act of writing is the beginning of a complex of gestures that includes its opposite number at the receiving end. Thoreau talks about writing continuously but about reading a good deal less, undoubtedly because the pressures of vocation affected him until the end of his life. When he does talk about reading, he frequently takes the approach of reading as a mode of experience, which means that what we have seen so far about writing as a matter of stance, as well as the relation of writing and stance to how being *is* in a place, is likely to be at issue when it comes to the act of reading. Indeed, these matters are so much at issue that they begin his major work, emerging in the introduction of his first important essay, "Natural History of Massachusetts" (*Excursions*, 37–72).

Emerson had asked Thoreau to review for the *Dial* a report on the flora and fauna of Massachusetts that had been issued by an agency of the state.[4] The essay turned out, unsurprisingly, to be only occasionally about its assigned subject, for it is preponderantly a laying out of some of Thoreau's views on nature in 1842. But even before he gets to the basic exposition of his ideas, he seeks to establish what he obviously saw as essential prior business, the question of what it means to read such books. He makes it difficult for himself by beginning with a radical separation between the weather around the reader and the weather he is reading about. That is, he separates the scene of reading from the subject of writing, and he does so with so much emphasis that we know we are being told something more than that it is pleasant to read about summer when the snow is piled up outside. For one thing, Thoreau echoes the beginning of "Tintern Abbey" when he says that in doing such reading he owes "an accession of health to these reminiscences of luxuriant nature" (37). In the second stanza of "Tintern Abbey" Wordsworth recalls how, "in lonely rooms, and 'mid the din / Of towns and cities" the reminiscences of beauteous forms had helped to restore his spiritual health. But the differences between the texts are as significant as any likeness, and they do a good deal to illuminate the varying modes that characterize the texts.

As we work our way into Wordsworth's poem, it seems that a hierarchy is shaping up, that, whatever the value of reminiscence, it takes a secondary place to the touch of the immediate scene. After all, the poem begins by extolling the glories of return, going on to record the speaker's pleasure in seeing the hedgerows and lines of smoke out there over against him, now more than the content of memory. Reminiscence of the sort he experienced in towns and cities is a welcome consolation, but he certainly needs no consoling as he looks out at this scene of wild seclusion. Yet if the poem seems to be leading us toward such valorization, it subtly, determinedly, shifts the weight of discourse into quite a different direction. As the restoration is pursued, it leads to another hierarchy and another kind of presence that encompass the wild seclusion and, indeed, everything else: it is that deep and pervading presence which is the life within all things. In pursuing these shifting hierarchies, the reader is made to experience not only a series of acts and turns of the mind but a process of valorization that has its own endemic ironies and ends by putting the reader right at the center of things. We not only read but perform, the play of mind, place, and value not only his but our own.

Thoreau's counterpart passage appears to be far more settled, showing no such ironic shifts. Indeed, the poem that makes up the bulk of the essay's introductory section ends with a predictable balance: "by God's cheap economy" he has been "made rich / To go upon my winter's task again" (38). There are, it seems, no surprises here. If we need to be restored ("I am singularly refreshed in winter when I hear of service-berries, poke-weed, juniper" [38]), then the condition we are in, whatever its special pleasures, is clearly less desirable than the one we are recalling. Now, if winter is less desirable, reading has to be seen as having a highly positive value, for reading is one of the sources of the material that restores. The other, as the poem shows, is memory itself, "the verdure of my mind," the larder within the self wherein is stored the stuff of summer, on which he can draw at any time. There are, then, two sources of saving reminiscence, one within ourselves, the other within the texts of natural history we read to foster reminiscence. And there seems to be only one hierarchy, that which places wintry experience into a secondary state. Writing and reading appear to be safely ensconced in a valued territory of their own, a series of cartographical moves having settled the map.

But that is not quite the case, as we can gather from what we have seen of the vagaries of the scene of writing and what we ought by now to suspect about reading as well. Writing is a reminiscence, the recorded recollection of a time that once had flourished and that, in the case of the seasons, will soon return. Perhaps what we need to do is agree that books of natural history have a certain advantage over books of human history: the latter look forward to no returning summers but only to pondering that which has been and never can be again. This distinction gives to the beginning of Thoreau's essay its warm and genial tone, for that beginning banks on the certainly of summer's return, his current state an interim between two warmer times. Human history has no such interim between comparable conditions, only unrepeatable states.

Thoreau made many versions of that point, particularly in *A Week*, where human history is often at issue. *A Week* shows Thoreau nearly as obsessed with human history as with writing, and when he puts the two together, they fuse into a perspective that opens up another context, an especially urgent one. For example, in the "Thursday" chapter of *A Week*, he works over some ideas about history and the comparability of states of civilization, and then quotes Sir Walter Raleigh, whom we have seen to be a much admired model: " 'We must look a long way back,' says Raleigh, 'to find the Romans giving laws to nations, and their consuls bringing kings and princes bound in chains to Rome in triumph; to see men go to Greece for wisdom, or Ophir for gold; when now nothing remains but a poor paper remembrance of their former condition' " (324). Remembrances so poor can hardly be compared to the "reminiscences of luxuriant nature" that, at the beginning of Thoreau's review, reading was shown to foster. But whatever the specific differences between histories of men and nature, comments like those of Raleigh *have* to echo into the histories of places like Massachusetts, and Thoreau hears those echoes plainly. Whatever the differences in subject, he knows that we are speaking of exactly the same process, the act of reading about events that, *because we can read about them*, are already part of history. All of the sanguine comments, the warm, summery tonalities that make the beginning of the review, can hardly go unqualified in the face of remarks like those Thoreau quotes from Raleigh. And we know that he hears their echoes because the introductory passage to "Natural History of Massachusetts" has its own qualifications that bring it precisely in line with Thoreau's qualified feelings about words and their reading.

Two aspects of the text carry the burden of those qualifications, one having to do with stance and the other with an unusual image. "Tintern Abbey" can help us here too. Thoreau's text takes in a single situation, one reader reading of summer in the midst of a heavy winter. Wordsworth's, on the other hand, takes in a pair of contrary states, one like that of Thoreau (Wordsworth in his lonely room), the other facing the remembered landscape five long summers after his previous visit. Wordsworth begins by talking of his return to the remembered scene, which is directly there in front of him in the poem's present tense. The speaker, in his turn, is clearly on a vantage point where he can see the countryside before him laid out as though on a map (he too works out a cartography for his particular needs). Thus, when he plays off images without and within, playing at degrees of presence and absence as complex as any in Thoreau, he can root the multiple seeing in the touch of the immediate scene. Thoreau's position at the beginning of his essay is most like that of Wordsworth as he was in the city, owning no rooted base, beginning at a secondary level, and proceeding from that stage. What appears in "Tintern Abbey" as a complex play of degrees of presence turns out, when it arrives at Thoreau's text, to offer only an emphasis on absence. Thoreau has only the secondary to deal with, only "paper remembrance" to offer, only a separation of the scene of reading from the subject of writing. With all their geniality, these introductory pages have no more to offer of the presence of the subject of writing than do the histories Raleigh describes. They show that a scene of reading exists only because there has been a bifurcation, an irrevocable severing. Whatever the anticipation of a return of the reminisced, the state that defines the scene of reading is, first and primarily, a state of perpetual absence. To put it in terms relevant to Thoreau's scene of reading, it can be seen as a frozen state, a flow now locked into ice. And those are precisely the terms Thoreau chose to see it in as he worked out the ramifications of reading as a state of absence. Even at this early stage of his work, he has a tense, profound awareness of all that is not there.

We can see that knowledge at work in an image the text singles out for particular emphasis. In the poem that begins the essay, Thoreau remembers "a busy rill, / Which now through all its course stands still and dumb / Its own memorial" (38). The rill in winter is frozen, a mute memorial to itself, a remembrance of itself. Writing is not mute, yet in natural and all other histories, it too is memorial, remembrance. What we can say of the descriptions of summer Thoreau reads in the natural histories is true not only of these texts but generically as well: the uncrossable gap inscribed into the scene of reading can also, it seems, be seen as a frozen state of things, the counterpart of the wintry rill. Whatever the contrary comments on texts and reading and nature that emerge from this clumsily put but really quite eloquent passage, the rill is part of a cartography that seeks to demarcate the contours of the scene of reading and link them to the rest of the map. The startling image of the rill is not only a piece of the landscape but an icy reification of the writing that can never be more than a memorial.

The sounds that emerge in the image of the rill are the voice of the subtext, that cranky, subterranean muttering which is always grumbling about matters like writing and reading and presence, always looking for a soft spot that it can poke through to get to the surface. It finds one here, in the image of the frozen rill. The gravestone is not the person, the obelisk not the battle. The frozen rill is a testimony, and so are natural histories. That is also what writing is, as Walter Raleigh declared when Thoreau brought him in for support. We stand in the scene of reading warmed by what the memorial tells of the tones of another time, warmed, in fact, by remembrance, though the memorial can be only chill.

• III •

This rounds off our look at the scenes of the essential pairs, teller/writer on the one hand, reader/speaker on the other. But in Thoreau's handling of these matters, writer and reader are not always the sole participants in such situations. Place itself is often an active element, often more than merely the locale of saying. Though not an especially active element in the occasion of reading referred to at the beginning of "Natural History of Massachusetts," it becomes intensely active in scenes like the one where Thoreau reads a handbill stuck on a tree in the midst of the Maine woods. Place may turn out to be not only a site of discourse but, itself, a speaker of discourse. It may also be a portion of that which is spoken. This tripartite package occurs in other figures around Romanticism; for some very different examples, see Hölderlin's middle and late hymns and Coleridge's early conversation poems, as well as texts as different as *Songs of Innocence* and *Waverly*. The scope and variety of such a grouping shows that we are dealing with something more than the usual business about nature as a source of symbols, either of its own organic life or of corresponding planes of existence. Thoreau is especially useful on the complexity of these issues because he went off to places as different as Cape Cod and the Maine woods to listen as well as to see. An important part of his business in such places involved instruction in the grammar and syntax of local discourse, and that often meant learning the discourse of the locale, what the place itself spoke and compelled him to hear. Much of the irony that appears in the records of those trips comes from the meeting of Thoreau's habitual discourse with that of the place itself, the Cape's barren, narrow flatness, the woods' dense and unending lushness. What turns up on such occasions is always a version of the competition for mastery among differing systems of discourse. One of them is always that which Thoreau brought with him, the other always that which he found to be the vernacular of the place. Since he was always, in such situations, seeking for sufficient speech, some of the struggles had to do with discoursing as a practice, an advanced and elaborate version of his habit of self-reflexiveness. Whatever else it takes as a subject, this is a speaking *about* speech, and it is usually quite revealing.

Among other things, it reveals the variety of discourse of which place is capable, a multiplicity that complicates Thoreau's encounter with place. When he comes to a place, he carries along with him established but flexible parameters of discourse. In his encounter with that place, he tests the new material against what he already knows, seeking to come to terms with what he now hears and sees. The success of such seeking is variable, and the stories of those attempts are among the most intriguing narratives that make up Thoreau's fable. He can, for example, face bare nature at the top of Mount Ktaadn and find himself quickly defeated, nothing within his thesaurus of discourse able to handle that barrenness. All he can do, ironically and pathetically, is speak of rocks as though they were sheep, seeking to inscribe a familiar pattern of discourse (probably reaching back to include traditional pastoral) into a turf that will simply refuse it. But precisely the opposite can happen in other versions of radical land, in places that are similar to Ktaadn but not nearly so overwhelming. Take, as another instance, a passage from the "Wednesday" chapter of *A Week* where Thoreau has been speaking of "pot-holes." These are holes in present or former riverbeds which were worn into the base rock by stones or pebbles that became lodged in a place, the action of wind and water forcing the stones to revolve and gradually cut those holes into the rock (247–48). Workers deepening the Pawtucket Canal in 1822 found potholes in ledges above the present riverbed, and others had been found nearly a thousand feet above the Merrimack and the Connecticut. This landscape was as old and elemental as the one on top of Ktaadn, but it produced none of the terrors that the top of Ktaadn did. Part of that relative ease came from the lesser extent of this bare, ancient rock; part from the fact that finding potholes did not involve a grueling mountain ascent and therefore did not raise expectations which the top quickly undid; another part from the fact that Thoreau had no problem in producing a mode of discourse that could handle the business of potholes.

Barbara Novak has shown in *Nature and Culture* how much such discourse was part of the available vocabulary of the time, how rocks were read as showing a "geological timetable" that offered clues to the primordial.[5] This practice was so popular and eagerly pursued that Novak can speak of geology as "the Great Myth of the nineteenth century."[6] That myth feasted on temporality and therefore helped to foster Thoreau's passionate preoccupation with traces of the ancient, with places that are *now* and that held what once *had been*: "In these very holes the Indians hid their provisions; but now there is no bread, but only its old neighbor stones at the bottom" (248). To touch at those very stones in those very holes is to come as close as one can to touching the verity of those who had used them. And one can do such touching because nature's discourse in this place is quite nearly literal, with the stones as engraving tools and the holes as the speech they wrote:

> The periods of Hindoo and Chinese history, though they reach back to the time when the race of mortals is confounded with the race of gods, are as nothing compared with the periods which these stones have inscribed. That which commenced a rock when time was young, shall conclude a pebble in the unequal contest. With such expense of time and natural forces are our very paving stones produced. They teach us lessons, these dumb workers; verily there are "sermons in stones, and books in the running streams." (248)

Thoreau conflates a series of ideas and images that make eminent sense together: the geological timetable; the stones as inscribing instruments; the holes as speech; the (mis)quotation from *As You Like It*. Together they create the discourse of this place, what Thoreau hears it say about times and traces and ways of producing speech; or perhaps what we hear is what he *makes* it say, the scene and what he knows falling so easily together that we are entitled to suspect the presence of several clichés. And indeed they are patently there, not only in the geological myth but in those lines from Shakespeare that had long been predictable in any situation where nature is seen as speaking.

But the recognition that discourse and temporality imply and implicate each other does not have to be received with quite the warmth, the overt affirmation, that it receives in these places. Novak and others have shown how Americans cherished geological formations in part because of the paucity of structures like castles, which could stand as touching places where traces of our history could be encountered. As Thoreau puts it just after the passage on potholes, "These, and such as these, must be our antiquities, for lack of human vestiges" (249). The older, then, the better; the more firmly inscribed in the past, the better; the more the inscription can tell of all that was so

far back, the better—in this case, at least. But Thoreau's profound
ambivalence about our relations to our contexts was never more subtly put than in the matter of natural texts and their relation to us. On
November 30, 1851, a cold and windy Sunday, he sat "on an oak
stump by an old cellar-hole and mused" (*J* 3:131). Permitting his
sight to wander toward the pines across the valley, "my eye finds
something which addressed itself to my nature. Methinks that in my
mood I was asking Nature to give me a sign. I do not know exactly
what it was that attracted my eye. I experienced a transient gladness,
at any rate, at something which I saw" (131). He goes on to describe
the pines on which his eye rested with pleasure ("on this my eyes pas-
tured"; a feasting was involved, as there often was in Wordsworth)
and rounds out the seeking for a sign by saying, "That, at any rate, is
what I got by my afternoon walk, a certain recognition from the pine,
some congratulation" (132). This is not exactly the biblical question
of signs, which ranges in scope and tonality from the Lord's insistence on offering a sign to the somewhat puzzled Ahaz ("Ask thee a
sign of the Lord thy God" [Isa. 7:11–14]) to Jesus' admonition to the
nobleman whose son was sick at Capernaum ("Except ye seek signs
and wonders, ye will not believe" [John 4:48]). Still, it has a significant
relation to the biblical pattern, which was almost certainly in Thoreau's mind during the scene on that November Sunday (in the "Sunday" chapter of *A Week*, he took up his own version of what others
were taking up in church). Indeed, the sign for which he asks and the
sort the bible propounds are metonyms in the field that takes in both.
And that the sign seeking should shift from asking divinity to asking
nature is one of his time's defining characteristics, the move putting
Thoreau into perfect consonance with the contemporary natural supernaturalism.[7]

But what Thoreau finds on this Sunday shows nothing like the clarity of biblical signs or the precision of the incisings of the stones in
the riverbed. The difference may have to do with what was asked for,
which—again a sign of the times—was far more intimate and personal, more the speaking of a Buberian "Thou," than the others we
have inspected. Thoreau's language is patently, deliberately vague:
"*something* that addresses itself to my nature"; "*Methinks* that in my
mood"; "I do not know exactly what it was"; "*something* which I saw";
"a *certain*" recognition" (my emphases). This is not the same as
Wordsworth's habitual covering of all possibilities, for example, in
"Tintern Abbey" ("If this be but a vain belief"), because Thoreau
leaves no space open to argue that it did not happen. It did happen,
but what made it happen and what came across to him are not, he

admits, entirely clear. The gladness that he felt is, he also admits, transient, of this occasion in this place.

And then, oddly and unsettlingly, Thoreau goes on without a paragraph break to meditate not only on what he saw but on the old cellar-hole beside the stump on which he was musing. The shifting of tone is as patent as his previous indefinition: "Where is my home? It is indistinct as an old cellar-hole, now a faint indentation merely in a farmer's field, which he has plowed into and rounded off its edges years ago, and I sit by the old site on the stump of an oak which once grew there. Such is the nature where we have lived" (132). His gladness is as transient as any settling-in that nature seems to offer, but it is tempered by his pondering of the equally transitory hole, once the ground and support of home, now nearly obliterated. Though the passage on potholes played with the relations of sign and temporality, potholes and cellar-holes, which are different modes of inscribing, have very different relations to the temporality implicit in every sort of sign. The potholes will last as long as the rock does; but the cellar-holes will last only until the next farmer fills them in. When nature speaks to *us*, the discourse and resultant gladness may be as transient as they are when we seek to inscribe home-places. It may well be that only when nature speaks to itself, inscribing holes for a sake that has nothing to do with us, that its discourse digs itself in.

This means that in extreme situations we may have to dig ourselves in by writing ourselves into the scene. Take, for example, the passage in *The Maine Woods* where Thoreau describes the rescue of a nearsighted friend who had gotten lost the evening before (262–63). One of the major moments of anxiety in his work turns up just before this passage, where Thoreau tells of his feelings during the night his companion was lost. His feelings are clearly inseparable from his sense of the immediate place:

> It was the most wild and desolate region we had camped in, where, if anywhere, one might expect to meet with befitting inhabitants, but I heard only the squeak of a night-hawk flitting over. The moon in her first quarter, in the fore part of the night, setting over the bare rocky hills, garnished with tall, charred, and hollow stumps or shells of trees, served to reveal the desolation. (261)

The next morning Thoreau "hallooed in a high key from time to time, though I had little expectation that I could be heard over the roar of the rapids" (261–62). But there *is* an answering shout, the completing of an aural circuit whose contours define the positions of Thoreau and his friend in this scene of vast indefinition. On the previous evening, the friend's nearsightedness had prevented the completion of a visual circuit, since he had not been able to see their Indian guide or the canoe, and that was the immediate cause of his getting lost for the night. He had sought, however, to leave the visual sign, taking an abandoned scrap of artifact and adding to it a piece of writing: "He had already stuck up the remnant of lumberer's shirt, found on the point, on a pole by the water-side, for a signal, and attached a note to it, to inform us that he had gone on to the lake, and that if he did not find us there, he would be back in a couple of hours"(263). There follows a quietly phrased echo of the previous evening's anxiety, the awareness that a wrong turn would have made looking for their nearsighted friend "like looking for a needle in a hay-mow." Clearly there was little chance of completing any circuit. That makes their next gesture a peculiarly knowing and ironic one: "We substituted for his note a card containing our names and destination, and the date of our visit, which Polis neatly enclosed in a piece of birch-bark to keep it dry. This has probably been read by some hunter or explorer ere this" (263).

There are several completions at play here, one especially brash. Given all their recent anxieties, the statement of their destination is brazen, even cocky. Yet it can also be read as asserting that *they* were *here* and had been so *at that time*, the only statement they could make with anything like assurance. Even more striking is the simple gesture of wrapping their card in birch bark, an act intended as protective but also one that showed signs of the previous evening's anxiety; they are using nature to enfold the supremely human just as nature had enfolded their friend the evening before. This act is homeopathic, using that which had caused trouble to ward off more of the same. But there is even more to the act because, as it completes itself, it also completes the circle of this self-contained subnarrative. Starting with the enfolding nature in which the friend had gotten lost, the text moves to two artifacts, clothing and writing, that have always served to define the human in the face of its natural opposite. There follows the brazen act of setting down their names (the basic Adamic gesture); then, as though acknowledging not only their arrogance but the context in which it appears, the text returns to the embrace of the natural, the birch bark enfolding all they can be certain of: their names, the date, and their destination.

This place in the vastness of the woods is obviously a scene of writing, more precisely of two such acts. The first is by the nearsighted friend, lost and making signs, the second by the assembled group, fixing themselves in time and place. It is also a scene of potential reading, again of two such acts, the first that of Thoreau and the guide, who might stumble upon the shred of shirt and the note attached to it, the second that of some hunter or explorer who might come across the card through which Thoreau and his companions name and locate themselves. Writing and reading are therefore cartographical gestures, acts of self-locating. They are precisely analogous to the shouting by Thoreau and his friend, which serves to pinpoint their positions as well as to clear a space in which their location defines not only their relation to each other but also their relation to place. This is the beginning of a map, the pinpointing of sites in the uncharted vastness. To put the action somewhat differently: the world imposes a set of events upon us, which causes us, in our turn, to impose points of reference on the world. We and the world happen to each other, the result a new anxiety but also the start of a demarcation and therefore a significant change in the character of the place. And all this is for the benefit of one radical act, an act that is surely among the most essential of all: this vastness needs to be mapped so that we can learn to *be* in the world with more clarity and certainty. What happens in this scene may well be a figure for all writing and reading, not just what happens here. From this point on, we shall consider writing and reading as acts through which we locate ourselves, their purpose to settle us more surely into the world.

This means that we need to ponder further the significance of place, especially place as a propounder of its own speech, not merely as a site for the utterance of others' discourse. This place became a scene of writing and reading because it became a place of anxiety. Anxiety compelled the nearsighted friend to leave his note, and precisely the same feeling, in company with several others, led the travelers to leave their card. But we must be very clear about the source and scene of anxiety; to mistake them would give a false character to the event. The main point is that the anxiety is within *them*: though Thoreau is always seeking to civilize these woods, he rarely slips into anthropomorphism, and he carefully avoids it here. What these woods speak openly, purely, is not anxiety as such but that which might cause anxiety, a capacity for creating absence—more precisely, for creating an interplay of absence and presence, enfolding and revealing, that is bound to create anxiety. To put it in a way we have seen at work in a variety of Thoreauvian contexts: this place is the point of meeting of two disparate, antagonistic discourses, one native, the other foreign. The first speaks of uncharted vastness, of absence and a grim embrace, the latter of modes of locating, assertions of presence that are also acts of clarification. The first is the speech of the Other, the latter purely our own. There is no separate speaker of the speech of the Other, yet that speech is elaborate and clear and comes from everywhere in this place. Place is therefore not only the scene of writing and reading but itself a wielder of discourse, speaking a unique mode of speech.

Consider, then, the travelers' irony in enclosing their card in a piece of birch bark. Their writing is enfolded by these quasi–book covers which mockingly partake in the binding and publishing of their text. The result is a volume in which we—our names, times, and places—are the subject of the text. And the text is protected by a piece of the same woods from which we sought protection by the making of such texts.

Nothing puts more clearly the shaky status of writing in these woods, its vulnerability in this place that is, at once, antagonist and shield. Writing needs all the protection it can get; at the same time, that bit of writing enclosed in birch bark challenges the unchartedness of this dense and dangerous place, arguing that we define ourselves by locating ourselves in place and time. The extent to which we place ourselves in the context of the alien is precisely the extent to which we add to our own definition. Map making is one more act through which we clarify what we are as well as where we are. Writing, in its turn, is a special kind of cartography, an appropriate line of work for this part-time surveyor and pencil maker. Wrapping one's card in some bark is, in one sense, a confession of vulnerability, but it is also an intentional act, and a forceful one at that. For if writing seems fragile in these overwhelming woods, it also performs assertive gestures, even pushy and arrogant ones, flaunting its own capacities while it seeks to flout the stern authority of the woods. Despite its relative fragility in this unforgiving context, it thrusts itself forward as a sign of the human, one that no other can match in import and exaltation. Of course the scrap of shirt is also a fragment of human presence, but its status within that discourse which puts forth signs of the human cannot match the capacity of writing within the same discourse. Nothing can match its ability to generate such meaning.

Thus, even in the inhuman woods one encounters a hierarchy in which writing has a place, another version of that ladder of valorization which writing cannot escape and in which it takes, as we have seen, a variety of positions. The one it takes in the Maine woods, the extraordinarily delicate balance of shakiness and exaltation, comes out wherever writing occurs in these woods, but it also comes out in other conditions where Thoreau ponders what is most human. In "The Allegash and East Branch," he had been watching a fire when he noticed a strange light coming from a piece of phosphorescent wood, chips of which he placed in his palm and showed to his friends. Its effect on him resonates at a number of levels: "I was exceedingly interested by this phenomenon, and already felt paid for my journey. It could hardly have thrilled me more if it had taken the form of letters, or of the human face. If I had met with this ring of light while groping in this forest alone, away from any fire, I should have been still more surprised. I little thought that there was such a light shining in the darkness of the wilderness for me" (180). Always alert to the potential for allegory, Thoreau acknowledges the import of the woods by seizing on the import of this ring of cold light. Most interesting is his association of light, the human face, and writing. As this light is opposed to the enfolding darkness of the woods, so is the human face opposed to this vast, nonhuman place. Of all the elements in the discourse that puts forth signs of the human, the face may come closest to writing in its capacity for signification. Thoreau thinks it does, yet light and all it stands for are up there with the best: "It could hardly have thrilled me more if it had taken the form of letters, or of the human face." The association of these three puts the point about writing precisely, its especially exalted status as our tool *and representative* in this place where everything else seems to be different from ourselves.

What, then, are we to do with Thoreau's ambivalence about writing as act and product? What are we to do with what seems elsewhere, often, to be its implacable secondariness? One routine passage in *The Maine Woods* asserts the superiority of the poetry and mythology of the trees to their human equivalents (229–30). Other than that, there is nothing that supports those passages in other texts where our current ways of writing are, at best, equivocal, mere holding operations until we get to the word of words and its great, serene sentence. Does Thoreau change his mind when he is confronted by the Maine woods (or their equivalent in the endless sands of Cape Cod)? Not really. The mode of the world he is in, and his way of being in that world, shift markedly among his various books, and especially between *A Week* and *Walden*, on the one hand, and *The Maine Woods* and *Cape Cod*, on the other. As there is shifting in the modes and his attendant ways of being, so is there shifting in his attitude toward writing. He does not change his mind about the secondariness of writing but comes to see writing as an especially valuable instrument for asserting human presence in a locale where such presence abides only with considerable strain. In a place like the Maine woods, where every scrap of civilization is welcome, and the most exalted are the most welcome, Thoreau cannot afford the luxury of his regular argument for writing's secondariness. In such places he needs all the help the civil can give. Indeed, we can work out patterns that show him eagerly searching for any evidence of the civil that might turn up in those places.

One conclusion is certain: Whatever its secondariness, one of the purposes of writing is to help us to achieve at-homeness in the world. The following chapter uncovers more of that purpose.

Chapter Three

INSCRIBING

THOREAU seems to be inconsistent on several important issues, arguing at one point that texts are radically autobiographical, at another that text and text maker should be, or are, distinct. It is not as though there were a chronological progression from one position to another, a narrative of mind changing. As in much else about Thoreau, there is no perceptible permanent reversal, no tale of a pilgrim getting to a place that has waited patiently for him. The fable in which Thoreau envisions himself as a pilgrim has other tracks in mind, other kinds of conclusiveness (insofar as it contains any conclusions at all). It shifts, backtracks, and sidesteps through a number of issues that dog Thoreau from the beginning of his work to its end—a dogging that is not a dialectic but is more like a systole-diastole play of elegant contraries.

Such moves bother some critics. Richard Bridgman, for example, spends a good deal of time in *Dark Thoreau* belaboring older readings of Thoreau that take him to be a democratic, nature-prowling moralist with particular thoughts about physical and spiritual economies. But such readings are no longer held without qualification in serious criticism, and never were so held in most of the best of the older studies.[1] Bridgman is especially assiduous in his search for situations where Thoreau contradicts himself, both in thought and personal attributes, and he argues from his examples that Thoreau avoided the implications of such contradictions: "his most crippling feature was that he dared not be a deeply reflective man."[2] Yet in fact we have seen Thoreau facing such issues with a determination more than equal to Bridgman's own: his uneasiness with binary structures and his persistent play with subtexts show no crippled knuckling under to the pressures of contrary states but a *searching out* of such states in order to find shapes to control ambivalence. Thoreau's task, like that of the Romantic ironist, was to make such tensions productive. If there is something in his work of "the siege of hateful contraries" suffered by Milton's Satan, there is also something in it of Blake's "Contraries," without which there "is no progression." In a very important sense, a good deal of Thoreau's work concerns a discourse on method, the sort that might lead eventually to what he calls "absolute or divine knowledge" but will certainly lead to a better mode of coping with the conditions that prevail.[3]

Take, once again, language and writing. If their centrality is evident, so too are their difficulty and stubbornness, their nearly triumphant resistiveness. It was with words as with so much else: Thoreau sought to live productively among the ambiguities and ambivalence endemic to the work of words and to all the other systems (his world owned several such) that harbored radical contradictions. That language can be both potent and shaky at once, simultaneously assertive and endangered, is shown with unmistakable clarity in the scene in *The Maine Woods* where the travelers wrap the name card in bark. Their gesture with the card pinpoints precisely the issue's tone and conditions.

In certain ways of immense significance to Thoreau's discourse on method, the ambiguities of written language extend to its status as metonymy, its position in a field that includes all sorts of counterpart practices. Thoreau's occasional praise of oral and written language reflects institutional compulsions, yet he is also compelled to show that he knows the production of meaning to be a more inclusive business than it is in *Walden's* chapter on reading. The scene with the name card located one issue perspicuously. Other instances from *The Maine Woods* help to expand the issue's context.

• I •

Sometimes a word sticks in the mind so much that it seems the appropriate sound when the need comes along to fill in a blank. That may happen even when it is not the obvious word, even when it has just been used in what seems quite another context. That happens about halfway through Thoreau's essay on the climb up Ktaadn. It was not long before the party came across evidence of loggers, traces of the civil such as logs tied to trees and a ringbolt drilled into a rock. He was particularly taken by the way in which every log was "marked with the owner's name" cut so deeply into the log as to be secure throughout the driving: "It requires considerable ingenuity to invent new and simple marks where there are so many owners. They have quite an alphabet of their own, which only the practiced can read. One of my companions read off from his memorandum book some marks of his own logs, among which there were crosses, belts, crow's feet, girdles, &c., as Y-girdle-crowfoot, and various other devices" (42). Through all the jamming and bruising of the drive, the logs hold on to what they are, and that, it seems, is another way of putting *whose* they are—note all the echoes of "own" in just these few lines. Absence and presence and ownership and identity play off against each other in a tension as tight and fierce as the jumbling of the logs. Each log is both the surrogate of the absent owner and a mark of his wealth. The log speaks for what had been present just as the card wrapped up in the bark said that the travelers had been there, and as the name on the card speaks also, and equally, of absence, so too does the mark on the log. These existential marks are institutional ones as well, signifiers of a civil structure, involving systems of exchange, that requires such marks and, in an important sense, speaks through them. On his later trip with Joe Polis, Thoreau remarked several times that this figure who touched on the primitive owned a good deal of property and was thinking of buying more.[4] Presence and absence and the savage, goods and the civil, cluster in still another grouping, each pushy and even belligerent because all the others are, and all this energy takes as its focal center the marks of the owner's name.

Yet the passage is curiously misleading; or, if that is too strong a word, the passage starts off with one sort of expectation and quickly but unobtrusively undoes it and compels us to consider other ways of performing what have always been familiar acts. Thoreau is precise when he begins the business of marks and names: "Every log is marked with the owner's name, cut in the sapwood with an axe, or bored with an auger." At this point in his exposition, we necessarily visualize "Smith," or the like, inscribed into the log in selections from our alphabet. Thoreau never openly tells us that this inference is mistaken. Rather, he makes us tell ourselves as the passage continues, and we hear about the need for a plenitude of marks to keep up with the plethora of owners. Business is clearly good, and the sign system had better be good in that way too. Business, in fact, is so good that old alphabets will not do (they may well have been quickly exhausted), and the loggers have had to shift into an arcane language, hieroglyphics understood only by the initiate. In effect, they have developed an institutional sign system, its signifiers too dense and complex for traditional bundles of signs. Thoreau's canniness does not become evident until several passages later, but at the least we are compelled to consider other possibilities of sign making for the same set of signifieds. These girdles and crowfeet are "marks," just as our own alphabet is. The term "marks," in fact, turns up three times in the passage, along with a single "marked," the term clustering about itself a rapidly developing set of observations on systems of inscribing.

The clustering continues a few pages later, all the play on "mark" finding another scene to work in when the travelers come across the site of an old logger's camp: "In the midst of a dense underwood, we noticed a whole brick, on a rock, in a small run, clean, and red, and square, as in a brick-yard, which had been brought thus far formerly for tamping. Some of us afterward regretted that we had not carried this on with us to the top of the mountain, to be left there for our mark. It would certainly have been a simple evidence of civilized man" (45). Signs and the civil come together in yet another way, this time having less to do with systems of exchange than with, once again, presence. It is not, however, the past presence of an individual (as with the inscribings on the name card and on the logs) but of a species in a place where it seems always on the verge of being thoroughly overwhelmed. Thoreau's sense of the relations of institutions and discourse takes on a different tonality here than it generally does elsewhere, because there is, in this instance, no sense of suspicion about power but, quite the opposite, a satisfaction in the power of the civil as it emerges in this sign, "our mark."

These nearly adjacent passages, linked through the play on "mark," complete a series of examples of the way we send out and understand signals about ourselves. At one end is the first reference to the owner's name. Ghostly but clear, it announces his name in the usual way and in the language he shares with so many of our kind. Moving out from that end of the spectrum, one finds the logger's hieroglyphics, a far more private system for a far smaller audience. At the far end is the brick, described in the most mundane terms— clean, red, square, as though sitting in a brickyard, a piece of potential construction "which had been brought thus far for tamping." The spectrum of marks ends with the familiar and comfortable. In one sense, the brick counters the arcaneness of the loggers' inscribings by bringing the spectrum around to an object that is almost comically commonplace. But in another, it counters what we consider the primary mode of signification, the alphabet through which we say our names, because it is an object, an unlettered thing, a very different way of stating that we have been *here*. Yet what it states is at least as rich as what could be said by the other modes in the spectrum. The brick is the emblem of humans as master builders. Putting it down on top of the mountain, "to be left there for our mark," would be as aggressive a comment as the other modes could make, its apparent slightness belied by its richness of reference. Once again, Thoreau finds a place in the line that goes from Blake to Stevens. His gesture with the brick finds its precisest analogy in Stevens's jar in Tennessee, set down in the slovenly wilderness.

This spectrum speaks of signs and their making and their function in distributing meaning. As such it touches at the center of *The Maine Woods*, which takes sign making as a major theme, one that holds the three essays together just as the nature of the woods does. That theme is so closely tied to the nature of the woods as to be, in several senses, inseparable from it. The circumstances in the Maine woods force Thoreau to ignore his pervasive uneasiness about writing: we must work with what we have in order to learn to *be* in the woods. In so working, Thoreau came finally to understand that modes of signification shift as situations shift, and that in such shifting, one develops a broader system of signs. The statement made in these passages goes for the book as a whole, and both statement and book serve to place our ordinary letters, the stuff of old hornbooks and modern spellers, in a far more encompassing context than they usually inhabit. In one way *The Maine Woods* redeems our writing, but in so doing it takes from writing its primacy and privilege and shows it to be a single element in a very considerable field.

Further, this statement has much to say not only about our literacy but about ourselves as persons both separate and civil. Every example in the spectrum has also to do with problems and perplexities of presence. By virtue of that linkage it puts ourselves, our texts, and our places into a package profoundly involved with systems of signification. That, too, goes for *The Maine Woods* as a whole, and, indeed, not only for this book but for every other book Thoreau wrote.

From now on in this study I shall use the term "inscribings" to indicate the entire field of which writing is a part. The term has a particular point: in *The Maine Woods* and elsewhere, much of what it refers to is literally incised, while that which is not literally is always metaphorically so. Play of an incisive sort turns up often in *The Maine Woods*, most of it based on the categories of the spectrum we have just inspected; but these further examples are more than mere elaborations, because Thoreau's fascination with discourse and sign making and their relations to the institutions we inhabit leads to all manner of speculations about texts and signification.

Take, for example, a passage a few pages after the spectrum, when the concept of "marks" is still very much on Thoreau's mind. As they poled up the river "some of the party read their own marks on the huge logs which piled up high and dry on the rocks on either hand" (52). Ten pages earlier we had seen one of the party "read off from his memorandum book some marks of his own logs" (42). At this later point they read them not just in books but in the things themselves. We have moved from the record to the act, from the dictionary to hands-on employment, a move toward a greater immediacy (recall the plays with "recording" and "recorded" in the *Journal* passage about libraries). But with immediacy comes uncertainty, unease, the tentative and the aleatory. It was simply a coincidence that they had passed by a jam of logs incised with their own marks. They and the logs could easily have been elsewhere; in fact, the logs were supposed to be. Their current condition was probably the result of a spring jam, and before they could be loosened they "would have to wait for another great freshet . . . if they lasted so long." So much for the security of our speculations. The chanciness of the meeting matches the chanciness of the operation in a fit too neatly put to pass by this master of the sardonic. And there is more that he does not miss: the play of property and presence broached at every point in the spectrum picks up the ironies of this aleatory affair and takes them into a complex of identities and geographies and spatiotemporal puzzles: "It was singular enough to meet with property of theirs which they had never before seen, and where they had never been before, thus detained by freshets and rocks when on its way to them" (53). In one sense, this is Thoreau practicing his cherished rhetoric of self-correction. The spectrum he had just drawn seemed both subtle and coherent, able to take in a range of semiotic possibilities that would form and contain the men's attempts to be at home in this world. But in fact it was not so comfortable, and neither were they—no more so than they would be on that later trip when they wrapped the name card in bark. Leaving a brick on top of the mountain as "a simple evidence of civilized man" hints at a pervasive uneasiness about their present modes of being. The subtextual muttering of that uneasiness can be heard at points such as the business with the brick, and it emerges in snappish frankness at occasions like those with the log at the freshet.[5] Thoreau is so far from being evasive about the import of what he sees that he draws out to the fullest its oxymoronic tinge. In so correcting himself, he puts with intricate precision what such inscribings have to say about the meaning and the difficulty of learning to be in such places.

Part of what they say has to do with the passage from memo to log, the secondary to the primary. The marks written down in the memorandum book take a far more comforting form than do the counterpart marks cut into the log for the sake of commerce. To go from the marks in the book to those on the log is to move from a place of ease to one where various kinds of unease seem to be always waiting to go to work. Further, Thoreau's comments on the puzzling relations among ourselves, place, text, and time are inspired not only by the unease but by what much of it is based on, the lack of broadly sustaining designs of order. In fact, his compulsion to create a wider field of inscribings is inspired by that lack.

The loggers' hieroglyphics help us to understand these points more fully. Within the chaos of these woods there is the beginning of the systematic. Within this place of the mainly untouched there is a line drawn between ourselves and a piece of the woods (a line of precisely the sort Thoreau and his friend tried to establish when they sought to regain contact). In this place of chaos and the discordant there is concord between some images in a book and some incisings on a log, images that not only record the marks on the logs but also represent all sorts of civil institutions. That such ordering has to do with various sorts of inscribing tells a good deal about the meaning of inscribing to Thoreau. Among other things, it shows that the expansion of the field to include many more activities besides what we usually call "writing" affects our use of those activities. If there is a variety among the inscribings that matches the variety of such needs, then the field of inscribings will have the utmost flexibility, the greatest possible usefulness in getting us to be at home in this or any place. Broadening the possibilities of discourse gives us, in all sorts of senses, a greater hold on things. In the previous chapter I argued that writing, for Thoreau, is in effect a form of cartography. That is all the more true for the broader field of inscribing, one of the supplest instruments shaped by this maker of all sorts of maps.

But Thoreau is also bedeviled by a frequently bitter play between desire and capability. Consider the bemused passage where some of the travelers meet with possessions they had never seen before, and do so in a place where they had never been before. The citizens of the site of conclusion are up visiting in the site of origin; absence and presence cannot seem to make up their minds about where they should do their business; we meet our representations in a very odd narrative where nothing seems to go as it is expected to go. And here, of course, is the complicity of the memorandum book, its guilt and requisite blame. Through its shape and organization, that book makes implicit comments about design and temporality, and those comments cannot hold up when we encounter the actual markings and the conditions of their context. We read the lines in the book from left to right, the pages go in the same direction, and we read the book from front to back. Part of the business of institutions is to establish such expectations of order and to affirm their rightness; indeed, they seek further to affirm that the question of what is orderly can be answered only by examples such as these, that is, by the institutions' own productions. Part of Thoreau's business in his pondering of institutions is to query their power to establish such criteria. Several of his comments on institutions, quoted above in another context, can help us here as well: "Statements are made but partially. Things are said with reference to certain conventions or existing institutions, not absolutely. . . . When facts are seen superficially, they are seen as they lie in relation to certain institutions, perchance" (J 3:85). Insofar as our expectations are based on the teachings of institutions, they can never quite match up to what emerges from the immediacy they must ultimately confront; and that implicit narrative structure which informs not only memorandum books but our natural and spiritual myths (Thoreau himself often dwelt on the concept of "westering") is fostered by all sorts of institutions which give shape to our lives. But the order the travelers find when they come across their logs is anything but front to back. In fact, it is doubtful whether any set of hyphenated words can counter the refusal of that order to settle down to anything understandable, anything so familiar as, say, a simple doubling back. Thoreau stands in the gap between the book and the logs, expectation and disruption, a progressive conception of things and the wildly skewed actuality. Desire and capability cannot quite coalesce. Our experience lacks connections at some very crucial points.

And yet, with all these difficulties that can never be fully mastered, Thoreau's establishment of a broader field of inscribings is a lucid and (given the nature of the opposition) relatively successful attempt to understand and cope with the inevitable gaps in experience. If ambivalence and ambiguity, a sense of indefinite suspension, are the requisite tonal components of the situation Thoreau sees, that gives the matter of inscribings a mottled tinge, but it does not make the matter confused or radically ineffective. In fact, the contrary is usually the case.

The passage has still more to tell us. One of the major characteristics of the ultimate discourse Thoreau envisions is its comprehensiveness, its ability to say it all. Any steps that advance to more encompassing modes of discourse are steps to the final one, and if the interim models are necessarily riddled with gaps, they still manage to prefigure the sense of expansive reach to be seen in the seamless conclusion. The issue of inscribings has added matters of immense significance to what we have learned so far about the components of Thoreau's fable. Like all fables, it is a narrative, but now we know that it questions aspects of narrativity, at least of the left-to-right sort. We are beginning to suspect that the ultimate sentence, though itself necessarily seamless, may have unseemly things to say when it finally says it all.

• II •

Thoreau was fascinated with pictographs. He comes back several times to the logger's crosses and crowfeet and makes a special point about an image to which Joe Polis gave concentrated significance. They had come to the Indian's camping ground, "one of his homes," and found an inscription in charcoal drawn on the trunk of a fir tree: "It was surmounted by a drawing of a bear paddling a canoe, which he said was the sign which had been used by his family always. The drawing, though rude, could not be mistaken for anything but a bear, and he doubted my ability to copy it. The inscription ran thus, *verbatim et literatim*. I interline the English of his Indian as he gave it to me" (199). Thoreau reproduces his copy of the image and also puts into a column on the page the interplay of English and "Indian," the column obviously meant to represent the verticality of the writing on the tree. The column is organized by dates, and Thoreau's eye must have been caught by the precision of their relations, two years apart and the days almost exactly the same: July 26, 1853; July 15, 1855; July 26, 1857. In a curious interplay that may have had to do with Polis's personal history, the first two entries were in the Indian's native language, the latest in English ("Io. Polis").

Recording of that sort was clearly a common practice with Polis. Later in the essay Thoreau tells how they set out from another camp, "the Indian as usual having left his gazette on a tree" (271). Such scenes have obvious relations to the event with the name card: with each, the affirming of a name creates a play of inscriber, text, place, and time, with all that such gestures signify for Thoreau's kind of cartography. But in this case there is something more, for time turns into histories of several sorts that necessarily intertwine. Take the passage we just inspected about the owners encountering their logs. Inscriber, text, place, and time come into that scene too, though with nothing like the stress on the *passing* of time that turns time into history. But it is precisely that stress that characterizes the scene where the travelers ponder the paddling bear and the columnar chronology. In fact, the passage reeks of history of a ritualistic sort. The precision of the timing of Polis's various visits makes those visits ceremonial, like the anniversary trips to a grave or a holy site. To confirm and expand that point, there is the totemic image of the bear, "which he said was the sign that had been used by his family always." Like all ritual figures, the bear partakes of the timeless. It is "always," and it stands fast where the family history cannot. That history, in its turn, is both unified and flowing, and as it flows, it absorbs the personal history they read, the one that moves down the trunk in its tale of Polis's visits to the place. Being and signification, temporality and text, take on a more intricate play than at most other points in the book, because *The Maine Woods* as a whole is less concerned with history than with the more immediate issue of getting to be in the world. This scene adds significantly to the field of inscribings that runs through *The Maine Woods*, and it stands out not only for its intricacy but for its special emphases. The field as a whole emerges with impressive fullness in the essays of *The Maine Woods*, for those trips compelled Thoreau to test out the breadth of such a field. That is why we have looked at that book first, though the essays come comparatively late in Thoreau's writings. Inscribings that dwell on history and temporality had in fact been explored in detail much earlier, particularly in *A Week*.

The kind of time that turns into history pervades *A Week* at every stratum, and it stretches out to include not only local histories but sweeps of ever-increasing grandeur. This permits all sorts of interplay between the narrativity of Thoreau's text and the narratives enfolded within it. Still, narratives have a "where" as well as a "what happens next," and one of the effects of Thoreau's cartographical gestures is to query the relations of those questions. He knew a great deal about the massacre and abductions that studded the histories of these places by the river, so that *A Week* becomes, in a very important sense, an establishment of the credentials of place, of its status as something more than a spot one happens to float by. Yet these acts of valorization come finally to take in more than any single spot, their purpose more inclusive than treating any particular place as a transparent palimpsest.

One instance can stand as a model for the rest. Thoreau begins his telling of the story of Hannah Dustan by playing on questions of presence, seeking, somewhat stiffly, to tie what he can see to what he knows happened at this place. It was "probably about this time in the afternoon" that two white women and a boy "were hurriedly paddling down this part of the river, between the pine woods which then fringed these banks" (320). Tying the tale to a specific place gives that tale, one may hope, a kind of credibility, the truth value that we associate (delusively or not) with immediacy. Place, text, and the touchable feed off each other in what the broker who brings them together hopes will be mutual enrichment. But the sense of strain is too evident on this page about Hannah Dustan to do much more than call attention to itself.

Thoreau continues the tale in conventional past definite discourse, through the point where the women and the boy perform their elaborate massacre, sliding, at that point, into a present tense whose clumsiness undoes his intent to enliven: "Early this morning this deed was performed, and now, perchance, these tired women and this boy, their clothes stained with blood, and their minds racked with alternate resolution and fear, are making a hasty meal of parched corn and moose-meat, while their canoe glides under these pine roots whose stumps are still standing on the bank" (322). The end of the sentence falls flat in its attempt to have us consider the problem of linking points in time, its relation to what precedes it merely stillborn. As the narrative continues, the present tenses pile up in patent uneasiness until, near the end of the passage, Thoreau tries another tack. This time the turn is less obtrusive, and it goes at least partway toward rescuing the slippage that had come to beset his story. "Sometimes they pass an Indian grave surrounded by its paling on the bank, or the frame of a wigwam, with a few coals left behind, or the withered stalks still rustling in the Indian's solitary cornfield on the interval. The birch stripped of its bark, or the charred stump where a tree has been burned down to be made into a canoe, these are the only traces of man,—a fabulous wild man to us" (323).

Thoreau understands that the relations of place, text, and time have a great deal to do with matters of narrative stance. First there is the shift in tonality as Thoreau has the travelers focus on shards and fragments, the few coals, the withered stalks, the charred stump. The tale of abduction and massacre turns into a parable of absence and presence as those states come to us through the "traces" that are still there: "the only traces of man,—a fabulous wild man to us." Thoreau's instincts have taken him to a way that works better than all the clumsy juggling of tense. He imagines the travelers doing what he himself finds it useful to do, ponder the meaning of pieces of a world, leftovers and remnants, that are synecdoches for that world, pondering, further, the relation of that world to our own. That we too are involved comes out in several elements in the passage. First there is the odd statement that this is "a fabulous wild man *to us*." That point has no relevance to the tale of Hannah Dustan, but it has the utmost relevance to the stage Thoreau has come to in his passionate search for method, for a way to get at what he has been seeking from the beginning of the passage, a tense temporal density. And in fact what happens next happens because of the impetus the shards and "to us" had established. The next paragraph blends the journeys of Thoreau and his brother, "who loiter here this autumn evening," with the journey of the survivors of the abduction, who "have already glided out of sight" while "the swift stream bear[s] them onward to the settlements." This time the interplay of two present tenses, pointing in rich coherence toward two different times, works wonderfully well. It does so because all those shards become points of triangulation between us and Dustan's party, which means that the Indians can become fabulous to us as well as to them. To put it another way, one that leads us directly into some of the deeper reaches of Thoreau's way of reading the world: the triangulations in time that the imagined remnants perform are precisely analogous in function to the way in which travelers separated in the woods seek to link up to each other. The imagined stumps and stalks and the hallooing of the travelers become instruments of location within the jumbles of woods and times in which we must find our place. One of the many reasons for the richness of this passage is the way it illuminates the relations among several cartographical acts.

The passage comes to an end with the wrap-up of the tale and a final focus on a specific concrete object that has stood long enough to tie the past to later times, old present tenses to new ones, through its firm substantial presence, its stubborn being-here: "The family of Hannah Dustan all assembled alive once more, except the infant whose brains were dashed out against the apple-tree, and there have been many who in later times have lived to say that they had eaten of the fruit of that apple-tree" (323–24).

The section on Hannah Dustan shows Thoreau's way of probing possibilities of method, turning them over and around until the pressure of his needs creates the appropriate tools, if otherwise none can be found. History comes too cheaply at the beginning of the passage, and it comes (if it comes at all) in a kind of desperation when he turns in the middle toward the ungainly presentation in a present indicative active. So much for dealing with the existent in such terms, with "these pine roots whose stumps are still standing on the bank." That this vaguely rendered scene takes part in a here and now is clearly not enough: compare the flaccidity of this passage with the sinewy accomplishments of the scene with the apple tree. The difference comes, of course, from what lies between them, the piling up of traces, the shards of what had been. What we, echoing Thoreau, have been calling by the term "marks" can also, in certain instances, be called "traces" as well. (Of course insofar as they are marks, they have a place in the field we have called "inscribings.") The imagined traces that appear along the bank—the frame of a wigwam or "the charred stump where a tree has been burned down to be made into a canoe"—live in a special kind of time that has been turned into history. Thoreau often uses the term "traces" to stand for that kind of "mark," the kind whose immediacy stretches back to a very far distance but touches at every point between us and that distance—which means, among other things, that touching at the trace, like eating the fruit of that old apple tree, comes to seem like a communion with origin as well as several points in between. Traces are ceremonial instruments that permit the one who ponders them to take part in an extensive continuum.

Given all that we have seen of the fable so far, these matters are clearly significant parts of its business. Not only does the fable involve a guest, but it is clear from the Dustan passage that it also involves a search for methods to perform that quest. (The ultimate modes of speaking that are among the objects of the quest are themselves methods. The fullest import of this point will come clear in the final chapter.) Communion with the past, which turns up in the business about traces and the old apple tree, makes equally eminent sense in terms of genre. That a fable could involve rituals should come as no surprise; many fables do, for they often turn to magic to make matters come out right. Nor, given Thoreau's long-standing interest in our engagement with place, should it be at all surprising that ritual gestures of this sort should be part of the field of inscribings. Such gestures are acts of self-location, especially location in time. We have already seen one instance in the Polis family totem, itself an active synecdoche that stands for the unity of a clan and each member's participation in all its past and present immediacies. Each time Polis puts down the date of his appearance at that camp he takes part in the whole history for which the totem stands, locating himself in his place within that history. (Of course each appearance adds to the history as well. It is characteristic of totems to be forever active, as alive in the present tense as they are in every past one.) In fact, Polis does no differently than those who "in later times have lived to say that they had eaten of the fruit of that apple-tree." What Polis and the others do is precisely what Thoreau seeks to do when he turns antique remnants into those marks that are traces. Thoreau's passion for traces ("passion" is not too strong a word, considering their prevalence in his work) has a good deal of shamanism about it—not especially surprising for one who once was tempted to eat a woodchuck raw so he could partake of its wildness.

We see this and much more in an especially resonant passage in the "Sunday" chapter of *A Week*. Thoreau works his way through issues of belief ("It is necessary not to be Christian, to appreciate the beauty and significance of the life of Christ" [67]) to systems of belief, institutional schemes that he quickly makes architectural. Most people, he argues, "have their scheme of the universe all cut and dried . . . which they set up between you and them in the shortest intercourse; as ancient and tottering frame with all its boards blown off" (69). The main problem with such edifices is that they get between us and the sky, blocking the light and the view, when all the wise man wants is the purest transparency: "The wisest man preaches no doctrines; he has no scheme; he sees no rafter, not even a cobweb, against the heavens" (70). Thoreau puts the point in terms that sound like a late assertion of Blake: "If I ever see more clearly at one time than at another, the medium through which I see is clearer."[6] That is why he has turned Abraham, Isaac, and Jacob into "the subtilest imaginable essences, which would not stain the morning sky." In Sunday terms, the position is radically, traditionally Protestant, stressing the immediacy of contact between oneself and heaven, or, more precisely, the perniciousness of schemes that prevent such immediacy.

And then there is the relationship of immediacy and authority. His readers, themselves the victims of similar schemes, are urged to "examine your authority," spell out its justification, reveal the sources of its power. Thoreau then opens a barrage on the builders of such schemes, bringing in elements we have seen in the relations of discourse and power, examining the way those elements tie in to certain kinds of cartography: "The perfect God in his revelations of himself has never got to the length of one such proposition as you, his prophets, state. Have you learned the alphabet of heaven, and can count three? Do you know the number of God's family? Can you put mysteries into words? Do you presume to fable of the ineffable? Pray, what geographer are you, that speak of heaven's topography?" (70). Words and figures and lines drawn on a map—the instruments Thoreau was to extol when he was surrounded by the Maine woods—are secondary tools at best, dependent on some metasystem that apparently does not exist. The passage offers no recourse against Thoreau's incisive questions. Behind the play of these discourses, there is obviously nothing but empty air, and that is precisely the kind of irony Thoreau cherishes most, the kind that, at once, removes and gives. Vacancy of the sort revealed by Thoreau's attack is just what the wise man wants. The space in back of those discourses turns out to be the purest form of transparency and therefore the most desirable medium through which seeing can occur. When the wise man clears the air, that act has, it seems, all sorts of salutary results.

And yet there *is* authority to be found among terrestrial things, though it is not among the shabby baggage of our schemes but in something more immediate and concrete, more precise and far more subtle: "in all my wanderings, I never came across the least vestige of authority for these things. They have not left so distinct a trace as the delicate flower of a remote geological period on the coal in my grate"

(70). This is as pure a version of the term "trace" as we shall find in Thoreau's work, and it adds a good deal to what we saw in the Dustan passage. For one thing, it indicates part of the reason for Thoreau's uneasiness and impatience with institutional discourse: this comment ties truth and authority to immediacy and tangibility in an unmistakable way. However delicate the trace of the flower, it bears a self-evident force. It is here, it is palpable, and it is an unimpeachable witness. It bears no institutional marks but only its own still-delicate shape—a delicacy that ought never to be confused with fragility, for it has survived beyond all those ancient and tottering frames of institutional schemas. Further, rather than getting in the way between us and old affairs, it links us directly to them in the most unmediated (if fragmentary) way. Universal religious structures can never be as convincing of the possibility of communion as are traces such as this.

It is thus that the field of inscribings can tie us to every temporal dimension, from the relatively recent past that held the doings of a woodchopper to the most ancient local events. In "A Winter Walk" he remarks on the "many traces from which we may learn the chopper's history" and on the way in which "this one chip contains inscribed on it the whole history of the woodchopper and his world" (*Excursions*, 121). Going back further in time, in a brilliant passage from the *Journal* of November 29, 1853, he dwells on an elaborately carved Indian pestle that is "affecting, as a work of art by a people who have left so few traces of themselves, a step beyond the common arrowhead and pestle and axe" (*J* 5:525). And he can go back even further, for he sees the nature of "traces" as such that they leave the way open to envisioning the scene of ultimate origin, the terminus a quo. Three weeks before Thoreau saw the finely carved pestle, he tells how he loves to see, "even in midsummer, the old water-line of the last year, far away from the edge of the shrunken stream." It reminds him of the floods of fall and spring and, through them, "of the origin of things, as it were, when water was a prevailing element" (*J* 5:485; cf. *J* 2:154). And there are living traces of those times as well, creatures at once inscribers and inscribed. In the "Wednesday" chapter of *A Week*, he speaks of "the smaller bittern, the genius of the shore." It is

> a bird of the oldest Thalesian school, and no doubt believes in the priority of water to the other elements; the relic of a twilight ante-diluvian age which yet inhabits these bright American rivers with us Yankees. There is something venerable in this melancholy and contemplative race of birds, which may have trodden the earth while it was yet in a slimy and imperfect state. Perchance their tracks too are still visible on the stones. (235–36)

The spectrum of inscribings can reveal what we most want to know about others as well as ourselves, their ways of being in places and therefore—the ultimate question for Thoreau at every point in his work—their ways of being in the world.

To go from language to writing, as we have done so far, has a plain inevitability. To go from language to writing to inscribings is not so plainly inevitable, though the evidence that is beginning to accumulate makes the inevitability as rigorous as in the more patent previous business. To take this progress further, into our involvement in the world, is to continue along a route that has a number of similar surprises as well as all sorts of indigenous compulsions.

It certainly had such compulsions for Thoreau. If the field of inscribings takes in ways of making meaning that are broader in kind and scope than those that "Reading" takes up, it takes in a good deal more than even the corrective to "Reading" in the first paragraph of "Sounds." The "language which all things and events speak without metaphor, which alone is copious and standard" (111), is itself only a segment of a much greater whole. It is one way among others of making meaning happen, one subject in a broad field. And it is with the ambiguities of "subject" that we are now particularly concerned. When I say that X is the subject of the sentence I just uttered, I could mean that X is the sentence's main actor, the subject who performs the verb. Alternatively I could mean that X is the sentence's subject matter. We may refuse to see these alternatives as mutually exclusive. Thoreau so refuses. Further, the fact that "subject" can also involve power and dominion—one is subject to forces that are greater than oneself, one is in a state of subjection—adds to the alternatives. And that there may well be a sense in which we are our own subject matter, makers of ourselves as well as the texts of which we are subjects (and perhaps makers of ourselves in and through such texts) is itself a subject worthy of our concern. Our involvement in the world has to do at every point with our making in the world, a making closely related to several of the senses in which we can be subject to ourselves.

Those shards Thoreau calls "traces" suggest some of the ways he understood this business. Traces permit us to take part in diachronic lines, touching at apple trees that the long-ago dead have touched, reaching into potholes where ancient Indians reached to store their tribal bread. In fashioning diachronic lines, we map out areas of temporality as surely and as effectively as the surveyor maps the farmers' fields outside Concord. Such mapping means locating ourselves with greater precision, for whatever else a map is about, it is always about where *we* are. And that, as it turns out, is true for synchronic lines as well as diachronic ones. If the immediacy of Stonehenge can stretch

us into contact with heroes of Ossian's sort (in *AW*, 344, he compares
the radical shapes of Stonehenge to what Ossian and Homer show of
the "essential parts of a man"), so does "a new and rare plant in Concord" lead Thoreau to think how "it grows alike on the bank of the
Concord and of the Mackenzie River, proving them a kindred soil"
(*J* 9:56). But it is not only riverbanks that have such lines drawn between them: "Through this leaf I communicate with the Indians who
roam the boundless Northwest."

At this point in his play with temporal cartography, some of the
deeper concerns of Thoreau's engagement with traces come clearly
to the surface. Thoreau is most taken with traces of the human. At
the end of each kind of line, synchronic and diachronic, stands a version of elemental man. It is not that the lines *necessarily* attest to the
human but that Thoreau sees them as doing so, here and very often
elsewhere. The practice is habitual, as though this act has as much to
do with the locating of others as it does with locating himself.

One of the ways in which Thoreau sought such multiple locatings
was through his quest for old cellar-holes. On May 12, 1850, he visited the probable site of the old Dustan house, one of the eight houses
burned on the day of the massacre and the abduction. All that is left
of the house is "a slight indentation in a corn-field, three or four feet
deep, with an occasional brick and cellar-stone turned up in plowing"
(*J* 2:7). Other "old cellar-holes in the neighborhood" are the likely
sites of the concurrent tragedies. There is a very important sense in
which his presence at that particular cellar-hole cleans up some of the
problems Thoreau had when he was recounting the Dustan episode
in *A Week*. The struggle to reach a viable stance toward the historical,
one that would sustain both its integrity and ours, had worked itself
out in a clumsy but sufficient way toward the end of the Dustan passage, and it had done so through his imagining of "traces of man."
What he sees of the Dustan house has the aptest sort of irony, for it
is precisely the same sort of remnant he had imagined in terms of
Indians several years earlier, and it speaks in the same way of the play
of absence and presence. What he had once usefully imagined he
confronts in actuality now, as though the need to resolve the struggle
in the Dustan passage from *A Week* were still working away at him
and could be resolved only through the palpable presence of something more than an imagined remnant.

That Thoreau tends to see cellar-holes as focal points of history can
be shown through the variety of uses to which he puts these shards.
In a passage written some months after his visit to the Dustan site, he
expresses that tendency in a form harmonious with a major discourse
of his time:

As for antiquities, one of our old deserted country roads, marked only by the parallel fences and cellar-hole with its bricks where the last inhabitant died, the victim of intemperance, fifty years ago, with its bare and exhausted fields stretching around, suggests to me an antiquity greater and more remote from the America of the newspapers than the tombs of Etruria. I insert the rise and fall of Rome in the interval. This is the decline and fall of the Roman Empire. (J 2:158–59)

Such harmony has its interest as we seek to understand his sense of discourses and institutions, and especially as we see how much he partook of public myth; but it is finally less significant than his relation to other sorts of speech that tell more cogently and potently of what it means to be in this world where he looks for location.

Toward the end of the "Monday" chapter, Thoreau goes over the history of Salmon Brook, which he describes as "a favorite haunt of the aborigines" (160). In fact, though, the history that interests him most has to do with Indians only indirectly, focusing instead on old John Lovewell, Indian fighter, farmer, and cobbler, who lived to be 120 years old and whose house "is said to have been the first which Mrs. Dustan reached on her escape from the Indians." The passage fascinates in part because of Thoreau's fascination with the personality of old Lovewell: "He was remembered by some who were recently living, as a hale old man who drove the boys out of his orchard with his cane" (161). What Thoreau knows of the man comes to him largely through written local histories, those secondary instruments that can fill us with facts and through which, if we click with the proffered material, we can raise some sense of the old "subject." Writers of texts about nature have trouble getting through to him—their words are unable to stretch beyond familiar home-places into those places of nature no word has managed to touch—but there seem to be situations where words can draw up within themselves the persuasive semblance of an old subject.

Yet however well words work, there are suggestions in this passage that they are not quite good enough, that they might well need support. The passage focuses persistently, obsessively, on other possibilities within the field of inscribings, especially the cellar-holes that stud Lovewell's landscape. The reference to white settlers near the beginning of the first paragraph comes close to identifying them with their traces, the wrecks of ubiquitous apple trees as well as "some dents in the earth, where their houses stood." Near the old Lovewell house is "the cellar and the grave-stone of Joseph Hassell," who also fell victim to the Indians. But what touches Thoreau most is the trace of old Lovewell that the earth still manages to hold: "I have stood in the dent of his cellar on the bank of the brook, and talked there with one whose grandfather had, whose father might have, talked with Love-well" (161). To stand in such a place and to talk with one person is, in effect, to talk with many, to take part in a line and through that line to reach toward the fullest sense we can get of the original in-scriber, the one who carved out the whole. The cellar-hole becomes a place where Thoreau seeks diachronic touching. Such an act offers Thoreau what no bundle of words can offer, what the inscription of the family totem offers to Joe Polis, participation in a line of which he is an integral part and to which his gesture makes its own contri-bution. When Thoreau stands in the dent of Lovewell's cellar, that is as much a ritual movement, a sacramental act, as Joe Polis's carvings on the tree. It is also precisely analogous to touching at the apple tree against which the Dustan infant's brains had been dashed out.

Yet even here we have to be cautious about claiming thorough suc-cess, as cautious as Thoreau obviously was: "whose father *might have* talked to Lovewell" is clearly a conditional statement, one that leaves it uncertain whether the reaching back has worked in any full and absolute sense. (There would never be a "might have" in the inscrib-ings of Joe Polis.) Even these moving traces of human presence might have indigenous limits. The line might have built-in lacunas that would make it less than perfect, less than absolute in its certainty that nothing has been left out. Of course we have to stress the "might," the play of possibility: the line could, after all, be pure, with every slot filled up though we shall never know for sure. We also have to stress that if there can be no absolute certainty, there is at least the family line ("grandfather . . . father") which Thoreau can observe. If there is a possible imperfection, there is at least a sort of link, a point that Thoreau can touch at simply by standing in the hole. And if it is only *some* sort of link, it is at least a link of a sort, and that will have to do under our current possible conditions.

Having access to a field of inscribings offered more to Thoreau than any single inscribing could; but this passage makes quite clear that even this favored kind of inscribing, the dents of old cellar-holes, in partnership with the kind to which he devoted most of his life, might still not be enough to get at what he wants in the fullest possi-ble way. He is still in a state of longing, which explains why he so often shifts the direction of his feelings from backward to forward, from origin to end, from what might turn out to be insufficient in-scribings to sentences he can conceive of (but not, at the moment, conceive) that are able to say it all. Versions of that shift appear in all of his major works.

Now that we have seen some of the import of old cellar-holes, some of their status as linking points, some of the attendant uncertainty that is likely to leave us with longing, we can appreciate more fully several elements in a passage we looked at in chapter 2. Thoreau had been out in the country, in a mood where he was asking Nature to give him a sign. It does, yet he is aware of a lacuna: "Where is my home? It is indistinct as an old cellar-hole, now a faint indentation merely in a farmer's field, which he has plowed into and rounded off its edges years ago, and I sit by the old site on the stump of an oak which once grew there. Such is the nature where we have lived" (*J* 3:132). Or as he put it some years earlier, near the end of *A Week*: "When a thing is decayed and gone, how indistinct must be the place it occupied!" (385).

Chapter Four

AUTOGRAPHICAL ACTS

OUR HISTORIES have shown all sorts of potential relations between ourselves and our texts, our being and our making, between that which Stephen Greenblatt has defined as "a sense of personal order, a characteristic mode of address to the world, a structure of bounded desires," and that which the *Oxford English Dictionary* tells us is derived from *texere* (to weave) and has many things to do with "that which is woven, web, texture."[1] One way we can speak of such relations is to conceive of the self as a tissue of impulses and prohibitions, a web woven out of what the world demands and grants, out of what we are willing to give and what we seek to contain. The link has partly to do with an image—the web—that is literal for the one and figurative for the other.

Georges Poulet has shown the extraordinary significance of the image of the self as web in the eighteenth century's conception of the nature of the self.[2] He focuses on the theme of the spider's web (*la toile d'araignée*), especially on what it provides of the sense of a circular structure with an extraordinarily sensitive consciousness sitting at its center, sending out tale-telling lines to touch at the world. Though this image seems to identify the self with what it has made, Poulet does not make precisely that connection. Since his major concern is with versions of the image of self, he does not extend the potential implications of the image to the weaving of a text, at the center of which one could speak of "une puissance receptive et cognitive" (receptive and cognitive powers).[3] Yet the essentials of Geneva-school phenomenology posit and assume precisely such a presence. Still, Poulet does not identify this presence with the author, because, as he says elsewhere, "the subject which presides over the work can exist only in the work," only, that is, as part of the text that is (woven/)-made.[4] Poulet's refusal to identify the self within the text with the self that made the text is a pretty piece of formalist playing with personas, oddly out of place within the criticism of consciousness, arguably inconsistent with some of that criticism's implications. Yet, despite these possible anomalies, the texture of his argument is itself a careful weaving of several disparate strands into a whole that, for the most part, holds neatly together, its purpose the ensnarement of an elusive center of consciousness.

One could call Poulet's criticism of consciousness a version of late modernism, consistent with the pervasive modernist sense of a Cartesian center at which consciousness sits, irreducible and entire. The study by Stephen Greenblatt posits a very different, quintessentially postmodern alternative in the relations of self and text; not surprisingly, Greenblatt lacks Poulet's confidence about the nature of self and ends in an uneasiness whose ironies reflect through a number of his more assertive comments. For Greenblatt, the essential sign of power is "the ability to impose one's fictions on the world," and given that definition, his study can be said to elucidate all sorts of power plays. He shows how Thomas More realized early in his career that the self which faces the world had better be well made, because one will have to live life as a "histrionic improvisation." This means that the self which faces the world is, in many senses, a text, for a figure like the historical More is, in fact, "a narrative fiction." Greenblatt is especially adept at showing a dialectic in More, the practice of self-fashioning countered in *Utopia* by attempts at self-cancellation. Another version of the play of self making and text making turns up in Thomas Wyatt and, especially, in the influence on Wyatt of the institutionalized inwardness of many versions of Protestantism. On the basis of Wyatt's psalms, Greenblatt argues that "there is no privileged sphere of individuality in Wyatt, set off from linguistic convention, from social pressure, from the shaping force of religious and political power."[5] Yet Greenblatt's uneasiness about giving the self away so totally to institutionalized power appears again at the end of his comments on Wyatt, where he openly takes back the self ("that which is hidden within") and gives it a good deal more than a mere semblance of autonomy: "Wyatt's great lyrics . . . give voice to competing modes of self-presentation, one a manipulation of appearances to achieve a desired end, the other a rendering in language, an exposure, of that which is hidden within."[6] Similar uncertainties appear elsewhere in Greenblatt's text. His ambivalence is our own, well earned in our own time, which cannot seem to relinquish Poulet's sense of a Cartesian center, yet has the strongest sympathies for arguments like those of Greenblatt.

But it is not solely our own, for one senses at least the *potential* for a kindred ambivalence in Thoreau's emphasis on the power of institutional discourse. Consider Thoreau's arguments in the "Sunday" chapter of *A Week* about the institutionalized inwardness that emerges on such days, about the vast cosmic schemas that frame such inwardness; consider, further, the very different modes of being in the world suggested by the traces of the fossil in the rock. Some of Thoreau's strongest passages suggest his awareness of the way that institutionalized discourse decides for us not only our acts but our being. The farmer who bears his entire farm upon his back not only owns values by which to live but also the mode of being through which to live those values. So, too, the cosmic schemas of the "Sunday" chapter lead us not only to what we shall live but how we shall do that living. Yet Thoreau is not nearly as deterministic as Greenblatt; much of the point of his witnessing has to do with our having somewhat more than "traces of free choice"[7] with which to do our living. In fact, his problems lie in quite a different direction. However much his Transcendental "centering" might make him sound like a proto-Poulet, Thoreau does not have the fullest possible confidence in what such a position implies. That centering is countered by a profound and pervasive sense of absence and incompletion, of that which is not yet here as well as that which has long since left, the latter strikingly clear in all that the cellar-holes imply. Much of the rest of this study will take up just those issues.

We can get to Thoreau's position in still another way, through the relations of self and text, exemplary of a kind, sketched out in Sacvan Bercovitch's *The Puritan Origins of the American Self*.[8] Though Bercovitch and Greenblatt offer very different readings of the nature of self, some of their basic points have significantly ironic relations: the Puritans, in Bercovitch's reading, sought for a mode of self-fashioning that would result not in an establishment but an effacement of self. Puritan biographical texts were designed to lead the readers' selves into a state of self-undoing. Bercovitch contrasts "the tradition of humanist personal literature," with its emphasis upon "the autonomous secular self," to the Puritan insistence that selfhood is "a state to be overcome, obliterated." For the Puritans, this meant living out a tense and bitter paradox. Bercovitch analyzes the modalities of self in Puritan texts and finds that their concern with the personal mode not only did not erase the self but, on the contrary, released its energies: "his labors are an assertion of what he loathes." The result is an automachia, the struggle for christic identity challenged by the mutually sustaining energies of self and text. Yet those energies can, at times, take on useful complications. The only true reader of the Bible is the one who, like Israel itself, has his "*telos* in the Christ-event." Interpreter and text confirmed one another in their mutual *imitatios*. That is one of the many reasons why Bercovitch can speak of "the synchrony of author, text and scripture." He traces the ways in which soteriology replaced Christology, with the new promised land confirmed as the locale of universal salvation. This development came to its fullest fruition in a line of texts and modes that Bercovitch calls "auto-American-biography," a line that offers "the celebration of the representative self as America, and of the American self as the embodiment of a prophetic universal design."[9]

Writing about representative selves, our own or anyone else's, involves the embodiment in the text of histories other than our own or even that of our ostensible subject, histories for which the story of any strong American individual could offer the representative type. To take it in the terms of my previous chapter, one inscribes within the text true and grand histories far greater than our own, histories of which our own offers the initial inscription.[10]

Bercovitch treats Thoreau in terms of "Emerson's method of American nature, where the fact mediates prophetically between redemptive history and the self, and so requires the perceiver to create himself in the spirit of the New World scripture, even as he interprets the American experience as a metaphor for the journey of the soul."[11] Self-creation in the spirit of Scripture has very close relations to the kind of self-fashioning that Greenblatt described in Wyatt and others; and it has the same effect, the splicing of self and text, though clearly with a very different view of how the self is constituted than Greenblatt has conceived. Bercovitch places Thoreau firmly in the tradition of his American Puritan predecessors, including Cotton Mather, in a brief argument based on Thoreau's symbolic, chauvinistic view of the American landscape and its promise, as well as his sense of the American self on its way to a glorious future.

Bercovitch is only partly correct in what he says of Thoreau. Much of what he described early in his study as "the tradition of humanist personal literature" can equally well be used to describe a great deal of Thoreau. Bercovitch paraphrases the humanist sense of self: "Leaving the question of sainthood to theologians, each of these writers declares the primacy of the single separate person, and justifies his self-study on its intrinsic merits, without pretense at religious or even moral instruction. He assumes that what he has thought and done will interest others because it is authentically *his*, the product of his own personality in all its rich uniqueness."[12] Not all of this applies directly to Thoreau, who certainly was interested in moral (not religious) instruction. But so much of it does apply, in such rich and intricate ways, that Thoreau has to be seen as a credible combination of Bercovitch's Puritans and humanists, Mather and Montaigne. One of the crucial paradoxes in Thoreau's paradox-seeking productions comes from the way he saw his acts as representative *and* unique. To put him exclusively on one side or the other is, therefore, not to see him as fully as we ought. (Of course, this is another instance of Thoreau's uneasiness with binary positions.) Further, much of what Bercovitch speaks of deals directly with matters of discourse, and his brief discussion of Thoreau leaves no room for qualifications of the sort Thoreau made about every form of discourse. Still, though Bercovitch says nothing directly about the relations of self and text that inform Thoreau's work, the background and context he offers suggest all sorts of possibilities for illuminating such relations. In particular, they serve to ground the very different views that we have seen in Poulet and Greenblatt in a strong domestic tradition that *had* to affect Thoreau's understanding of the play of self and text, as well as his understanding of the nature of each. Many of his concerns take part in a lively and intricate history that extends from at least the Renaissance through Thoreau's time to our own.

• I •

Thoreau's dialectic of self and writing is actively involved in the making of historical texts. Take, for example, the discussion of such making in the "Monday" chapter of *A Week*. In a variation on the tenets of American Adamism, one of whose primary attributes is a tense and arrogant focus on the contemporary moment, Thoreau argues against the efforts of historical societies: "Critical acumen is exerted in vain to uncover the past; the *past* cannot be *presented*; we cannot know what we are not. But one veil hangs over past, present, and future, and it is the province of the historian to find out, not what was, but what is" (155).[13] Historical societies are institutional representatives of a grand cultural discourse that exalts temporality, tending to define what we are, as nations and persons, in firmly temporal terms. Thoreau spoke that discourse eloquently, as he does on those occasions when he seeks out American "antiquities." But such reverence for what is perceived as the unbreakable continuities among the various stages of time can quickly be turned around. It can then be turned against such established institutions as schools and historical societies, whose prestige and power are predicated on such a reading of time. Those shifts occur regularly in Thoreau. In moods like the one in this passage, he scorns any reaching back, either because it has nothing to offer to backwoods Adams or—more subtly, as in this passage—because lacunas are forced upon us as the immediate slips back into an irrevocable otherness. Once again, he is working at questions of absence and presence, this time with an American Adamite shrug and most of its attendant tones: "Time hides no treasures; we want not its *then*, but its *now*" (154).

It is the precisest kind of logic that leads Thoreau into a closely related question that takes in history and absence and the presence of the history maker. At the conclusion of the passage in which he complains about the practices of the historical societies, Thoreau goes on to talk about these problems as they appear in other modes of writing: "Biography, too, is liable to the same objection: it should be autobiography. Let us not, as the Germans advise, endeavor to go abroad and vex our bowels that we may be somebody else to explain him. If I am not I, who will be?" (156). Biography is history that aims at the elucidation of a self, but the subject of self, Thoreau argues, ought to include the maker's as well. Indeed, the text ought to contain an interplay of selves, that of the subject, that of the maker, and that of the maker himself as subject. (Consider, again, all that "subject" entails of syntax, theme, and power.) We ought to be writing about others in such a way that we are, at the same time, writing about ourselves, putting ourselves into the text to make certain that it tells of a *now* as well as a *then*. The text as a scene of writing ought to take as its *staffage* the two essential selves (the essentials of the two selves) that occupy its landscape. In one sense, this is related to Thoreau's remark that "we cannot know what we are not" (155). But biographical histories seem to bring out special reasons for putting that argument forth. Thoreau rejects Germanic empathy in precisely the same way he would have rejected the Keatsian sort, though where Keats feels the impingement of other selves on his own, Thoreau senses the potential of an unsettling vacuum within.[14] There is a kind of unease in Thoreau that Keats never had, something approaching a fear about leaving those inner contours empty, about the resounding hollowness that might ensue: "If I am not I, who will be?" Once again he ponders absence, this time of a frightening sort.

By the time Thoreau got to the introductory pages of *Walden*, that queasiness had been (temporarily) put by for quite a different position, one so important to his sense of what he was about that he put it forward bluntly at the beginning of the book. He will, he says, use this book to answer all those questions about the time he spent at the pond; and if that makes him seem frivolously self-involved he is, in fact, being franker than most who write: "In most books the *I*, or first person, is omitted; in this it will be retained; that, in respect to egotism, is the main difference. We commonly do not remember that it is, after all, always the first person that is speaking" (3). Every time we write, we write about ourselves. Every mode of text, whatever its ostensible subject, is inhabited by self, impregnated with its discourse. All voices are our own, and every life we describe is our own in some form of disguise. By this point, the issue has become a far more complex one than the versions we saw earlier, for now it has turned into a question of several senses of occupation: to what degree do I occupy the texts that I make; to what degree does my occupation as writer keep me occupied with myself, with *my* self as subject? The issue, so put, is no longer the relatively straightforward one that it had been in *A Week*, the insistence that every biography ought to be autobiography. "Ought to be" has become "is," the possible is now the requisite, and not only for the lives of others but for any mode that emerges in the making of a text.

Thoreau's stance at this point should not be confounded with what used to be put forth as a High Romantic egotism that sees all aspects of experience as sites for self-preening. For one thing, such readings of Romanticism have very little to do with the actualities of the texts of the time. (Those readings are most meaningful as part of the history of readings of Romanticism.) For another, such confusion patently ignores the way in which puzzles about the relations of self, text, and place turn up regularly in Thoreau, their persistence the clearest indication that those matters seem to be getting at something basic about the way he reads the world. We ought not to be surprised that no single track of interpretation can handle these radical issues or even the events which point toward the existence and character of the issues. That is another way of reminding ourselves that at any point in his writing, we are likely to run across Thoreau's uneasiness with binary solutions. We run into it again on the matter of the self's occupation in and with texts. Language cannot be taken with open, innocent trust, yet we seem to entrust our selves (*must* entrust our selves, Thoreau says at several points) to what we make out of words. Texts, we also saw, often localize an absence, a curious business when one also wants to argue that texts are, by nature, autobiographical. No absolute yes or no can frame anything so basic as questions of "occupation," however we take the term.

To the degree that the self so occupies, we can speak of what it does as a mode of self-inscribing, self-writing, autography. The sum of Thoreau's comments puts the imprint of self into the substance of a text, whatever the status of the subject, whatever the textual mode. It is not only, he argues, that we write *about* ourselves—most often we do not do so directly—but that we write ourselves *into* the text. In and through the act of writing, we seek to establish ourselves within the text, seeking, finally, to inhabit the text, to find a home place within it. Seen in these terms, the text becomes a site for the self to occupy, one locale where it seems likely to find a place to be. The self-locating for which Thoreau so frequently argues has a patent relation to the self-fashioning Greenblatt describes; but the autographical acts accomplished by More and Wyatt do not seek to establish the text as a place for the self's location in the way Thoreau's acts do. Neither More nor the other autographers of his time would have thought of the text as such a place: they take their texts as a way to *meet* the world, not as a place to *be* in the world. (Autographical acts—which can be acts of self-constituting as well as acts of self-locating—are taken differently at different times, depending not only on varying conceptions of the self but on the changing contents of our theories of the text. This is another way of saying that we cannot universalize Greenblatt's argument, any more than we can do so with the one I am making about Thoreau.) Thoreau conceives of writing as a process of mixed intentionality, since it not only records and interprets but establishes as well. Writing is therefore a kind of mapping in which we find out important facts about matters of self-location through the very same act that places the self where it is. It is as though Thoreau, the surveyor, were not just verifying certain demarcations but *making them for the first time*, even as he marked them out. The congruence of the main activities through which he chose to earn a living—making pencils, surveying places—becomes even more apparent in the light of what writing means to him, and the congruence of those activities with our radical compulsion to make a place for ourselves in the world also becomes more apparent. In their turn, those congruences point not only to an overriding coherence but to a complicity of self and writing that comes close to being an intrigue.

One can add history to that pair and make a complicitous, intriguing triad. Every form of inscribing we have seen up to this point—we need think only of cellar-holes and fossils—has ultimately to do with our contact with the earth, specifically, with the places of such contacts and the times in which we made them. Literal inscriptions make these matters graphic, but they are no different in what they do from the less literal kinds. Insofar as I write myself into the earth, I practice autography. Insofar as I write when I do, I find a place in a historical context as well as a physical one. And insofar as I inscribe absence into a text, I continue to inscribe history, engraving my awareness of what is no longer there. Autography therefore invokes not only a *where* but a *when*. (If we recall Thoreau's desire to have history take in a *now* as well as a *then*, some of the temporal complexities of the act of autography will quickly become apparent.) No form of self-inscribing (no form of *any* inscribing) can be separated from history, made autonomous and atemporal. In fact, we can ask ourselves the question from quite the opposite direction: can any form of history be separated from autography? Thoreau thought not, and he had his reasons why.

• II •

Before we turn to a more detailed examination of Thoreau's sense of
the literary text as an autographical site, we need to understand more
fully what autographical acts have to do with inscribings in general,
and especially with the sort we looked at in the previous chapter.
Take, for example, the following passage from "The Allegash and
East Branch." Thoreau and his companion and Joe Polis, their Indian
guide, have been making their way through the woods. After an especially difficult passage, Polis goes on with their canoe while Thoreau and his companion continue to walk.

> We did not at once fall into our path again, but made our way with diffi-
> culty along the edge of the river, till at length, striking inland through the
> forest, we recovered it. Before going a mile we heard the Indian calling to
> us. He had come up through the woods and along the path to find us,
> having reached sufficiently smooth water to warrant his taking us in. The
> shore was about one fourth of a mile distant, through a dense, dark forest,
> and as he led us back to it, winding rapidly about to the right and left, I
> had the curiosity to look down carefully, and found that he was following
> his steps backward. I could only occasionally perceive his trail in the moss,
> and yet he did not appear to look down nor hesitate an instant, but led us
> out exactly to his canoe. This surprised me, for without a compass, or the
> sight and noise of the river to guide us, we could not have kept our course
> many minutes, and could have retraced our steps but a short distance, with
> a great deal of pains and very slowly, using a laborious circumspection. But
> it was evident that he could go back through the forest wherever he had
> been during the way. (*M W*, 251)

What the Indian did in the forest has the most potent sort of relation
to what Thoreau says we do with a text. Consider the travelers' situation, as well as the meaning of *The Maine Woods*, in Thoreau's writing as a whole. The travelers are trying to find their way through a
scene that gives little help, that in fact gives only the rivers and an
occasional old path. The Indian helps himself, and he does so by literally imprinting his steps into the turf. As he does so, he creates a
trail, demarcating a piece of that which before had been trackless
chaos, establishing the traces of a human presence—most precisely,
his own presence—into the surface of the forest. In a quite literal sense,
he inscribes himself into the scene. Whatever else the scene becomes,
it comes to be a place where the self has located itself by making its
representative image part of what we see, part of what we learn to
read. The Indian is therefore not only a self-inscriber but also a self-

reader; indeed, he is a much better reader than his Anglo-Saxon companions. He imprints in order to interpret, creating a circle of interpretation as he goes back over what he has made. Thoreau is fully aware that language and writing are complex sign systems with a high degree of privilege and a profound grounding in institutions. That awareness precludes his making an exact metaphoric relation out of what he inscribes on a page and what the Indian inscribes in the turf. Yet what the Indian does in the forest is patently analogous to writing as Thoreau so often describes it. In fact, those acts are synecdochical, each a representative gesture that can stand for the general field that contains them both. Each is, quite literally, an autographical act.

Thoreau collected such autographs with an unceasing passion, his fascination deriving in part from his awareness that what we ordinarily call writing is one of several elements in a much larger context. What he said about writing on the first page of *Walden*—that all texts are in the first person and reveal the qualities of their maker—he says in much the same terms about other sorts of inscriptions, especially the tracks he comes across in the turf or in the snow. Most tracks are not as deliberate as the ones Joe Polis made, but they all have the same function for one who knows how to read autographic inscriptions. Thoreau seeks out tracks because they represent the traces of a being that has gone about its most basic and necessary work, its acts of encounter with the world. Those tracks not only verify that the encounter had occurred but denote the precise point where foot and earth met and intentions were enacted. It is as though the foot or the paw were an extension of being and one could go from the traces in the turf back to the mind of the one who was making the tracks.

As early as in "Natural History of Massachusetts," Thoreau showed what he was after, this time by following a fox. Part of his fascination, he says, comes from observing the fluctuations of the fox's tracks, which create a line of beauty satisfying in itself but also satisfying in its harmony with the place where the tracks are made: "When the ground is uneven, the course is a series of graceful curves, conforming to the shape of the surface" (55). But there is something more at play here than independent beauty, because the fluctuations of the tracks are the external correlation of the moves of the mind that made them, the play of the tracks the result of the play of a mind in this place. "I am curious to know what has determined [the trail's] graceful curvatures, and how surely they were coincident with the fluctuations of some mind. I know which way a mind wended, what horizon it faced, by the setting of these tracks, and whether it moved slowly or rapidly, by their greater or less intervals and distinctness;

for the swiftest step leaves yet a lasting trace" (*Excursions*, 54–55). All that we have seen in Thoreau's use of the term "trace" takes part in this extraordinary occurrence.

Thoreau rejected empathy for the very good reason that it would require a temporary cessation of self in order to examine the being of another. But when he becomes a reader of tracks, he can hold on firmly to what he is while he works his way back from those traces to the wendings of the mind that made them. With this ideal arrangement at work, he can afford to let himself go, feeling his way into a fox's life with no sense of danger to his own being because it is firmly anchored in its own established place. In February 1854, he recorded in his journal the pursuit of another fox: "I followed on this trail so long that my thoughts grew foxy; though I was on the back track, I drew nearer and nearer to the fox each step. Strange as it may seem, I thought several times that I scented him, though I did not stoop" (J 6:101). He can act as Keats acted with the sparrow who was pecking around in the gravel, that is, take part in the creature's life and do as the creature does.[15] And he can do so because he is not replacing himself with the fox but adding foxiness to himself, extending the range of what he can know. Through this "track of a wilder life," he can get to the mind of the fox whose imprints he sees and learn the scent of foxy ways, sense the contours of foxy thoughts. The fox's self-inscriptions are as much a first-person product as any of the words we write. And the uneven ground that reveals the graceful curves of his course is as much a scene of self-locating as the moss where Joe Polis left the imprint of his foot. As Thoreau reads these scenes, the fox, the Indian, and the writer of *Walden* are all makers of texts.

It may be that one of the reasons Thoreau could take on foxiness was that he had to deal with paw prints, not the tracks made by a boot, that is, there was nothing between him and the trace of the pure paw, the imprinted record that spoke of foxiness. Some comments in the *Journal* for July 21, 1851, substantiate this point:

> I see the track of a bare human foot in the dusty road, the toes and muscles all faithfully imprinted. Such a sight is so rare that it affects me with surprise, as the footprint on the shore of Juan Fernandez did Crusoe. . . . It is pleasant as it is to see the tracks of cows and deer and birds. I am brought so much nearer to the tracker—when again I think of the sole of my own foot—than when I behold that of his shoe merely, or am introduced to him and converse with him in the usual way. I am disposed to say to the judge whom I meet, "Make tracks." (J 2:328)

When we touch the turf with a shoe, its imprint will leave the clearest sort of evidence of the precise point of encounter; but that imprint will still leave the reader of our tracks at least one layer away from ourselves as possessors of "a bare human foot," of all that about ourselves which is on the nether side of civility. Tracks inscribed by shoes may well be visible correlatives of the moves of the mind that made them, the alphabet of its speech, pointers of intentionality. And yet when Thoreau is deeply taken by the impression of a foot, "the toes and muscles all faithfully imprinted"; when he compares the pleasure he feels to the one that ensues when he sees "the tracks of cows and deer and birds"; when he says, simply and movingly, "I am brought so much nearer to the tracker"; when he refers to his feelings as he thinks of the sole of his own foot, knowing better than anyone else what the imprint of that sole offers ("I should not talk so much about myself if there were any body else whom I knew as well" [W, 3]); then we get through to a greater understanding of what Thoreau was after in his search for tracks in the turf.

In a passage from the *Journal* nearly two months later, these questions still much on his mind, he compares cart paths to footpaths and what it means to follow each: "One walks in a wheel-track with less emotion; he is at a greater distance from man; but this footpath was, perchance, worn by the bare feet of human beings, and he cannot but think with interest of them" (*J* 2:456). A path worn by bare feet holds more of a trace than one worn by shoes, not to speak of wheels. Such a path puts us as close to where Thoreau wants to go as such traces can get. Implications of that pattern can appear in the strangest places. When he is tempted to say "make tracks" to the judge whom he meets in a social situation, he is in effect asking the judge to come out from inside civility, the speech of the secondhand. Social conversation is like speaking to a shoe, not a foot. As we are swallowed up in our shoes, so are we swallowed by civilities, by all that seeks to suppress that which would give off our radical reek, just as the fox's tracks give off foxiness. That strange, synesthetic reading through which we sense the traces of foxiness works to its fullest capacity only when we who "make tracks" make them the purest available traces of what Thoreau seeks to know.

A passage entered in the *Journal* for March 28, 1859, very late in Thoreau's career, holds a compact, coherent expression of these and related issues (*J* 12:88–93). He had been thinking of publishing the story of his searches for arrowheads, the bare-turf counterpart of his search for tracks in the snow. The arrowheads' ubiquity generates a like abundance of imagery: they are like seeds, like "the dragon's

teeth which bore a crop of soldiers," like "stone fruit" (90). Finally he
gets to where his intuition has been taking him all along, the sense of
the arrowhead as a trace that brings him "nearer to the maker of it
than if I found his bones" (90–91). At that point, his perceptions of
arrowheads begin to fuse with his established imagery of inscribings:
"It is humanity inscribed on the face of the earth, patent to my eyes
as soon as the snow goes off . . . the best symbol or letter that could
have been transmitted to me. . . . It is no single inscription on a particular rock, but a footprint—rather a mind-print—left everywhere,
and altogether illegible" (91). In the same way that the fox's tracks
had given him a sense of the mind that made them, so do the arrowheads become the products of a long-gone consciousness: "They are
no fossil bones, but, as it were, fossil thoughts, forever reminding me
of the mind that shaped them." And as he goes on, the full meaning
of the pursuit comes into the open and into play: "I would fain know
that I am treading in the tracks of human game,—that I am on the
trail of mind,—and these little reminders never fail to set me right."
Thoreau's puns are not always so pertinent: the play on "mind" and
"reminders" (note also "reminding" and "mind" just above), with the
reiteration of "re-," emphasizes the reemergence of these traces of
mind, their flouting of temporality through their status as imprints
and the earth's ultimate status as a palimpsest, a many-layered text.
Toward the end of the passage, continuing the reiteration and all that
it points to of inscribings as texts which re-mind, Thoreau fuses the
extremities, foot and head, once again: "The footprint, the mind-
print of the oldest men" (92). In so doing, he not only affirms the
existence of a spectrum of inscribings, he also confirms the inter-
changeability of the elements within the spectrum, their metonymical
status: the arrowheads can stand at either end or at both.

These tracings are modes of working in the world that are ultimately
modes of being in the world. To put it most precisely, they are modes
of being in the world whose purpose is to inscribe being into the
world. Whatever their specific function, all of these modes give body
to forms of autographical discourse. For example, we saw in the previous chapter that the building of a house begins with the digging of
a cellar, and that the digging of a cellar is as literal an inscribing of
traces into the earth as is the making of footprints. Now we also can
see the meaning of the act with which we begin our houses. To stand
in an old hole which is all that remains of a house is to do the best
one can to turn history's *then* into *now*, to touch at the gesture in
which someone dug a mark into the scene. Here too what Thoreau
seeks is the purest autographical expression.

Certain kinds of occasions turn up as exemplary instances. In the "Thursday" chapter of *A Week*, he tells of a brazen act of self-assertion that occurred in the 1720s in the wilderness near Haverhill. He quotes the local historian:

Soon after [the first team was driven through the wilderness] one Ayer, a lad of 18, drove a team consisting of ten yoke of oxen to Penacook, swam the river, and plowed a portion of the interval. He is supposed to have been the first person who plowed land in that place. After he had completed his work, he started on his return at sunrise, drowned a yoke of oxen while recrossing the river, and arrived at Haverhill about midnight. (303)

The boldness of the act ensured that the young originator would forever have his name associated with these initial incisions. His act of plowing becomes a mode of inscribing himself into the turf, of turning the turf into a text and the landscape into a scene of writing. In so doing, he acts out an old metaphor for writing. Ernst Robert Curtius has shown the antiquity of the image of plowing as writing, its lineage going back at least to Plato and found in allusions in Latin literature that made their way into the Middle Ages.[16] Thoreau does not refer directly to what he surely knew well (Curtius points out that the compound *exarare*, "to plow up," was used frequently by the Romans, without any sense of the figurative, meaning "to write" or "to compose"). And, indeed, he would not have had to develop the allusion in order to make the point precisely, since the congruence of plowing and inscribing, unusually patent in this passage, would be inevitable for him to see, given his bent of thought on these issues.

Indeed, this striking incident of ground breaking is by no means the only one that equates plowing with the act of writing. *Walden*'s chapter on "The Bean-Field" makes the same point throughout, and Thoreau begins *A Week* with the point made so explicitly that when we come to the report about Ayer and his arrogant plow, we are ready for the full import of his act of opening the earth.

You shall see rude and sturdy, experienced and wise men, keeping their castles, or teaming up their summer's wood, or chopping alone in the woods, men fuller of talk and rare adventure in the sun and wind and rain, than a chestnut is of meat, who were out not only in '75 and 1812, but have been out every day of their lives; greater men than Homer, or Chaucer, or Shakespeare, only they never got time to say so; they never took to the way of writing. Look at their fields, and imagine what they might write, if ever they should put pen to paper. Or what have they not written on the face of the earth already, clearing, and burning, and scratching, and harrowing, and plowing, and subsoiling, in and in, and out and out, and over and over, again and again, erasing what they had already written for lack of parchment. (8)

The complex intertextual life of Thoreau's extensive canon ensures that such passages resonate at multiple levels, showing how the act of inscribing takes in a good deal more than the books we write and publish, but also showing how that act, whatever the mode it uses, seems always to be concerned about our confluence with our texts.

And because it is so concerned, we can get to the fullest import of acts like those of Ayer, the eighteen-year-old plowman. When he swam the river with his oxen and engraved his trace in the virgin turf, he performed a version of the process through which the alien becomes our own and we get to be at home in what was the other's world. He claims a place in that world by inscribing his trace into the turf, but in so doing he unwittingly claims it for more than himself alone: there is a very important sense in which he was a representative figure, engraving our trace as well as his own into the turf across the river. Acts of precisely that sort turn up repeatedly and passionately throughout Thoreau's writings, especially in *The Maine Woods*, his most extended statement of the confrontation with the alien other. All the clearing and plowing and building of cabins that occur in the essays on Maine are claims made by the human upon the inhospitable thickness of the forest, claims for the species as a whole as well as for the plowman who dug his trace into the territory's turf. And such claims can appear in landscapes with conditions totally unlike the dark density Thoreau found in Maine. Though the other takes on a very different landscape in his book on Cape Cod, Thoreau records analogous gestures in that equally alien place, knowing that our needs will always remain, whatever the conditions of the turf. At this point we can see how the act of plowing becomes, for Thoreau, a ritual gesture, a consecratory move performed at a multitude of levels and for an equal number of reasons. What Ayer did so graphically in the forest around Haverhill turns up persistently in Thoreau, the vocabulary of the discourse taking all manner of variations but the import of the discourse always precisely the same, whether in plow cuts or cellar-holes or the tracks of a paw or a foot. Ayer's graphic act confirms what Thoreau asserted about the autographical qualities of writing, but it does more than confirm, because what we saw to be true about writing turns out also to be true about all these related incisings. Every autographical act is a gesture through which we seek to domicile ourselves. Whatever the variety of modes or the multiplicity of locales—turf, sand, snow, or the white paper of *Walden*—our compulsion to cut texts for ourselves has to be taken as a way of enacting our radical desire for a place of inexorable grounding. The making of a text has ultimately to be seen as a way of seeking to be at home in the world.

Sometimes points can be observed with particular precision in negatives, that is, in lacunas, absence, unknowing. Here is a *Journal* entry from December 25, 1853: "The effect of the snow is to press down the forest, confound it with the grasses, and create a new surface to the earth above, shutting us in with it, and we go along somewhat like moles through our galleries. The sight of the pure and trackless road up Brister's Hill, with branches and trees supporting snowy burdens bending over it on each side, would tempt us to begin life again" (*J* 6:27). One way of envisioning origin is to consider it a trackless time, with no imprints around to pinpoint attempts to fix traces into the world. Thus there is the impossible temptation to begin imprinting all over again, from that state of uninscribed purity one can never quite seem to forget.

Here is another entry, put down just over two years later: "Sometimes a lost man will be so beside himself that he will not have sense enough to trace back his own tracks in the snow" (*J* 7:109). Whatever our capacities to inscribe ourselves into a scene, the possibility of panic, of a curious kind of division that would put us beside ourselves, means that the newly fragmented awareness might not be lucid enough, single-minded enough, to recognize the signs of its former, more desirable condition.

Absence awaiting presence, absence of a former presence: both attest to the profound and abiding needs that reside in the touch of traces.

• III •

There is a way of talking about such traces that helps us to explain many of their complexities and, in so doing, uncovers additional ones. It takes in what we have seen of that stubborn, incomplete presence which attests to an absent completeness, one that continues, despite its absence, to approach us through the trace. We can be helped in understanding Thoreau's ways of handling traces by considering some implications of C. S. Peirce's concept of the index.[17]

The kind of sign that Peirce calls the icon refers to its object insofar as it resembles the object. That is, it stands to the object in a condition of similarity, and if there is no object to which the icon can refer

(Claude's paintings of imaginary castles would be useful examples of that), it tells us what such an object would be like were it to exist. We are dealing, then, with that which may have the only existence it has within the iconic image of its potential actualization. An index, on the other hand, points to an actually existent object, one that has to be, or have been, in order for the index to be what it is, to do what it does. Peirce speaks of the index as having "a real connection with its object," the terms "real" or "actual" on the one hand and versions of "connection" on the other sounding repeatedly throughout his comments. The idea of connection emphasizes the index as pointer, as that sort of sign which compels the sign reader's attention toward the object to which it refers:

> A weather cock is an index of the direction of the wind; because in the first place it really takes the self-same direction as the wind, so that there is a real connection between them, and in the second place we are so constituted that when we see a weathercock pointing in a certain direction it draws our attention to that direction, and when we see the weathercock veering with the wind, we are forced by the law of mind to think that direction is connected with the wind.[18]

The coercion is, as Peirce says, blind, because we unthinkingly turn our attention to the direction and therefore to the object indicated by the index. When one says words like "this" or "that," one's auditors do not have to think actively of the continuity between the demonstrative pronoun and its object. Unless we are playing tricks on our auditors (consider what indexes mean to a magician or a sleight-of-hand artist), there is an emphatic existential connection between the index and its object, and the auditors instinctively follow the energies of that connection.

To put it another way, the index is a sign not only of truth (the object indicated really exists) but of location (it is here or in that direction). "Here" and "there" are indexes, and so are "now" and "then." And insofar as the index locates the object, it also brings it to our minds, connects it with us here and now, for the index is "a sign, or representation, which refers to its object [. . .] because it is in dynamical (including spatial) connection both with the individual object, on the one hand, and with the senses or memory of the person for whom it serves as a sign, on the other hand."[19] Thus, insofar as the index is a statement of connection, and insofar as we are involved in the indexical transaction, the index connects the object to what and where we are. It establishes a continuum among object, sign, and ourselves. However distant the object (it may be a few feet away or in the next county, an element of last week or of several centuries back), the index undoes distance. (That it can also, most emphatically and *at precisely the same time*, affirm such distance is a point I shall make presently.)

One other aspect of the relation of index and icon is implicit in Peirce's remarks and has considerable significance for our understanding of Thoreau. Consider the following comment: "Psychologically, the action of indices depends upon association by contiguity, and not upon association by resemblance or upon intellectual operations." The index is a sign that ties by being part of a context. The icon is a sign that ties through likeness, similarity, resemblance. In these aspects, their relation is like that of metonymy and metaphor, and in fact Peirce says that some forms of icon represent "a parallelism in something else" and thus "are *metaphors*."[20] If we keep in mind Jakobson's comments on the relations of metaphor and metonymy, Peirce's distinctions between icon and index can tell us a great deal about how we are in our worlds.

One more point must be added. The index may be an entire thing in itself (Peirce's examples of the hygrometer or weathercock are each existential wholes), but because it is part of a context, it is necessarily incomplete. It is a portion of a complex that includes the situation in which index and object are connected.

What, then, does all this mean for those marks we have been inspecting in this and the previous chapter, especially those inscriptions that are the results of autographical acts? What does this have to do with the tracks of the Indian or the fox, with those cellar-holes that so fascinated Thoreau that he deliberately sought them out and even sought to stand in them? When he stands in such a hole, he is touching at a trace of what once was there, a fragment of the whole that once occupied the place. In so touching, he establishes a continuum—in Peirce's terms, "a real connection"—between himself and the original scene; such a continuum has within it none of the iffiness of the comment that he makes when he stands in the dirt of Lovewell's cellar and talks with one "whose grandfather had, whose father might have, talked with Lovewell" (*A W*, 161). If that oral continuum may well have been broken, there is no breaking the ineradicable continuity, the "real connection," among object, sign, and observer that comes into being when Thoreau steps into the hole and completes the connection. Such traces are indexes, which means that autographical acts are, in their very nature, indexical gestures. These traces are therefore signs of the truth of the object (unlike an icon, it had to exist) and of where the wholeness of conditions like Lovewell's ménage had been in place and time. The tracks of Polis or the fox are pointers toward previous acts and bring in all of the implications associated with those acts; bring them back, that is, toward us. As participants in the continuum established by these indexes, we not only take part in the unbrokenness of the continuum but can see through to the original acts and their attendant conditions. Lovewell's cellar-hole points not only to a long-gone house but to the place of the hole in the way Lovewell sought to be at home in his world. The cellar-hole can therefore invoke the meaning of that act and the relation of that meaning to our present versions of it. The self-inscribings that had to result from young Ayer's arrogant plowing would do much the same things, which is why Thoreau imagined them with such passionate intensity.

So far, so fine and comforting, but the old wholeness of these ancient inscribings is not their entire story. By their nature, these Thoreauvian indexes are localizers of absence, versions of a basic set of his mind (we have already seen that set at work in aspects of his handling of language). If there is always a "real connection," it connects with that which can no longer be present. That is, the cellar-hole is a survivor, a shard, a fragmentary remnant of what was once an entire context. And so, in their ways, are the tracks of man and fox, the remains of Indian settlements Thoreau imagines Hannah Dustan had seen, those arrowheads whose collecting was one of Thoreau's regular acts. (The shape of the arrow as pointer lends all sorts of ironies to these issues and may well have been part of what intrigued Thoreau.) The existential pathos in his treatment of such survivors must stem from his recognition, only occasionally verbalized, that his indexes also point to the biggest hole of all, the blackest there is.

Thus, if these Thoreauvian indexes affirm nearness or presence—what the continuum looks like right now, how it is manifested here—they also affirm distance, the otherwhereness of the original context, its necessary and permanent absence from us. All indexes, Thoreauvian and otherwise are, *at one and the same time*, both fragmentary and continuous. Thoreau's models of that sign are tensely, concernedly so. However complete within itself, however perfect a footprint or cellar-hole, it is a surviving piece of an absent condition. The localizing of an absence never makes that condition less than absent. But this too is not the entire story, for we cannot forget the fact that, *because* it is so localized, we can tap into the continuum of which the index speaks, which speaks through the index.

These aspects of the Thoreauvian index concern more than this sample of inscribings, because they relate to, and affect, his attitude toward writing as well. Given that autography is by nature an indexical gesture, it is clear that the result of writing must be in some sense indexical, certainly in the way it leaves marks that are traces. The question that ensues has to do with the object of these pointers, what there is at the originating end to balance the reader at the other end. All logic leads us to conclude that out at the originating end is some aspect of the "auto" that is in the idea of autography. We are, it seems, returning to the matter of the relations of ourselves and our texts, that nagging query that has been haunting autography's subtextual life. Through nothing like a coincidence, we are also getting closer to some further implications of Thoreau's understanding of writing as necessarily autobiographical.

He had made that point, we recall, on the first page of *Walden*: "it is, after all, always the first person that is speaking." In fact, the introductory paragraph is a passage of extraordinary significance, one of the cruxes of his writing. It functions primarily as an allegory of self-locating, acting out the practice in terms of two related events, a pair of echoing inscribings. The first is the business about building beside the pond, the second the more immediate business of telling about the first one and, at precisely the same time, getting a book underway that narrates a part of one's life. The first event is always-already-past, the second a practice that becomes immediate whenever we read the page. Both are prime instances of autographical acts.

One of the most important aspects of the introductory paragraph is the order in which it presents its material. This is Thoreau at his requisite canniest: he knows that what he is about to do will have all manner of major consequences.

"When I wrote": distilled, as it is, to a set of basic elements, this could have been a subtitle of the book. In its privileged introductory position, it establishes what Thoreau wants us to see as an essential condition. The phrase emphasizes, in sequence, the sense of temporality and then the subject of the phrase and then what the subject did that, of all his possible business, must have been the most important, or it would not be so prominently stationed. Time, act, maker, and product appear to fit together in a most efficient way, with all sorts of valorization. Yet he does not place himself before (prior to, more prominent than) the period of time involved (he could, after all, have begun the book by saying "I wrote the following pages when . . ."); rather, he has it precede him and therefore include and encompass him. The subject, then, is to be taken in several of the senses we have seen, subject *of* and subject *to*. He is the subject within a phrase and, also, the being subject to time. His place in this phrase shows that these two aspects of "subject" can in no sense be separate: to be one is to be the other. Further, writing, as these words indicate, is clearly a temporal act, one that has as much to do with us within time as with time within us. The remainder of the passage, and, in fact, of the book that follows, works out all sorts of implications attendant upon this initial phrase.

"I lived alone": the "I" comes in for the second of its five appearances in this paragraph (there are also two "my"s and a "myself"). We are six words into the book, and "I" has appeared twice. If it is the subject of the introductory phrase, its thumping reiteration seems to argue, even this early in the game, that "I" will be the subject *matter* (our third meaning of "subject") of the material that follows. Of course, that is no surprise in what every reader knows will be an autobiographical book. Thus, there must be something more than this obvious conclusion, and if we are not told exactly what it is, we have certainly been alerted to watch for it carefully. Further, if the reiteration of "I" singles him out in a special way, separating him as a subject of interest from all the other potential subjects, he is also separated in still another way. It is the way Keats had in mind when "forlorn" drew him back from the nightingale to his "sole self." "Alone" tolls within these words just as "forlorn" did within Keats's, although the tone is not nearly the same. Though "alone" specifies only one aspect of how he lived then (at this point we can say only "then" because we have not yet been given a "there"), it must be an aspect of great significance because it precedes everything else he could say about how he lived. In fact, it comes directly after "I lived" and is clearly next in importance only to that.

What follows shows precisely how the act that he describes (settling in beside the pond) and the act he is now performing (getting this book going) are closely related acts that are metaphors for each other and metonyms within a larger context. To see what Thoreau is about here, it helps to keep in mind the pervasive Transcendental impulse to treat the self as center. That act is often visualized spatially and, therefore, fits right in with Thoreau's various modes of mapmaking: "Wherever I sat, there I might live, and the landscape radiated from me accordingly" (*W*, 81). The first sentence has, so far, established him as such a center, giving us, for specificity, no more than the elemental "I lived alone." "In the woods" spreads out from that radical condition to tell where, of all the possible places in Concord, he was. "A mile from any neighbor" continues that centrifugal spreading into further specificity, acknowledging for the first time that there are other things within the world than himself, the woods, and these pages. A balance has been achieved; at least, some would call it a balance. However elemental a world, it is essentially a complete one because it has within itself not only him but a requisite Other. He has, it turns out, been building a world in this place at the beginning of his book, the sequence of that building one of the most extraordinary things about it, its completeness within such brevity an equally extraordinary fact. Thoreau has been working at his version of Genesis, and has been so successful and has gotten so far along that he has even established an Other without losing any pieces of himself, a rib, for example. If we look at this passage in terms of the act of self-locating, we have to admire the dexterity with which he has given himself a place to locate himself, and that in the very process of performing the self-locating.

Once the building of a world has been completed by this inclusion of others, he can turn back to himself and tell of another object of building, the house that he built himself. The passage continues and affirms much of what he had set down earlier in terms of himself: the third "I" comes in (and we are not yet at the end of the first sentence) while "myself" not only echoes "alone" but helps to establish the tone of singularity with a certain discreet bragging (one of the many reasons why the title page of the first edition has him playing the part of Chanticleer). And there is also, now, the establishing of some very basic analogies, components of this allegory of self-locating that takes in all manner of making/building and shows self-locating to be closely associated with such building. The building of a house is obviously an act allied in kind to that building of a world we have seen to be part of the function of these introductory lines. But "built" is also the third verb we have seen in their sentence, preceded by "wrote" and "lived." Building one's house is obviously an act of self-locating, and so, as we have seen so many times, is "wrote." And nothing could, of course, be more self-locating than "lived." In a very important sense, then, "built" becomes the reification of all we have seen up to this point, the synecdoche of the whole, the narrative of the allegory. As it sketches a dwelling on this map, it becomes a palpable confirmation of all that these words have been saying. It is Adam calling to himself and saying to himself, "Here I am." Here, as elsewhere in the paragraph, we are given instructions for reading the text that is to follow. We are also getting at the fullest import of some of the major acts it records.

As the paragraph continues, the mapmaking intensifies. So far there has been one major repeated pronoun, its possessor never yet named though at the same time never in doubt. "I" is a "shifter," a word that stays empty until we fill it with content. In this introductory sentence, it is asked to do an extraordinary job. For one thing, by filling the shifter with "I = Henry David Thoreau," it serves as a place of self-location for that tripartite naming, a place for it to inhabit within this rapidly developing text. This means that by the second of the introductory words, we have not only a "when" but a "where." That does not quite negate (though it certainly has to qualify) my earlier point that, this far in our discussion of these introductory lines, we do not yet have a "where." We still do not have one in terms of a proper noun of the kind printed on every sort of map— Los Angeles, Yugoslavia, Tenth Avenue, Antarctica. What we do have is the "I" that contains "Henry David Thoreau" and therefore finds a place for something that goes by that name. We can define that location more precisely: it is the pronoun in itself, and the syntactical order of the phrase that contains the pronoun, and the syntactical order of the sentence within which the phrase occurs, and the place of the sentence within this introductory paragraph, and the place of the paragraph within the text as a whole. That is, the "I" and what it contains are located in the text that lies (perhaps in more than one sense) before us. Thoreau uses the shifter to perform the same act he performs at every point in his engagement with life, an act of self-locating. And because he sees that gesture as an autographical act, writing is linked once more to so much else that he admires, that he seeks so hard to emulate.

The tour de force is not yet over. Thoreau's play with uncapitalized nouns ("the following pages," "a house," "the woods," "any neighbor") had gone as far as he dared to take it. He wanted the kind of grounding, the sense of localized attachment, that only a proper name can give. As a surveyor, he knew how much we need the unequivocalness of the proper name, and as one who had gone (and was to go) through several scares in the Maine woods, he knew how much the precisest mapping makes our lives that much more bearable. He was, in effect, a kind of Antaeus who needed to touch at precisely *this* earth. Consider, for example, "the following pages," a phrasing that can refer to only one batch of pages. Such a phrasing, however specific, cannot have the particularity of "Walden Pond" or "Concord" or "Massachusetts." This is precisely the difference between reading "the following pages" and reading "*Walden*," signifiers that cannot point to the same aspects of the signified. It is just such differentiating that Thoreau wants us to see when he finally comes to naming something *un*shifting and capitalized. We are, once again, playing with modes of self-locating, locating with the finest precision what we have so far seen, *de*shifting it, as it were. By our naming the place in which it all happened, the place becomes even more of a local habitation.

Thoreau's obsession with modes of self-locating occurs at every level of this text, thematically and syntactically and even in the nature of its nouns, in their spirited, nervous interplay. It is no more than deadpan accuracy to say that this primal activity may well turn out to be the primary subject of the pages which follow. To put the point in a related way: the text has so far shown us (we are *still* not through with the first sentence) how autographical acts can occur in a dazzling array of ways and at an equally dazzling series of levels. Whatever the ultimate subject of the pages that are to follow, we can be certain that such acts will infuse it at every level and most likely at every point of the narrative that is to come. And that, we can be certain, will also be true of the underlying fable. We are now getting to know the geography of its deepest reaches.

The sentence is finally drawing to a close, and it does so by means of some richly sardonic play with echoes of preceding words. I pointed out in another context that the first paragraph as a whole plays with variants of "life": "lived," "living," "lived," "life." What we saw Thoreau doing with the levels of nouns he does also with these variants on "life." "I lived alone" has, as we have seen, all sorts of extraordinary import, existential, phenomenological, linguistic. "I lived there two years and two months" has some of the resonance of the other "lived" but adds matters of temporality and puts more emphasis on the meaning of the word as "resided." "In civilized life" brings in other contrasting elements, leaving little of the special resonance that sounds in the initial "lived." That leaves "earned my living," which we now can hear in the way it ought to be taken, with almost none of the resonance in the opening "I lived." "Earned my living" has everything to do with questions of self-support and little or nothing to do with questions of self-locating. It says "thus I got by," while the other says "thus I *was*."

There is another, related twist, the play on "only." To begin with, the statement contains an implicit bifurcation, the separation of hand labor and mind labor. The bifurcation is neat and will do for an entering wedge, though we know enough by now to guess that so binary a statement will never satisfy Thoreau. But there is still more to "only," for it not only intends to distinguish between various kinds of labor but to valorize them as well. Not only did he choose not to earn a living with his mind but in fact it took only some labor of his hands to earn a living. Sardonic if not quite precise (he says several times elsewhere that he could not earn a living with his mind), this too is a binary play that will not hold up to inspection. Still, there is much more to the matter than such a simple squaring off, for "only" echoes both "myself" and "alone," recalling both of the terms in import and the latter in sound as well. Yet if they are kin, they are not nearly doubles. "Only" picks up a great deal of the willed singularity and solitude in "alone." It also picks up some of the bragging (an act usually performed with others in mind) that sounds from "myself." If "only" is not quite a summary word, it does all that one word can do to end this sentence properly by pulling within a smaller frame much of its essential thrust. The requisite incompleteness of this culminating word ought not to dim our admiration for all that it manages to do.

What it does here in particular is inscribe the fact of his oneness into a variety of acts. Yet, because of the differing concerns of these various modes of oneness, it locates the "I" within them in somewhat different ways, situating it differently because of the differing relations of the "I" to others that share its world. It seems that we cannot depend on oneness always to look or be the same, any more than the play with variations of "live" will always have the same result. "I," that primary shifter, will surely be forced to shift according to the kinds of living we do as well as to our feelings about those acts we choose to perform alone. What we have come forcefully to see is the extraordinary variability of the world within which the "I" has been seeking to locate itself. Obviously that asks of the "I" an equally extraordinary flexibility. We see no set of conditions in which "I" can afford to sit still.

The introductory paragraph ends with two not-quite-flat-out sentences, the first ("I lived there two years and two months") somewhat less innocent than it seems. As I pointed out above, it puts more emphasis on the sense of "resided" than did the earlier appearance of "lived." It does that in part by being relatively precise about the amount of time involved (though in fact Thoreau was there for two years, two months, and two days), which is more specific and far less resonant than the quite remarkable "when" that begins the paragraph and the book. It does for time what the naming of the pond, the town, and the state had done for space, creating an Antaean pinning down. Yet it is as much as instruction for reading as any other aspect of these lines, for the text that is to follow could be (and has been) read as though its actions took place within a single year. The conclusion to be drawn seems simple enough: as we read, we are to watch what Thoreau urges us to watch in "Natural History of Massachusetts," facts blossoming into truths, mere dates turning into transcendental readings of time. Yet these new games with time cannot be permitted to pretend innocence. The autographical acts that form the substance of the paragraph inscribe the "I" not only into the places that syntax makes, not only into the variety of places that echo in the variety of levels of nouns; they also inscribe the "I" into the various kinds of time distinguished by differing terminologies such as "when" and "two years and two months." "I" has differing functions in these differing kinds of time, functions as different as those that sound out from the two appearances of "lived," and out from the related but very different "alone," "myself" and "only." We are being put on the alert in regard to temporal matters, told to be watchful about what happens to "I" in various kinds of time, for it cannot be the same in every one of those kinds. The flexibility the "I" requires with the various forms of "live" and the various modes of oneness has to be carried into its relations with the temporal schemas in which it seeks to inscribe itself. To put the point most precisely and with the merest hint of chill: "I" has to consider the possibility that there is no single temporal scheme, no unitary mode that encompasses all the possible kinds.

Yet the end of the paragraph seems to be brought in quite deliberately to counter this impression, for it affirms a cyclical scheme: "At present I am a sojourner in civilized life again." At one level, this act of recurrence announces the primary structure of *Walden*, the circular shape of the four seasons. It also informs the *re*reader of *Walden* that the introductory paragraph functions within this text like the "argument" of older texts, a sort of précis for the whole; and as though to counter the uneasiness about temporal schemas that runs as a subtext throughout the paragraph, it offers a reminder for the rereader that the cycle the text is going to present is the surest, the most dependable, of all temporal forms. In fact, the final word adds comfort to that gesture: the paragraph that begins with "when" ends with the pleasantly rhyming "again," form affirming function, sound confirming sense. What we have is a tale of recurrence, maybe even the kind of Quest Romance that leads the "I" back to where it came from but with its condition profoundly enriched. That is the scheme that underlies much of the natural supernaturalism of the time, as well as what Meyer Abrams has called the Greater Romantic Lyric.[21] Other terms can frame the recurrence and offer additional sorts of support: for example, the paragraph seems to offer a neatly Aristotelian narrative with an unmistakable beginning, middle, and end, the most comforting framework imaginable for all the inscribing performed by the "I," its autographical gestures, its acts of self-locating.

But to make things so snug and comforting would be to make them inconsistent with everything else we have seen in Thoreau, not only in this paragraph but in his work as a whole. If the last sentence is the key to the announcement of a basic sequence, the key clicks in the lock with the sound of "again." Yet what kind of certainty does he assert when, in the very same sentence, he puts himself forth as a "sojourner," the OED's idea of a temporary (for-the-day) resident, a lodger without deep roots in this place of civilized life? If recurrence promises completeness through the fashioning of an enclosure, a to-talizing that makes up an enclosed temporal space, there is the con-comitant and continued reopening, the fracturing of sequence, that goes on in "sojourner." One of the major effects of that noun is to turn the fact of recurrence into no more than a tentative state. As a result, this sentence reveals a dialectic of doing and undoing, se-quence making and fracture making, one that has the profoundest affinity to the mode of Romantic Irony as it is theorized in Friedrich Schlegel and acted out in Byron's *Don Juan*.[22] One of that mode's main characteristics is a deep antipathy to stasis that emerges, most of all, in a fierce refusal of closure. The appearance of a like dialectic in *Walden*'s introductory lines puts into proper (and unsettling) per-spective those lines' claims for sequence, and since the paragraph as a whole stands as an "argument" to *Walden*, it puts into the same per-spective any claims made by that book. It is not that the sequence of the seasons will cease to do its business but that the participant in that sequence is only passing some days there, is, in effect, a passer-through. That is how the nature of the sequence comes to function within the context of the shiftiness of the shifters, the extraordinary variability in syntax and noun, the incompleteness of "only" despite the efforts to make it whole. It is only as we see the equivalent rest-lessness of the participant in the sequence, only as he contributes to the unmaking of closure, that the assertion about sequence comes to be seen for what it is, no more than a single element in an ongoing dialectic.

And if there is incompletion at so many levels of the paragraph, there is a parallel condition in the "I" whose self-locating is, in a very important sense, the purpose of it all. Consider Thoreau's under-standing of the nature of language and writing. If writing is, by na-ture, a secondary affair, then the words that make up writing must point to an absence. The "I" that commands these lines will therefore have difficulty claiming *immediate* wholeness for itself, that is, a pres-ent totality always sufficient to itself. If writing is the locating of an absence, it is the recording of one as well.

But whether that absence is itself complete, a pure and autono-mous lacuna, may now be called into question. The answer to our problem probably lies in the fact that we are speaking, at once, of *both* the recording and locating of absence. What we are hunting is, there-fore, a mode of understanding that makes sense of a variety of Tho-reauvian statements as well as a variety of his practices. Those prac-tices and statements include his awareness of incompletion and the concomitant pressures of absence, but they also include his ongoing passion for self-locating as well as his regular argument that all texts are, or should be, autobiographical. Absence is therefore incomplete, and for several precise reasons: all of this work of the "I" is a series of autographical acts, gestures of self-locating; and autography is, by nature, a making of indexes; and indexes are, by nature, both fragmentary *and* continuous, locaters of absence that participate in the continuum that ends at the index. Insofar as the "I" is an index (and it is very much one indeed), it speaks simultaneously of the absence of what is pointed to *and* the presence of the pointer, a pointer that stands at the end of a line that has to be whole for the pointer to work at all. Only thus can it establish the "real connection" on which Peirce repeatedly insists; only thus can it be an index at all. This means, of course, that the continuum touches at the immediate—if only fragmentarily so—because that is where the index is located. Words like "absence" and "presence," however shaded and refined, cannot hold all that happens in the Thoreauvian index and therefore in the "I" that begins the text by telling us what went on when he wrote the following pages. Flat-out assertions about either state cannot work in the Thoreauvian context, and they would be just as unsuccessful in commenting on the index, for it, as we recall, both affirms and undoes distance. Autographical acts may be Thoreau's most complex gestures in the passionate self-locating that we have called all along his seeking to *be* in the world. Those gestures were never more complex than at the beginning of this book that tries to say it all.

Part of what it tries to say has to do with the functioning of the "I" not only as index but as metonym within the sociomoral framework. Such a place will inevitably be complicated by the fact that it is always the "I" that is speaking. Consider these comments from the second paragraph, expounding on the idea of the inevitable first person: "I should not talk so much about myself if there were any body else whom I knew as well. Unfortunately, I am confined to this theme by the narrowness of my experience." Of course we are to take this as the inescapable narrowness of everyone's experience, not only Thoreau's. His fullest meaning shows up several pages later: "Nature and human life are as various as our several constitutions. Who shall say what prospect life offers to another? Could a greater miracle take place than for us to look through each other's eyes for an instant? . . . I know of no reading of another's experience so startling and informing as this would be " (10). This means that all we read and write is necessarily restricted, for this passage of speculation is finally no more than a subtly teasing "what if," impossible to realize. Now we see more of what Thoreau means when he speaks of the requisite first person: whatever else it is, it is a sign of inadequacy. However expansive the spectrum that enfolds our self-inscribings, it also contains an inescapable limitation, our inability to get beyond a first-person condition.

But "inescapable" may not be, after all, quite the way to put it, for the dialectic the sequence develops is not yet fully accomplished. There is still another move waiting to be played, a move that accepts the limits imposed by his requisite narrowness but works with them in such a way that the limits become largely irrelevant. Consider the position Thoreau assumes vis-à-vis the audience he has in mind, that curiously mediating stance, part aloof and part participatory, part prophetic and part exemplary. The first few pages of the book show that he is prepared to describe our situation and to chide us from a distance, far enough away that he can see us in the context of exotic Brahmins, close enough that he can see us bearing barns upon our backs. And he will keep up this intricate balance throughout the text which follows, for if he is to tell us repeatedly what we ought to know and do, he will offer, in his own person and through his own repeated actions, as clear an instance as he can of how we ought to do it. He becomes, thus, a synecdoche, acting for all of us in revealing our surprising capacities, what can happen through a wedding of insight and power. The mocking loner becomes a representative figure, much like Ayer the teenage plowman or all those woodsmen in Maine who acted for all of us in inscribing their signatures into the turf.

Consider, too, his position as Cavellian prophetic figure. The prophet is a person who is among us and of us, yet who takes a special stance between men and God, speaking of each to the other. He does what Hölderlin saw himself doing as poet-prophet in "Wie wenn am Feiertage," standing out in the storm to catch and temper the lightning of the gods. Here too is a figure who comes to represent us all in an encounter whose dangers will be no surprise to him. In Thoreau, the figure stands between us and "the world." "Nature" is, in this context, too delimiting a term, unless we take it as Emerson does to include all that is "the NOT ME."

Consider, further, Thoreau's attitude toward the place where all this will occur. He will say something "not so much concerning the Chinese and Sandwich Islanders as you who read these pages," his New England neighbors. "I have travelled a good deal in Concord": which is to say, as he says at the beginning of the final chapter, that he has come to know the whole world by knowing this place so well. After all, the image of the Brahmins universalizes our penance as precisely as any homegrown image. It is a metonym that locates us sardonically in the universal scheme of self-flagellation. What this finally adds up to is a precise equivalence in function of Thoreau and

Concord, each a representative of the larger context, a microcosmic stand-in, the examination of which will yield truths for New England living.

In so establishing himself and his home town as exemplary instances, Thoreau manages to ease the noose of the limitations inherent in the requisite "narrowness" of our experience, its inevitable fragmentariness. He lives within those limits, in fact cannot do otherwise, but does so in such a way that they rarely become claustrophobic, the noose rarely so tight that it leaves no room for play. He knows the limitations of language as well as anyone of his time, yet he can so maneuver the play of pronoun and sequence in the first paragraph of the book that "I," text, and time come into precisely the relation he wants—which is not to say that it is the most desirable relation he can think of but that it is the best he can now achieve. He knows the limitation of his and any experience, his and any place, yet he can so maneuver his prowlings around Concord that he can talk sense about Brahmins to busy local blacksmiths.

All of which is to say that the easing of such nooses may well be part of the business of autographical acts.

• IV •

There are hints of a cosmic allegory in Thoreau's meditations on autography, no more than suggestions but enough to let us glimpse the allegory's contours and how it would fit into his radical fable. Two of its manifestations can serve as the coda for this chapter and the bridge to what follows.

In a passage from the "Monday" chapter of *A Week*, Thoreau compounds lakes and sentences. He had been speaking, in the previous paragraph, of ancient Hindu writings, the Dherma Sastra and also "the laws of Menu with the gloss of Culluca" (150). He begins the next paragraph by speaking of sentences, then shifts unexpectedly into some local events. Woodcutters had felled "an ancient pine forest, and brought to light to these distant hills a fair lake in the southwest; and now in an instant it is distinctly shown to these woods as if its image had travelled here from eternity" (151). The connection comes clear at the end of the paragraph: "So are these old sentences like serene lakes in the south-west, at length revealed to us, which have so long been reflecting our own sky in their bosom." The last part of the sentence is curious if taken by itself, but not if taken in the light of what we have seen of autography as well as related suggestions in this and other texts. These sentences are like lakes which reflect our sky in their bosom; these lakes are like sentences which enfold us within themselves. As our sky is inscribed in the lake, so are we inscribed in these sentences. Part of this surely intends that undoing of temporality Thoreau sought so often to perform, and of which the business of inscribing is one more manifestation. Part of it also intends an echo of the question of inscribing, with all sorts of additional echoes of questions of temporality and that very odd inhabiting of which and to which we are "subject."

This marriage of sky and water, which seems both to bring us into being and to find a berth for us, turns up occasionally in Thoreau, most eloquently in some passages about Walden Pond. The pond is at one time blue and another green, for "lying between the earth and the heavens, it partakes of the color of both" (*W*, 176). It unifies by accepting the inscribing of the colors from above as well as our own local color. There are other inscribings as well. On a fine day in the fall, he finds it soothing to study "the dimpling circles which are incessantly inscribed on its otherwise invisible surface amid the reflected skies and trees" (188). But one can go even deeper than this, down from that surface and into the deepest acts of inscribing. The lake is "earth's eye; looking into which the beholder measures the depth of his own nature" (186). Among such beholders are those who come in the spring, ostensibly to fish for pouts: "they plainly fished much more in the Walden Pond of their own natures, and baited their hooks with darkness" (130). Put in such a sequence, these passages sketch a cosmic geography that goes from the farthest out to the farthest within, expressing in its sweep a continuum of inscribings that reach back into Romantic traditions and certainly beyond those.

And if we return to the paragraph in *A Week* in which lakes are compared to sentences, other patterns become apparent and reveal a further set of connections. The paragraph begins this way: "Give me a sentence which no intelligence can understand. There must be a kind of life and palpitation to it, and under its words a kind of blood must circulate forever" (*AW*, 151). We saw the earliest version of these lines in a *Journal* passage that bears repeating:

> I should like to meet the great and serene sentence—which does not reveal itself—only that it is great.—which I may never with my utmost intelligence pierce through and beyond—(more than the earth itself)—which no intelligence can understand—There should be a kind of life and palpitation to it—under its rind a kind of blood should circulate forever—communicating freshness to its countenance. (*J* 1:375)

The great and serene sentence, the ultimate inscribing, will reflect us as surely, but even more fully, than Walden or any other pond, or any sentences from Menu as well as any we now can make. The cosmic marriage of earth and sky that gives us a place for ourselves prefigures the ultimate writing and therefore, inevitably, the ultimate locating.

Chapter Five

A SPACE FOR SADDLEBACK

THE LOGIC of this study derives, in part, from the logic of Thoreau's thought on some very basic questions about being at home in the world. From language, to writing, to the field of inscribings of which writing is a part, to the functions of autography as a mode of self-inscribing—each of these actions or consequences implies and implicates the others, all of them together creating a tight and rigorous complex. The complex is remarkable in part because, after some hesitant sputtering that sometimes slips into sentimentality (seen as late as in several sections of "Natural History of Massachusetts"), it quickly matures and stays surprisingly consistent through the rest of Thoreau's work. We saw that consistency as early as in *A Week*. Thoreau had drawn up the main lines of the complex by the time the book was completed, that is, during his stay at Walden. For the rest of this chapter, we shall look at *A Week* as a model of many issues, among them the possibility of irony and self-parody, the flexing of a metacommentary.

There are all manner of oddities about *A Week*, and much of the commentary has been devoted to pointing them out. Some have to do with the grab-bag quality of the book: Henry Seidel Canby said that it was "perilously like a library of the shorter works of Henry Thoreau," though Canby went on to say that the poor reception of *A Week* has to be attributed as much to a failure in its audience as to anything in the text.[1] Many commentators since Canby have come to accept the structure of the text, arguing, for example, that its order is based on association and a careful interweaving and development of themes.[2] Still others think of the book as an especially dense version of Transcendental writing, what Lawrence Buell calls "an exploration of one's own higher latitudes," whose purpose is to help one live better at home.[3] Toward the end of his historical introduction to the Princeton text of *A Week*, Linck C. Johnson surveys the shift in twentieth-century thinking about the book, from early readings of its "formlessness" to what he calls, in more recent critics, a "congratulatory view."[4] Writing since Johnson's essay, H. Daniel Peck points to the temporal firmness of *A Week*'s ordering, especially when compared to *Walden* and *The Maine Woods*.[5]

Many of these recent views are plausible; some, like Buell's and

Peck's, are quite convincing in their central efforts; yet most are based on readings of the modes of traditional discourse that appear in *A Week*—classic styles of history writing, various sorts of circling, trips to the natural source—and what they tend not to do is take into consideration Thoreau's questioning of such discourse. That he uses it richly, fruitfully, and often to compelling effect is a point that modern criticism has helped us clearly to see. But that he usually finds the discourse to be unnervingly insufficient—perhaps, finally, incompetent—is the next point to be taken, and that has not been done.

An unquestioning acceptance of the patently regular patterns that form the substance of *A Week* cannot control the bundles of anomalies—some simple, some bogglingly complex—that also inhabit the book. Take, for example, the relation of the title to the content. The trip from which the narrative is taken was, as we know, a two-week excursion, condensed in the text to one for much the same reasons that the two years at Walden Pond came out to be one in the book. Yet the oddity has to do not with the condensation itself but with what was condensed out, or down to a minimal existence. In point of fact, they divided their time equally between land and water trips; and that is precisely what the title does *not* say.[6] Perhaps the title is arguing that the essence of the text is watery, not earthy. Peck shows how the point of view is developed from a position out on the river, with all the implications deriving from such a position. Still, the land trip was not erased completely. Near the end of this good-sized book, Thoreau sketches a two-page record of their hike up Agiocochook, a trip to the source of "the river to which our native stream is a tributary" (314). He goes outside of the titular framework to bring into the textual framework a clearly crucial event, yet what he chooses to say could hardly be briefer. There are other, attendant difficulties, especially with the tone of the event. At least half of the record of the ascent is involved with the description of "a soldier lad in the woods" marching with nervous pomp to his muster, shivering "like a reed in his thin military pants" (313). Such an introduction would qualify any climax. Here it can lead only to a mocking understatement.[7]

Thoreau knew precisely what he was producing at this point: "we would," he says, "be faithful to our experience" (313). The hike may not be part of the week they spent on the river, but Thoreau obviously takes it as part of the meaning of that week. It therefore had to appear somewhere within the framework, even if it had to be brought in from the earthy outside. His handling of his narrative is designed to get him closer to "a true account of the actual" (325). Such loyalty to exactitude characterizes all his works, even when they reshape the relationship of the events on which they are based. As he puts it in the "Friday" chapter: "I have no respect for facts even except when I would use them, and for the most part I am independent of those which I hear, and can afford to be inaccurate, or, in other words, to substitute more present and pressing facts in their place" (363). Those present, pressing facts are the stuff of sufficient fictions, fictions surely supreme.

Those who argue for the orderliness of *A Week*, for its carefully designed artifice, have come to be far more convincing than those who shrug at the text. Yet this is still not to say that every element in *A Week* clicks comfortably into place once we recognize commanding shapes. Take, for example, the "Tuesday" chapter. It begins at an earlier point in the day than some of the other chapters, with a noisy predawn excursion to hunt for firewood. By the time they clean out their boat and get themselves ready, it is 3:00 A.M. They push off into the fog that seems to envelop them every morning, trusting, as Thoreau says, "that there was a bright day behind it" (179). After quoting a historian on the prevalence of such fogs, Thoreau remarks on their extent and on the limits of the larger fogs that go beyond river valleys. He then says, "I once saw the day break from the top of Saddleback Mountain in Massachusetts, above the clouds. As we cannot distinguish objects through this dense fog, let me tell this story more at length" (180). And he does so, for ten of the most compelling pages in his writings. Yet the story he tells has peculiarities about it. *A Week* is the record of a river journey taken in the fall of 1839. The ascent up Saddleback Mountain (now known as Greylock) took place in 1844, though the text never mentions that point (any more than the title mentions the week they spent on land). Thus, Thoreau describes a hike up a mountain while the narrative still has them floating on the river, and he gets to tell of the hike by interrupting the record of a journey that took place five years earlier. Why does he do it precisely at that point—which is, as it turns out, almost exactly in the middle of his narrative? Why, indeed, is it in *A Week* at all?

• I •

To answer those questions properly we need to begin by examining the shape and process of Thoreau's narrative and how they come to be. "Concord River," the introductory chapter, goes over the physical and historical context of the river and works out the mode in which the book asks to be read. Though the chapter is not part of the narrative of the trip, it has the same function as those introductory lines in meditative poems that tell us where the meditator is located, establishing a place from which the journey of the mind will begin. George Herbert, whom Thoreau quotes several times in the text, wrote a number of such poems.[8] Wordsworth practiced a version of the technique in "Tintern Abbey" and the "Immortality" ode, and Coleridge did the same in his Conversation Poems.[9] This chapter's link to meditative beginnings of the sort Thoreau knew well offers a considerable hint about the qualities that will follow. But Thoreau cannot resist ironizing and exalting at once. He turns "our muddy but much abused Concord River" into a counterpart of history's most famous rivers and then, irony gone underground, into an image of the stream of time. Thus, before we enter into the main body of the narrative, the text itself offers suggestions about how to read it. At the same time, it demonstrates how our minds can turn the facticity of our experience into images of radical truth. As the introductory chapter moves through a discussion of the river in all its literal contexts, it transmutes the river into "an emblem of all progress, following the same law with the system, with time, and all that is made" (12). The chapter, it turns out, is about ourselves as well as the river, about processes of mind as well as processes of nature.

It seems inevitable, then, that the text will lead us in two directions at once, down the river and into the mind. The travelers are hardly on their way, just passing the remaining abutments of the North Bridge, when the two directions come into play. "Our reflections," he says, "had already acquired a historical remoteness from the scenes we had left" (17). Separating rapidly from his immediate surroundings, his thoughts go off to an encounter with the events of 1775, his mind engaging with the past while his body and the boat go forward with the flow of the present. His body takes part in the rhythms of nature while his mind finds other rhythms, unavailable to the body. Thoreau's statement about the historical remoteness of their reflections comes in at this initiating point to clarify an essential issue, what meditation means to the relations of mind and body. We will be seeing a bifurcation in which one fork goes inevitably seaward while the other goes where it wants. It can go to the season when the North Bridge was rumbling with intimations of war, or back to the earliest beginnings of "the Musketaquid or Grass-ground River," which is "probably as old as the Nile or Euphrates" (5). Bound inexorably to the present and its rigorous forward thrust, the body is caught in the rhythms of nature; but there are no inevitable directions in the mind, seaward or otherwise. We are beginning to uncover the contours of a map that contains several kinds of geography, and Thoreau is careful to point out what we can do in each of them.

These pages show still more. After quoting some of his own poems and remarking on the sinking of the sun and the subsiding of the village murmur, Thoreau spends some time on a detailed description of the foliage on or near the water. This is Thoreau the naturalist, focusing on the immediate and contemporary, on what he can notice by opening his eyes. His mode here is observation, and it differs very clearly from the mode of meditation. Meditation can take us anywhere; observation stays right here. In meditation, the mind goes in one direction and the body in another. In observation, mind and body focus on the same place and time, the here and now, and any speculations that the mind makes are speculations on the world around it. It is the product of a meeting of mind and body in the immediate moment. But meditation can occur only when the mind moves within itself and away from immediacy.

This interplay that is offered so early in the text is as important to the life of A Week as any other elements within it. One of the essential oscillations in the book, it is repeated with varying cadences for the rest of A Week. This text is therefore not only about Thoreau as river traveler or even as mental traveler, either role offering ample precedent in the cultural history he knew. One of the major feats of A Week lies in its ability to be, at once, about both kinds of traveling—which means, in effect, to be also about a third that not only encompasses the other two but, refusing a binary choice, suggests a richer and better way. That third is, of course, the simultaneous performance of what seemed to be a set of alternate choices. Here, as elsewhere, A Week lays down the lines of some basic Thoreauvian practices. In the "Village" chapter of Walden, Thoreau remembers those times when he would walk back to the cabin late on dark nights, "dreaming and absent-minded all the way, until," as he says, "I was aroused by raising my hand to lift the latch" and was "not able to recall a single step of my walk" (170). Here he is doing that strange third thing, performing both kinds of traveling at once, the body following its instincts with a life that is seen as separate from and independent of the mind. It can function without the mind's attentiveness while moving easily, comfortably, through the spaces of the wood. The mind pursues its business through its own kind of spaces, returning to the spaces the body inhabits when it is ready to touch the world again. The same process occurs repeatedly in A Week: Thoreau will get his thought going at some point on his river trip, let his mind go about its business, and then return to the river, although farther downstream from the point where he started.[10] Though the several kinds of traveling happen in different places, they happen at the same time and to the same person. Each is therefore part of the capacities of Henry David

Thoreau, and their relationship in the book appears to be offered as an allegory of their relationship in him.

That sounds very fine and satisfying at this point in the narrative, establishing a grand surmise for the journeys in the rest of *A Week*. But we have seen enough of Thoreau to suspect that this parallelism of self and text will turn out to own ironies that make the surmise uneasy. *A Week* is so far from being the muddle that some have called it that we could (should) end by admiring the canniness of its practices, especially its practice of subversion.

For that surmise had been made uneasy during the process that was laying it out. At the beginning of the "Saturday" chapter, Thoreau describes the boat he and his brother had built the previous spring, the boat that was to take them down and up the two rivers. Here too the text plays with a variously dimensioned allegory, though this time with implications that turn the other one quite around. Built like a stable fisherman's dory, the boat was "painted green below, with a border of blue, with reference to the two elements in which it was to spend its existence" (15). That point prefigures exactly those passages in *Walden* where Thoreau speaks of the pond as a link between heaven and earth: "Walden is blue at one time and green at another, even from the same point of view. Lying between the earth and the heavens, it partakes of the color of both" (*W*, 176). In so partaking, it offers a fusion of the green nature we live in and the blue heaven we aspire to. That is the fusion of the demigod, who finds within himself that marvelous illogic in which radical differences find a way of working together. Defined in other terms, both pond and boat offer an outline of total desire put into a total form, in the case of the boat, offering a shape that permits it to work fluently in several elements at once. If fashioned with proper attention, the boat should be a perfect blend; and even though theirs is not quite so (it was "hardly of better model than usual" [16], Thoreau and his brother came close enough at least to comprehend perfection:

> If rightly made a boat would be a sort of amphibious animal, a creature of two elements, related by one half its structure to some swift and shapely fish, and by the other to some strong-winged and graceful bird. The fish shows where there should be the greatest breadth of beam and depth in the hold; its fins direct where to set the oars, and the tail gives some hint for the form and position of the rudder. The bird shows how to rig and trim the sails, and what form to give to the prow that they may balance the boat, and divide the air and water best. These hints we had but partially obeyed. (16)

Partial obedience is enough to make a working version of the blend, a form of that ideal instrument which can take us through the elements that determine the ultimate shape of what we want to be.

One way of conceiving that shape has its profoundest roots in traditional discourse, that is, in the way we think of our ideal selves in terms of combinations like that green-blue blend of swift fish and strong-winged bird. Conceptions of that sort run all through *Walden*'s descriptions of the pond and our relations to it: if the pond is "intermediate in its nature between land and sky . . . many men have been likened to it but few deserve that honor" (*W*, 188–89; 192). However few they are, the pond remains an ideal image of ourselves, as does the boat. That Thoreau and his brother chose to paint the boat in those colors shows a more-than-subliminal awareness of the import of the blend. And in fact he had hinted openly at the ideal, the placement in a single framework of flesh and spirit, just a few lines before this, at the beginning of the text: "for Concord, too, lies under the sun, a port of entry and departure for the bodies as well as the souls of men" (15). By the time we get to the spelling out of the colors of the boat, the meaning of those colors is beyond any doubt. Bright and early in the text we are given still another surmise about ourselves and how we are constituted.

And it is precisely because these surmises come at the same crucial point in the text, little more than a page apart and at the beginning of the setting out, that the ironies have their way. That surmise which has to do with varieties of bifurcation, the traveling of the mind and the traveling of the body offering a parallel to the capacities of Henry David Thoreau, cannot sit comfortably with the other surmise, the one that finds *its* allegory in the workings of the boat. At the onset of its narrative, *A Week* puts forth two contradictory ideals, each of which has its basis in all manner of traditional discourse. The ideal of bifurcation, the splitting of soul and body that privileges the former both in its freedom and essential divinity, finds one of its strands of history in the business about the Brahmins that turns up at the beginning of *Walden*, just as a journeyman version turns up at the beginning of *A Week*. The opposing ideal of the blend puts Thoreau firmly within the traditional discourse we have noted. And if, in certain ways, he stands midway between Blake and Stevens, Thoreau's boat furthers Blake's notion that "man has no Body distinct from his Soul for that called Body is a portion of Soul discerned by the five Senses. The chief inlets of Soul in this age."[11] To proffer this pairing of contrary readings at the beginning of the narrative is, finally, to insist that the making of a choice may be impossible to resolve. And yet it is surely the ultimate matter when we come to ponder our ways of being in the world, for if we, as forked animals, take biforking as our basic condition, we shall be in the world in a very different way than if our condition is a blue-green blending. The only viable approach is to take Thoreau as, again, seeking to be faithful to our experience. Its only viable result is a position of ambivalence—not a refusal to make a choice between the pairing of surmises but a recognition that no choice can honestly be made without massive equivocation. If "Concord River" stands as a prologue to *A Week*, putting forth, as prologues do, suggestions for ways of reading, the first three pages of the narrative put forth some other options, less blatant but equally traditional, less easy to fix and hold.

And as though to confirm the dilemma these options force upon us, Thoreau has trouble making up his mind on several issues deriving from them. To take one representative pairing: in the "Wednesday" chapter, he repeats a story about a woman who discovered traces of an old hunting camp while looking for pennyroyal. The thought of that healing plant leads him to the healing arts, to the relations of priests and physicians (their roles interchangeable in even the most civilized countries), and then to the typically Thoreauvian paradox that, despite their likenesses, "the one's profession is a satire on the other's, and either's success would be the other's failure" (257). He ends the passage with the complaint that, though "men believe practically that matter is independent of spirit," in fact "there is need of a physician who shall minister to both soul and body at once, that is to man." The human comes to be defined according to its blend of blue and green, its pure unitary state. Subliminal echoes of the boat as "amphibious animal" call back to the text's beginnings for linkage and support, and beyond them to the sounds of one old discourse. But the text makes other calls toward the end of the same chapter. Sitting on the bank, eating their supper, the travelers come to think of universal laws, of Syria and India, Alexander and Hannibal, and they arrive at the conclusion that "this world is but canvass to our imaginations" (292). Men endeavor with infinite pains "to realize to their bodies" what ought to be realized to the imagination, "for certainly there is a life of the mind above the wants of the body and independent of it." So much for that aptest medicine which would minister to the truly human by attending to body and soul together. So much for a colloquy of discourses: it seems that the choices the text proffers can end only in cacophony.

Of course it would be much easier if the text offered either/or, blue-green or bifurcation; but it does not, and given Thoreau's antipathy to the binary, it would be surprising were the text to do so. One might consider such a choice as in fact a metadiscourse offering perfectly clear alternatives between two opposing readings of the relations of soul and body. As readers of the histories of such speculations (those histories are one of the sites where the metadiscourse works), we know what such choices would look like. But Thoreau flatly refuses to accept these blocked-out alternatives, perhaps because such choices create a neatly unified structure, the wholeness that results when a pair of perfect opposites ends up in a self-contained microcosm. Nowhere is Thoreau's uneasiness with such autonomous packages more patent than in his refusal to accept such a choice, and in what that refusal does to our reading of *A Week*. For in presenting the possibility that each alternative has a legitimate claim upon him, Thoreau undoes the wholeness that either/or makes and puts it all into suspension, the result, the discontinuity that comes from irresolution. Instead of a binary whole, there is radical incompletion. This too we shall have to attribute to his passionate wish to "be faithful to our experience."

All of this puts *A Week* into some very difficult trouble—a warring of text and subtext, of subterranean mutterings and the bright chirpings of accepted discourse—that gives the text a deep and especially vigorous life. The trouble has to do with some of the major formulations that make up the text, the cycles in particular but also several tendencies stemming from the generic function of the text as travelogue. Consider, for example, the business of directions. When the travelers pushed their boat away from the banks of the Concord "and dropped silently down the stream" (15), they were setting out in a seaward direction, going down the river to the point where it joins the Merrimack. To continue the text's suggestions on how it ought to be read, their trip down the Concord concurs "with time, and all that is made," a passive, acquiescent gesture that puts them into harmony with the most basic level of nature. At noon on Sunday, they entered the Merrimack through the Middlesex locks, making a turn in direction and mode that would take them upstream to New Hampshire. Once again we are led to accept the logic of the text's suggestion: if the trip downstream involves a concurrence with nature, the trip upstream would have to involve its opposite, a decision to go against the natural direction, a decision that could be acted on only through a considerable exercise of will. This imposition of will upon the tendencies of nature is characteristically Thoreauvian, a gesture that, in other contexts, he saw as eminently human. Every time a farmer turns a swamp into a meadow, every time a woodsman makes a clearing in the forest, someone has imposed his will upon nature and turned it into something useful for the human.[12] This we can call the humanizing imagination, the sort he saw so often with the loggers in

The Maine Woods, the sort that finds it purest Transcendental expression in Emerson's *Nature*. Its requisite opposite would be the naturalizing imagination, that desire to shape one's life as part of the natural order, the impulse that drew Thoreau to think of devouring woodchucks and, when he was up in Maine, to admire Indians who could talk to muskrats. The naturalizing imagination seeks to lock us into nature, the humanizing looks at nature as our opponent in a struggle—which ought not to be taken to mean that we are *anti*natural but that we are seeking to impose ourselves upon the natural order, perhaps to do something that nature will not ordinarily permit. It will not, for example, permit us easily to go upstream in search of the place where the river begins. To do that we have to be *contra*natural. Thoreau's journey on the rivers can therefore be taken as an allegory of the workings of two kinds of imagination, two opposing modes of encountering nature.

Put so baldly, this is, of course, a reductive scheme at best, not least because of our uneasiness with terms like "naturalizing" and "humanizing." We can assume that Thoreau establishes the scheme in its simplest form so he can complicate it sufficiently and bring it closer to the truths of our experience. His awareness of the play of directions and the import of that play turns up often in the text, for example, in this passage from "Tuesday," where they are resting from the heat of the day: "When we made a fire to boil some rice for our dinner, the flames spreading amid the dry grass, and the smoke curling silently upward and casting grotesque shadows on the ground seemed phenomena of the noon, and we fancied that we progressed up the stream without effort, and as naturally as the wind and tide went down, not outraging the calm days by unworthy bustle or impatience (222–23). Going upstream "naturally" can happen only in fancy, just as Thoreau can go back in time to the events of 1775 only in acts of the mind. The contranatural imagination involves not only acts like making clearings in the forest but also our capacities to counter the temporal flow and our capacities to counter the flow of the tide.[13] Of course, those last two capacities have a long, archetypal linking, but their placement alongside acts like redeeming a meadow or placing bricks in a trackless forest is by no means an obvious one, and it complicates the issue considerably.

For example, countering the flow of the tide in a blue-green boat that stands for the wholeness of flesh and spirit makes for a clear and pristine allegory, putting together as it does both the struggle we have to make against the contranatural flow and a perfect sort of instrument with which to make the struggle. Relating these two concepts seems almost inevitable, and Thoreau accepts the temptation.

But the blue-green idea is only one way of reading the relations of body and soul, as we saw in the binary choice between blending and bifurcation. So—to bring in the alternative that always shadows the blue-green one—how does one go up toward the place where the stream begins its flow if body and soul cannot work in comfortable harmony? If their harmony is less than perfect, will that hamper the ascent? Thoreau, as we shall see, accepts that possibility too.

To add to these complications, we have to keep in mind that there are several mountain ascents referred to in *A Week* and that the climbing of a mountain necessarily involves precisely the same processes, the going up and down that describes an ascent and return, that appear in the other activities that crowd under the heading of the humanizing imagination. Indeed, it is only when we acknowledge the homology of these processes that much of the richness in *A Week* becomes apparent.

We are now ready to return to the problems we posed ourselves earlier—why the climb up Saddleback Mountain is where it is in *A Week*, why, in fact, it is in the text at all.

The Saddleback episode is actually a single element in a rich and complex sequence, one of a series of mountain ascents referred to in *A Week*. We shall have to consider several ascents in order to establish some answers to our questions about the point of Saddleback. Still—and this, we are coming to realize, is typical of Thoreau—the sequence stretches to include scenes outside of *A Week*, especially those in the early essay, "A Walk to Wachusett." That stretching will surely have an effect on how we read the series, but it is also an object lesson in how we ought to read Thoreau; we need to establish the proper contextual focus. We gain our fullest understanding of the Saddleback ascent only when we see it in the context of Thoreau's earlier work.

"Wachusett," which was published in *Boston Miscellany of Literature* in January 1843, records a four-day walk begun on July 19, 1842, with Margaret Fuller's brother, Richard.[14] As so often with Thoreau, the text begins with instructions for reading, though this time the reading will extend through Thoreau's first book (which is not, of course, to say that Thoreau planned it that way but that as he worked out *A Week* the continuity became apparent and then developed and thickened as the text progressed). Here is the first sentence of the essay:

> Summer and winter our eyes had rested on the dim outline of the mountains in our horizon, to which distance and indistinctness lent a grandeur not their own, so that they served equally to interpret all the allusions of

poets and travellers; whether with Homer, on a spring morning, we sat down on the many-peaked Olympus, or, with Virgil and his compeers, roamed the Etrurian and Thessalian hills, or with Humboldt measured the more modern Andes and Teneriffe. (*Excursions*, 72)

A great deal of literary history works through the intertextual life of this sentence, not only eighteenth-century saws about distance lending enchantment to the view, and the related context of saws in which dimness and the sublime reinforce each other, but also a broad sweep of literary mountains from the earliest classics to more recent traveling. Most important, however, is what the sentence says about the related ways in which we read landscapes and texts. To start off with distance and indistinctness means, in this context, to make space for sufficient fictions, adequate to illuminate a range of relevant truths. We have not only returned to Thoreau's point about being true to our experience but are looking ahead to the beginnings of many chapters in *A Week* where fogs are the first element we face in the "morning" of the piece. The most elaborate of those beginnings is the one in "Tuesday," the chapter that takes Thoreau up Saddleback Mountain.

Other hints of a flexibility that undoes the day-to-day appear as the text gets underway, the first a clumsy phrasing from the doggerel poem (rejected by Margaret Fuller for the *Dial*) that stands near the head of the text:

I fancy even
Through your defiles windeth the way to heaven;
And yonder still, in spite of history's page,
Linger the golden and the silver age;
Upon the laboring gale
The news of future centuries is brought,
And the new dynasties of thought,
From your remotest vale.

(75)

Westering leads to heaven, but it is a very curious heaven that holds within itself not only the golden and silver ages but future centuries and other discourses ("new dynasties of thought"), a place where origin and end fuse without confusion, so that going toward the one comes also to mean successfully going toward the other. That establishes a surmise whose echoes we shall be hearing elsewhere in the sequence on mountains.

The second suggestion of flexibility makes plain Thoreau's insistence on the efficacy of certain fictions. Their walk took them through the town of Sterling and past the banks of the Stillwater, "where a small village collected" (82). Thoreau's habit of associating westering with wildness, and the wild with that which either has not yet been named or is named by those who are wilder than these travelers (cf. 78), takes over here as well, not only in the names of the river but of "this village [which] had, as yet, no post-office, nor any settled name" (83). He goes on to describe how "in the small villages which we entered, the villagers gazed after us, with a complacent, almost compassionate look, as if we were just making our *debut* in the world at a late hour. 'Nevertheless,' did they seem to say, 'come and study us, and learn men and manners.' So is each one's world but a clearing in the forest, so much open and inclosed ground" (83). Though this is especially effective in the context of the trip to Wachusett, it actually comes from a journal entry about a trip made four years earlier in a very different place:

Portland to Bath-via Brunswick-Bath to Brunswick-May 5th—
Each one's world is but a clearing in the forest-so much open and inclosed ground. —When the mail coach rumbles into one of these-the villagers gaze after you with a compassionate look, as much as to say "Where have you been all this time, that you make your début [*sic*] in the world at this late hour? nevertheless, here we are, come and study us, that you may learn men and manners. (*J 1:45)

When and where things happen are less important than what happens, for the latter may be a fiction in terms of *this* place and time but can become a sufficient synecdoche for an abiding and prevalent condition. In this light, an earlier remark in "A Walk to Wachusett" seems to offer a justification for what is actually an adequate lie: "So soon did we, wayfarers, begin to learn that man's life is rounded with the same few facts, the same simple relations everywhere, and it is vain to travel to find it new" (78). Once we accept this idea, such synecdoches make sense, for they tell the same radical story and may well be more efficacious than what was actually there. We shall see the same efficacy in the "Tuesday" chapter of *A Week*.

There is, however, no question of substituting something else for the ascent of Wachusett Mountain, for Thoreau can make what he needs out of the materials at hand. He prepares our reading of the ascent with some fairly fancy writing about getting to be at home up there:

As we gathered the raspberries, which grew abundantly by the roadside, we fancied that that action was consistent with a lofty prudence, as if the traveller who ascends into a mountainous region should fortify himself by eating of such light ambrosial fruits as grow there; and, drinking of the springs which gush out from the mountain sides, as he gradually inhales the subtler and purer atmosphere of those elevated places, thus propitiating the mountain gods, by a sacrifice of their own fruits. The gross products of the plains and valleys are for such as dwell therein; but it seemed to us that the juices of this berry had relation to the thin air of the mountain-tops. (84)

They seek a sacramental libation to put them in tune with the mountaintops, acknowledging that they come out of the plains and may well carry part of the plains within them as they go up. Literary, somewhat stuffy, approaching affectation, these and similar lines seek carefully to control a distinction of locales that has within it the potential for considerable unease. Yet the comfort is not quite complete, for some subtextual mutterings still manage to make it to the surface, partly through comments on how the summit is "removed from all contagion with the plain" (87), partly through others on their passage over the heights where "the follies of the plain are refined and purified" (92). Their upward mobility has a redemptive dimension. We can gauge the degree of its potency by the degree of fanciness in the language, going on the assumption that such elevated language is there to contain the threat of contagion, to distance them from its touch in precisely the same way that the ascent distances them from the pollution of the plain. The homology of the ascent and of the language that makes it happen ("elevated" works for both) is evident and precise. Still, however successfully "Wachusetts" keeps down the subtextual muttering, it cannot do so completely. The travelers' need for a libation grows clearer to the reader as the text grows more familiar.

This puts into perspective Thoreau's comments on the place of mountains in the general scheme of things (91–92). On the summits, one arrives at a pervasive sense of unity, for we can see how the hand "which moulded their opposite slopes [made] one to balance the other." From this we go on to learn how the least part of nature refers to all space, how the rivers answer to "the general direction of the coast, the bank of the great ocean stream itself." And all that elaborate ordering works around "a deep centre" that holds the whole together. (That center appears, with different suppositions, in Poe's *Eureka*.) One can see all this only when one climbs to the summits, and even then not right away. No wonder that we seek to leave the place of contagion behind, purifying ourselves as we ascend: only with such purity can we attain such a vision. A long tradition claims this to be the only possible condition in which such seeing can take place. Further, we need that condition to perceive how we ourselves relate to that radical shape, how not only "the least part of nature" but we too, in our bearings, refer to all space. To be able to see is to be able to partake, that is, to achieve that sort of at-homeness where we are in absolute relation—no hesitation or rebuff, no incompleteness, no place or sight blocked off—with all that there is to be seen.

Of course when they descend, there has to be a kind of letdown, a condition connected with the travelers' return "to the abodes of men," as they turn their faces to the east, finding themselves "almost at home again" (93). Those circular travels put them into a most ironic oneness with the conditions of the plain, and they find themselves going mindless: "At length, as we plodded along the dusty roads, our thoughts became as dusty as they; all thought indeed stopped, thinking broke down, or proceeded only passively in a sort of rhythmical cadence of the confused material of thought, and we found ourselves mechanically repeating some familiar measure which timed with our tread" (94). The ascent had called from them the fullest stretch of being, but the descent and return home ask only a homologous descent on the Great Chain of Being, approaching the condition of mindless dust. Oddly, they say nothing in their walk over the plains about the contagion of the plains, the need to purify themselves. They realize the need for cleansing (of all that the dust is, surely) only when they travel in the other direction. They know nothing of the threat of staining while they are in the place of staining. Thoreau speaks of how their climbing and descending are "perfectly symbolical of human life" (95), of how the desultory life of the plain needs some "mountain grandeur" in it (96). But a bit of allegory making and a comforting moral conclusion cannot subdue the subterranean grumbling that mandates not only the putting aside of impurity but even the defensive language in which that putting aside is described—the kind that echoes at the end in the allegory of human life and the insufficient moral. The framework of the experience rendered in "A Walk to Wachusett" is not especially stable, whatever its claims to the contrary. It is precisely that instability that *A Week* was to pick up.

And in fact it was ready to do so when it took into the "Monday" chapter (162–66) a condensation of "A Walk to Wachusett." Thoreau includes the introductory lines of "Wachusett," which are on distance and indistinctness and how they serve to interpret "all the allusions of poets and travellers." He is equally careful to include the comments about scaling the blue wall at the horizon, "though not without misgivings that thereafter no visible fairy land would exist for us" (165). Except for a version of the poem, nothing of the rest remains, the result of which is to leave the surviving prose excerpts speaking largely of readings and fictions, and hinting (without resolution) that there might be disappointment ahead. Subtle and somewhat ominous, the shift carefully defines what "Wachusett" had come to signify for Thoreau since its publication in 1843. Though the new version says nothing about the contagion of the plain, it suggests that *something* could stand in the way of their glimpse of a "visible fairy land." The subtext lives on in these unresolved speculations, putting into *A Week*'s pondering on mountains a potential for uneasiness, based on a potential for incompletion, that was never to leave the text.

Other elements in these pages suggest further subversions. "A Walk to Wachusett" took some notes out of the *Journal* for 1838 and wove them, without acknowledgment, into the report of a trip he made in 1842. *A Week* reverses direction, taking sections of the essay and weaving them, without acknowledgment, into the report of a trip he made in 1839. Further, *A Week* sets the impression that the poem was contemporary with the trip on the two rivers, quoting directly from the essay but in a way that clearly refers to the travels *A Week* is describing: "Standing on the Concord Cliffs we thus spoke our mind to them" (163). Taking out of the essay what now seems to him most significant, Thoreau grants a dark hint to contagion and blatantly plays with fictions that subvert "regular" temporality, especially its insistence on rigorous, determinate order. That is a very odd thing to do in a book built so openly on self-contained cycles, and it necessarily affects the way we read the sequence on mountains and maybe even the book as a whole. The reader who comes to *A Week* with a reasonably good memory of Thoreau's previous work (and considering the paucity of sales, many of its readers must have been such) hears a voice emergent in this passage which speaks in countertones to the overall voice of the text. In effect, this is to say that "A Walk to Wachusett" is, to certain elements in *A Week*, a pre-text for what is to follow, and it remains in the background as a shadow text that has a great deal to say about crucial aspects of the book.

Of the seven chapters in *A Week* that have to do directly with their trip, five refer to the fog or mist with which the day's atmosphere begins, one speaks of how "a warm drizzling rain had obscured the morning" (15), and only one ("Wednesday") says nothing about such impediments to vision. Readers of Thoreau know that morning means to him a diurnal re-originating where all opportunities begin again (see, e.g., *W*, 88–89). Since each chapter of *A Week* begins with the condition of the morning, textual and diurnal origins take an in-

terlocking relationship, each mirroring the other and ultimately becoming indistinguishable from it. And since fog or mist turns up at
all but one of these points of beginning, it seems reasonable to conclude that Thoreau connects these varied scenes of origin with difficulty of vision.[15] That those beginnings also suggest—somewhat more
than subliminally—the origin of the world appears not only in many
of the passages about mornings as fresh starts but in this passage
from the *Journal* written a decade after the writing of *A Week*: "It is
one of the mornings of *creation*, and the trees, shrubs, etc., etc., are
covered with a fine leaf frost, as if they had their morning robes on,
seen against the sun. There has been a mist in the night. Now, at 8.30
A.M., I see, collected over the low grounds behind Mr. Cheney's, a
dense fog (over a foot of snow), which looks dusty like smoke by contrast with the snow" (*J* 8:74). This pure illustration of that conflation
of themes is by no means the only one in the canon.[16] The chapters
and days of *A Week* begin with a set of significations that can end only
at origin, at the first lines of *Genesis*, which show precisely the same
complex questions of origin occurring at the beginning of a text, with
darkness spread over all.

That reference has more to speak of than the intertextual life of
Thoreau's various beginnings. Something of the fullest meaning of
their traveling in *A Week* comes through in the "Thursday" chapter,
in remarks directed not only to traveling in general (these comments
prefigure those in the late essay "Walking") but to their actions in the
two weeks that *A Week* disparately covers. "True and sincere travelling," he states, "is no pastime, but it is as serious as the grave, or any
other part of the human journey, and it requires a longer probation
to be broken into it" (306). It is so solemn and serious a matter because "the traveller must be born again on the road, and earn a pass-
port from the elements, the principal powers that be for him." The
play with originatings that starts each chapter of *A Week* is linked
with—prefigures and supports and ultimately defers to—the one
form of rebirth that is the most important of all, the one that has to
("must be") take place within ourselves. The multiple beginnings in *A
Week* and the act of traveling that informs it need to be taken together
in order to gather the fullness of each and the profoundest meaning
of the whole.

That meaning comes out more openly in the story of the ascent of
Saddleback than at any other place in the text, a point which goes far
toward explaining both the emphasis on originating and the unusually dense fog that appear at the beginning of "Tuesday" (179–80).
At the same time, that introductory passage suggests broadly what is
to follow. It quotes from two poems, one by Tennyson and one by

Thoreau, the former (from "The Lady of Shalott") heading the chapter with a reference to traveling "thro' the fields the road runs by / To many-towered Camelot." (That there are hints of the Romance in all of Thoreau's excursions is a point we can begin to explore in this passage.) Thoreau's poem, however, speaks not of ends but of origins and dwells especially on a contranatural traveling that pits them against temporality and puts them always at the point of beginning:

> Rivers from the sunrise flow.
>   Springing with the dewy morn;
> Voyageurs 'gainst time do row,
> Idle noon nor sunset know,
>   Ever even with the dawn.

(179)

An odd, uneasy illogic pervades the meeting of these pieces of poetry: if the travelers are always even with the dawn, knowing nothing of the stages of the diurnal narrative, how can they get to a Camelot, the goal of every Romance? In fact, they will always be on the way, the journey always incomplete, Camelot never quite in sight.[17] We have already seen how the subversion of "regular" temporality that occurs in the excerpt from "Wachusett" calls into deep question the cycles that inform *A Week*. Here is more of the same questioning, a subversion of temporal sequence that has to cast into doubt not only the efficacy of cyclical journeys but, especially, the desirability of completion. Yet it seems as though a desire for arriving somewhere is also at work in this passage, in part in the Camelot business, in part in the passage's interplay of obscurity and clarity, one that combines hope and surmise: "Though we were enveloped in mist as usual, we trusted that there was a bright day behind it" (179).

Perhaps there would be, but the Tuesday-morning fog was to be the densest of their journey, so dense that Thoreau adjourns the narrative of their river excursion for another that tells of a trip up a mountain. Part of the reason he tells the story is to compare the extent of fog on the two journeys. The one on the river is less confining than it appears: "That which seemed to us to invest the world, was only a narrow and shallow wreath of vapor stretched over the channel of the Merrimack from the sea-board to the mountains." But other conditions seem less bound to the contours of the earth: "More extensive fogs, however, have their own limits" (180). No other chapter in *A Week* is prepared as cannily, elaborately, as this. That is because what follows controls so much of the meaning of the book.

Thoreau places part of that meaning squarely before us at the beginning of the narrative, drawing on some of his habitual play with language. He "had come over the hills on foot and alone" and "began in the afternoon to ascend the mountain" (180), noting the few scattered farms along the way. "It seemed," he says, "a road for the pilgrim to enter upon who would climb to the gates of heaven" (181), the hints of allegory not so blunt as at the end of "Wachusett" but sufficient to produce the point. Yet Thoreau seems to think otherwise and goes on to put together the comments about solitude and askesis into one punning sentence: "It seemed as if he must be the most singular and heavenly-minded man whose dwelling stood highest up the valley" (182). We are eased into our reading of the ascent with some familiar themes and practices, Thoreau's solitude and wordplay already known from the early essays, his theme of askesis known from the densest cultural history. Further echoes of the Romance combine with his own preoccupations: "gradually ascending all the while," he is taken by "a sort of awe, and filled with indefinite expectations as to what kind of inhabitants and what kind of nature I should come to at last" (181). And thereupon come some surprises, the first a figure unparalleled in Thoreau's work and, given the nature of that work and his views on sexuality, frankly astonishing. Having reached the last house but one, he considers returning to it after the ascent and staying for as much as a week, "if I could have entertainment" (182). That last word rings very oddly through the sentence which immediately follows, describing the inhabitant of the house:

> Its mistress was a frank and hospitable young woman, who stood before me in a dishabille, busily and unconcernedly combing her long black hair while she talked, giving her head the necessary toss with each sweep of the comb, with lively, sparkling eyes, and full of interest in that lower world from which I had come, talking all the while as familiarly as if she had known me for years, and reminding me of a cousin of mine. (182)

Considering what we have seen of patent echoes of the Romance, this figure makes all sorts of sense and has a long, rich set of counterparts from the beginning of the mode. In medieval forms of Romance and their immediate successors, she would be one of the impediments to the success of the quest, what Homer began with Circe.[18] Indeed, her query about "that lower world from which I had come" gives her precisely the right aura to fit her into that Romance pattern. Of course, nothing like those diversions could happen in this context, yet her quite unexpected appearance not only offers further echoes of the ancient mode he was practicing but also prepares Thoreau for other unexpected answers to his query about people and places higher up the mountain.

Still, even this bit of the unforeseen (given Thoreau, of the unforeseeable) is not, it seems, enough to make him uneasy. At that house he had determined to take the less frequented way, in part, he says, because it was shorter and more adventurous, in part also because it would be his "own route," the way of the different drummer. And as though to confirm the extent of his confidence, he ends this long paragraph with one of his purest examples of Transcendental self-centering. After scoffing at what to others would seem an arduous way up, he goes on, it seems irrelevantly, to scoff at the idea of getting lost:

> If a person lost would conclude that after all he is not lost, he is not beside himself, but standing in his own old shoes on the very spot where he is, and that for the time being he will live there; but the places that have known him, *they* are lost,—how much anxiety and danger would vanish. I am not alone if I stand by myself. Who knows where in space this globe is rolling? Yet we will not give ourselves up for lost, let it go where it will. (184)

Considering all that mountain ascents mean to Thoreau, the point is not irrelevant at all. Such ascents have a great deal to do with being at home in the world, as we have already seen suggested and will see further on in substantial, confirming detail. The question of being-in-place has, of course, much to do with being at home in the world. This aside finally argues that we are at home wherever we stand because we are our own homes. Though much of what we have seen from the Tennyson passage on cannot quite support such confidence, the full ironies of this statement were not yet ready to emerge.[19]

Others were, however: up at the top, Thoreau digs out a well with his hands and some sharp stones, eats his rice with a wooden spoon he had whittled on the spot, then meditates on the "naturalness" of advertisements he found in the scraps of newspaper other travelers had used to wrap their prefashioned lunches. But his own nature gives him some minor trouble up there, for the pile of wood he collects to keep himself warm ("not having any blanket to cover me" [186]) is not, finally, sufficient. He packs the boards around him in such a way that, in a single gesture, he manages to warm himself up and also tune into the deeper reaches of the askesis, the leaving-the-world, which has been the form of his pilgrimage: "I at length encased myself completely in boards, managing even to put a board on top of me, with a large stone on it, to keep it down, and so slept comfortably" (186). Ever alert to the themes of traditional discourse, Thoreau acts out a dying to the world, playing on the ancient likening of bed and coffin, sleep and death. In so doing, he shifts into a register that prepares both him and us for the experience that is to follow.

In that experience, the quasi-coffin becomes the saving plank in a way that looks strikingly forward to the conclusion of *Moby Dick*: "But now I come to the pitch of this long digression.—As the light increased I discovered around me an ocean of mist, which by chance reached up exactly to the base of the tower, and shut out every vestige of the earth, while I was left floating on this fragment of the wreck of a world, on my carved plank in cloudland; a situation which required no aid from the imagination to render it impressive" (188). The morning fog that began the chapter prefigured this massive fog which—the light in the east steadily increasing— "revealed to me more clearly the new world into which I had risen in the night, the new terra-firma perchance of my future life." The trip to the top of the mountain had taken him to a new beginning, a re-originating more potent than any of its prefigurations because it happened on a height to which he had climbed and happened after a night spent wrapped in boards. (It is hardly extravagant to hear echoes of this scene in the last scene of *Walden*, where the "strong and beautiful bug" emerges from under "many concentric layers of woodenness" into a new morning life [*W*, 333].) Old places are put away—"there was not a crevice left through which the trivial places we name Massachusetts, or Vermont, or New York, could be seen"—and so, perhaps, is old time: "I still inhaled the clear atmosphere of a July morning,—if it were July there." And as these are put away so also is the uncleanness of the old world below: "As there was wanting the symbol, so there was not the substance of impurity, no spot nor stain" (188).[20] No wonder he sees himself as if on a platform, staring out at a prelapsarian world (189), and that here at this midway point he envisions an ascent to the goal of all spirit, his origin, and, he hopes, his end. All of the re-originating has led, finally, to this, all of it offering impetus to a climb toward the place of absolute beginning that is also the absolute goal. A few pages before, at the end of the "Monday" chapter, he had prepared for this experience by describing how the sound of a distant drum had led him out of his habitual thinking into an awareness of the health of the universe: "Suddenly old Time winked at me, —Ah, you know me, you rogue,—and news had come that IT was well" (173). But Time does not stay ("idle Time ran gadding by / And left me with Eternity alone"), and he moves directly into an experience of the Timeless, "that everlasting Something to which we are allied, at once our maker, our abode, our destiny, our very Selves" (193). Those last words speak of the Ultimate as, at once, origin and goal. The next step would have to be an attempt at a more permanent union, a reaching to end at the place of beginning. The Saddleback episode offers a vision of such an attempt.[21]

That vision culminates in an epiphany, the shining forth of the sun of "this pure world," a sight unknown to "the inhabitants of earth" below who "behold commonly but the dark and shadowy under-side of heaven's pavement" (189). In a move of extraordinary subtlety, Thoreau exults in his good fortune, praises what he sees, and—by recalling the spatiality, the sense of up here and down there that the passage had nearly forgotten—surreptitiously prepares for what is to happen next.

What happens should be no surprise, given the efficacy of the subtext, in "A Walk to Wachusett" and the excerpts from that essay that had been imported into *A Week*. Inherent in the climb up Wachusett had been the fear of the plain's contagion. The excerpt continued that deeply ingrained threat. Up here on Saddleback, where his vision is most extended, most fully played out in all its exultation, the subtext demands and gets its own piece of the action, its chance to play itself out. In fact, what the subtext does is compel the journey to take a cyclical shape rather than the unswervingly linear one that had been the form of his utmost desire:

> But alas, owing as I think to some unworthiness in myself, my private sun did stain himself, and
>
>> "Anon permit the basest clouds to ride
>>
>> With ugly wrack on his celestial face,"—
>
> for before the god had reached the zenith the heavenly pavement rose and embraced my wavering virtue, or rather I sank down again into that "forlorn world," from which the celestial Sun had hid his visage. (189–90)

The evening before, he had "seen the summits of new and yet higher mountains, the Catskills, by which I might hope to climb to heaven again"; but for now he had to descend, and he soon found himself "in the region of cloud and drizzling rain, and the inhabitants affirmed that it had been a cloudy and drizzling day wholly" (190). A whole history of visionary returns echoes through this passage, especially those that touch on the loneliness of the visionary who had seen but could not be believed, who had drunk the Milk of Paradise alone.

Thoreau has his own ironies to add to that history. He needed to return to the place of contagion, as he was still too much a creature of darkness, rain, and stain to complete the askesis; yet the touch of that very place made the askesis, for the moment, impossible. It was not the epiphany that failed: he had seen the light ("its own sun") in its own place, and "never here did 'Heaven's sun' stain himself." It was the askesis that failed, its frustration the fault of his private sun and its own stain of contagion. Up on Wachusett, they had sought a pure libation, and now we can see its point. Only thus could they remove the effects of the plain from themselves.

Other ironies take into their purview some of the deeper structures of *A Week*. The questioning of cyclical forms appears once again, this time with an undertone of melancholy that will reach out to affect the text's inner shape and, necessarily, its tonality. The act of ascending and descending describes a perfectly cyclical pattern, one that echoes all those cycles—day, week, season, and more—that give *A Week* its dominant form; yet he makes it clear at this point that he can dispense with such chiming in. From the point of view established in the world of rain and stain, he has sketched an ideal shape, an image of completion; but in terms of the way of seeing he knew of from above the clouds, there is only incompletion, the breaking off of a pattern that required only ascent. Cycles are wonderfully efficacious by one set of standards and sadly inadequate by another. One of the results of this impasse is to leave him in a state of suspension between differing ways of moving and their opposing valorizations. Another, the most potent, is to subvert the very concept by which this text claims to function. Halfway through *A Week*—just about half in pages, precisely half within the week that the text shaped out to be—stands a scene and an experience of extraordinary prominence. The import of that scene had been carefully prepared, and its effect on the book whose center it commands is to profoundly, permanently unsettle all of the claims of certain old discourses about the need to round things out. Nothing about *A Week* is more important than this undoing. The events on Saddleback Mountain embody a major statement about being in the world, and they have the gravest effect upon Thoreau's understanding of what such being means. For the remainder of this study, we shall be pondering other scenes that deepen that understanding.

One of these is the ascent of Agiocochook, the point and purpose of which are now a good deal clearer. That ascent is a climb to the *natural* source, the place where the stream begins, one end of that natural cycle which carries the waters to the sea and then up to the clouds and then back again to the source on top of the mountain.[22] A cycle is the inevitable frame for such a sequence. The ascent of Saddleback Mountain has a different source in mind, the primal beginning that is also the absolute end, and if that goal is reached, the narrative needs nothing more to be essentially complete. Each of these ascents is all that the other is not, and Thoreau felt compelled to bring both into the text in order to bring out the fullest meaning of each. Agiocochook by itself is only a *partial* truth, and the same can be said for Saddleback. Only with both together can the potential totality of experience (a totality envisioned rather than achieved, always about to be but so far incomplete) be properly understood.

To shift the focus to the individual climbs, Agiocochook and Saddleback must have each other in order for each to be fully itself, in order for both to satisfy the need for the fullest fidelity to Thoreau's worldly experience. Saddleback supplements Agiocochook, adding a dimension to the text that Agiocochook alone cannot possibly offer. Making that point, though, we also need to acknowledge that the parity between the ascents is now beginning to slip: whatever the homologous shapes of these mirror image journeys, there is no question of giving them equivalent valorizations. We have noted how much of the passage on Agiocochook involves the silly figure of the strutting soldier boy, but consider also what follows in the passage:

> Thus, in fair days as well as foul, we had traced up the river to which our native stream is a tributary, until from Merrimack it became the Pemigewasset that leaped by our side, and when we had passed its fountain-head, the Wild Amonoosuck, whose puny channel was crossed at a stride, guiding us toward its distant source among the mountains, and at length, without its guidance, we were enabled to reach the summit of AGIOCOCHOOK. (314)

The stream that becomes their river is shown to be only a trickle that can be easily stepped over. To compare this to the massive breadth of the "seascape" above the clouds is to put the experience on top of Saddleback, whatever its frustrations, within an even more exalted aura, its sublimity that much more awesome.[23]

Which brings us back to the first half of our original question, why Saddleback is where it is in the text of *A Week*. Another way of putting that question is to wonder why Saddleback is precisely *when* it is, which means to question not only why it occurs when it does in the text of *A Week* but also why it turns up in the record of a trip that took place at another time. Agiocochook had to be where it is in the text because that is when it happened in their journey up the river. Saddleback appears at the beginning of the "Tuesday" chapter, in the center of the recorded journey, for other good reasons: it insists on its centrality to the experience the journey records, much of the coding that goes into the concept of "center" coming into play in the episode. If we think of the text as a landscape (Romantic epics like *The Prelude* encourage us to do so), we can envision Saddleback as an eminence placed at its center, and Agiocochook as a smaller and less exalted eminence placed near the end.[24] To shift discourses slightly, the "actual" ascent comes halfway through the actual journey, the "symbolic" ascent halfway through the journey as finally described;

which is another way of saying that the placement of Saddleback is really an instruction for reading.

But what then of the *when*, Saddleback out of its time? Much of the use to which Thoreau puts facts has finally to do with his compulsion to play havoc with those dominating cycles that claim to command *A Week*. By setting this prominent action precisely when it is, five years away from the sequence in which he gives it so significant a part, Thoreau skews the regular temporality on which those cycles depend and therefore undermines the ultimate source of authority through which they seek to substantiate their claims. We saw something similar happening with the excerpts from "Wachusett," which are more devious than Saddleback because Thoreau so works the text that the excerpts seem contemporaneous with the journey in which they are placed. Saddleback is more open and therefore more arrogant in what it does and says about all those (equally) arrogant cycles. There is a very important sense in which *A Week* never recovers from the effects of the Saddleback episode. From that point on, it becomes difficult to speak of closure with the confidence it demands. What *A Week* has come to show is not the impossibility of closure—it happens on a regular basis—but, what is a good deal worse, its relative insufficiency, its ultimate, insulting impotence. At a subsequent juncture, we shall see how this refusal of total obeisance to the closures in the text carries into the way Thoreau chooses to conclude the text.[25]

Two final points: one a connection, the other a question. What we have seen and shall see in *A Week* about the uneasiness of closure, the subversion of the cyclical, the skewing of temporality, tells us a great deal about the fable that runs through Thoreau's corpus. What we have seen is, in fact, a major contribution to the fable. We know that the word of words and the great, serene sentence cannot finally be found here, whatever their precursors in moments like the magnificent paragraph that gets *Walden* going. (It is not, we saw, impossible to make words work, only very, very difficult.) What *A Week* shows of the inability of closure to say all that needs to be said has a great deal to do with the fact that the ultimate ordering of language is not yet to be found but always about to be. We can read the Saddleback episode as an allegory of that inefficacy, and of all sorts of others as well. If Thoreau had had the spiritual wherewithal, he could have transcended Saddleback, even in this life: that, it would seem, is the claim the episode makes, such wherewithal having to do with purity, of course, but also with the tools one needs to make such a trip. Among those tools is the capacity for self-transcendence that will take him beyond stain; but it is clear that such capacity needs at least one prior tool in order to realize itself fully, the supreme language that will serve to get him to where he is going—a place that, to no surprise, is the one where that language resides. That bitter paradox is hard to live with, yet he cannot live without it. *A Week* gives us not only more of Thoreau's fable but more of what it feels like to live within its terms.

That is the connection; what follows is the question, which has finally to do—as does everything else in this study—with how, in Thoreau's experience, one gets to be at home in the world. What kind of at-homeness (what *degree* of at-homeness) can one achieve in the world below the clouds, this place of contagion and stain? Given the tentativeness of things, it would be a difficult kind, surely, incomplete at best whatever the glorious moments that turn up in Thoreau's experience. One thing we have certainly seen in the conditions of the fable, one thing any careful observer of the tonality of the corpus cannot help but notice, is a persistent dissatisfaction that sounds all through the corpus, despite those glorious moments. Put in terms of the fable, the inaccessibility of the ultimate word and its sentence means that whatever Thoreau does here can never be more than tentative. Whatever the moments of gold, the at-homeness that is possible in the world below the clouds is ultimately ephemeral, which means that we are always on the way to somewhere else. That perpetual going-on goes far toward explaining some of the radical gestures in this corpus based on excursions. How can we put together the passion for the excursions that one chooses to make ("A Walk to Wachusett," *A Week, The Maine Woods, Cape Cod,* "Walking") as well as the other excursions within which one is carried (all those cycles that inhabit the corpus, especially those in *A Week* and *Walden*) with the passion for at-homeness that is equally Thoreauvian and always under strain? Some answers to these questions will come from the closer look at the acting out of at-homeness that we shall take in the next chapter.

Chapter Six

WRITING HOME

I N NOVEMBER 1835, Thoreau applied to the town of Canton,
Massachusetts, for a teaching position, and was interviewed by
Orestes A. Brownson, the town's Unitarian minister. Brownson
recommended him for the job, and Thoreau received from these
events not only his first teaching experience but other boons as well:
he and Brownson studied German together, enough, apparently, for
Thoreau to establish a solid foundation in the language.[1]

By late October 1837, when he began to keep a journal, Thoreau
had mastered enough German to translate a section of Goethe's journey to Italy, recording his entry into Trent. On November 15, Thoreau wrote into the *Journal* his rendering of part of that section, of
which these are the opening lines: "And now that it is evening, a few
clouds in the mild atmosphere rest upon the mountains, more stand
still than move in the heavens, and immediately after sunset the
chirping of crickets begins to increase,—then feels one once more at
home in the world, and not as an alien—an exile. I am contented as
though I had been born and brought up here, and now returned
from a Greenland or whaling voyage" (*J* 1:11). Two days later Thoreau wrote down the substance of one of his own moments of present
joy in lines that echoed Goethe exactly but also defined a thrust of
intent that was to occupy him obsessively for the rest of his life. That
passage ends, "The smothered breathings of awakening day strike
the ear with an undulatory motion—over hill and dale, pasture and
woodland, come they to me, and I am at home in the world" (13).
The lines from Goethe had taken Thoreau's interest because they
touched on desires that, even here at the beginning of his career, he
sensed to be fundamental to his way of being in the world. When he
echoes the lines two days later, in the context of his own joy in place,
his own feelings of at-homeness, the echo confirms that touching.
Here, early and plainly, appears a preoccupation so profound that it
went far toward determining Thoreau's sense of vocation as well the
passions attending that sense. Rarely was the act to seem so easy to
accomplish as it did at that early time.

The intertextual life of the quotation from Goethe was by no
means over, however. An extended version appears near the end of
the "Thursday" chapter of *A Week*, this time with picturesque prefa-

tory material on the flora and the inhabitants, and with a slight re-
writing of the crucial phrasing: "then feels one for once at home in
the world, and not as concealed or in exile" (330). The passage that
follows finds Thoreau and his brother back on the river and records
a scene in which the whole world looked fluviatile: "all things seemed
with us to flow; the shore itself, and the distant cliffs, were dissolved
by the undiluted air" (331). All things, that is, joined in a liquid oneness, including their thoughts, which "flowed and circulated." At the
hub of that oneness stand (reading the sentence in all its possibilities,
since all are at play within it) man, these travelers, and every individual: "Let us wander where we will, the universe is built round about
us, and we are central still." This bit of poetic prose (the cadences and
rhymes suggest that it might have been intended for a poem) appeared first in the *Journal* for August 28, 1841, nearly four years after the rendering of Goethe (*J* 1:323). Its reappearance now, and at
this point in the text, is of more than casual moment. Coming as it
does after the passage on Goethe in Italy, which had also hung on for
long, this Transcendental centrality profoundly affects and supports
the feeling at the heart of the translation about being at home in the
world. Thoreau's linking of these passages in the text of *A Week* shows
how the persistent question of at-homeness invades even the com-
monplaces of Transcendentalism. After all, if we are always central
to the order of the universe, we are at home wherever we go; we are,
in effect, our own home. That was one of the most comforting
thoughts Thoreau was ever to have. We shall come across it repeatedly as we push these issues further.

There is one more point to note in the translation from Goethe:
the *Journal* passage spoke of being "*once more*" at home in the world;
the later version in *A Week* speaks of being so "*for once*" (in both cases
translating *einmal*).[2] But much more is involved here than a more accurate translation. The difference in the renderings is existentially
momentous, so much so that it calls into question his earlier confidence about at-homeness and even the comforting centrality that
puts us at home wherever we go. To say that *for once* we are at home
has to qualify that comfort, even before we hear of it. The pairing of
these passages suggests that the place of at-homeness in *A Week* is by
no means an easy one. It is certainly not consistent.

These comments come near the beginning of a sequence of statements and speculations that concludes *A Week*. The sequence itself
begins with other comments on Goethe made a few pages earlier.
Thoreau takes Goethe as a kind of early Transcendental traveler because he is one of those who "make objects and events stand around
them as the centre" (326). (The phrasing prefigures precisely what

would be said a few pages later about our being "central still.") It is one of Goethe's chief excellences that "he was satisfied with giving an exact description of things as they appeared to him, and their effect upon him." His Italy is fully of this world, "a solid turf-clad soil, daily shined on by the sun, and nightly by the moon. Even the few showers are faithfully recorded." But part of Thoreau's purpose is to describe certain inadequacies in Goethe, his education having a "merely artistic completeness" so that "Nature is hindered." Goethe himself seems to have guessed at this: Thoreau quotes a passage from the autobiography where Goethe speaks of how "only the undefinable, wide-expanding feelings of youth and of uncultivated nations are adapted to the sublime, which, whenever it may be excited in us through external objects, since it is either formless, or else moulded into forms which are incomprehensible, must surround us with a grandeur which we find above our reach" (327–78). Goethe's powers have to do with a loving grasp of the actual, the finest of focusing on what we can touch. His insufficiencies have to do with his lack of another power, a capacity for a kind of expansiveness that ends up in formlessness; ends up, that is, with what cannot be offered by a detailed rendering of objects, with what is beyond our touch.

Putting this in terms of other preoccupations that turn up in *A Week*: first, the distinction we noted earlier between observation and meditation clearly is kin to the pairing of capacities in the Goethe passage; second, all that we saw of foggy, formless beginnings is now shown to be an element of the sublime, the indefinable, the expansive; third, surrounded with "a grandeur which we find above our reach," we repeat another scene of insufficiencies, the frustration on the summit of Saddleback. Here and elsewhere in the text, we see that the incomplete askesis never left Thoreau's awareness, that it was always there to be evoked in a pertinent situation. Now, however, we pick up something really quite new, efforts at valorization. In the passages on Goethe, the capacity to render the immediacies of experience is shown to be useful and important but not, finally, the best we can hope for. It is the product of the Artist, not the Man of Genius, who is driven more by his unconscious than by the careful and precise seeing that the Artist can do so well. We have no difficulty in identifying the Man of Genius with those who are capable of adapting to the sublime.

All of this puts into puzzling perspective one of the conclusions Thoreau comes to a short while later, near the end of the "Friday" chapter, when he is, in effect, wrapping up the book. He complains that no men "live yet a *natural* life," that men need to be "*naturalized, on the soil of the earth*" (379). Then, in a striking echo of the Saddleback experience, he scorns what we have become: "When we come down into the distant village, visible from the mountain top, the nobler inhabitants with whom we peopled it have departed, and left only vermin in its desolate streets. It is the imagination of poets which puts those brave speeches into the mouths of their heroes" (379). And this leads to a disquisition on how we need to be "earth-born as well as heaven-born," for "here or nowhere is our heaven." Earlier in *A Week*, Thoreau had made assertions about the need to "live, betwixt spirit and matter, such a human life as we can," about the fact that a healthy mind with a steady job "will not be a good subject for Christianity" (74). But this late comment goes a good deal further, for to say that our heaven can *only* be here is (discounting even Thoreau's habitual extravagance) to ground us firmly in the world in a way that Goethe would have understood. But this assertion comports quite strangely with the statements about Goethe's way as the inferior way of the Artist. It comports even more strangely with the patent echo of Saddleback, a strangeness made precise in the fuzzy logic by which Thoreau moves from that echo to—in only a few lines—the establishment of at-homeness in this place on which we stand.

Rarely in Thoreau's work do we see his ambivalence dramatized so patently as it is on these pages. The pulls and pushes and tugs that keep him going in alternating ways work openly at this point, making any single position very difficult to hold. Yet they lead, at the end, to one position that plays all kinds of havoc with the cycles that dominate *A Week*—havoc we have already seen working its skillful devastation, subverting the text with all sorts of subtextual energies. Now, near the end, the subtext comes to the surface, taking over the text's direction and rejecting the cyclical play with an acceptance of open-endedness that, among other things, makes the Goethean kind of at-homeness an insufficient one. That kind is good only for the here and now that Goethe cherished and described so well. It is not good, finally, for end-of-the-line acceptance.

Even a brief sketch of the subsequent passages shows how the assertion that "here or nowhere is our heaven" comes finally to be rejected, and that happens even after its components are (eagerly, urgently, lovingly) spelled out.[3] Within less than a page, Thoreau speaks of the "stupendous masses of clouds" that look like "the battlements of a city in the heavens," and of how he is "hardly worthy to be a suburban dweller outside those walls" (381)—a phrasing that clearly echoes his dejection as he turned to descend Saddleback, an emotion also explicit in the echo from Saddleback heard a few paragraphs earlier. Such feelings reject unequivocally any suggestion of a heaven around us. That sense of unworthiness uttered, Thoreau tries another tack, a somewhat more conciliatory one. Music has unusual effects, its sounds and some attendant odors implying, "perchance, that we live on the verge of another and purer realm, from which these odors and sounds are wafted over to us." Less than a page later, he goes on to speak of a quasi-Blakean transformation of the senses that would permit us to "behold beauty now invisible," for "may we not *see* God?" (382). To so transform the senses that we could *see* even God is to make our heaven here; and why, indeed, given such transformation, should it be anywhere else? But that is the final utterance of the impulse to have our heaven accessible around us, and if it places Thoreau, once again, within the Blake-Stevens line, it has no further echo in the few pages (less than a dozen) that it takes to conclude the text. What follows has to do with anecdotes of astronomy, the point of which is the desire to burst "the fetters of astronomical orbits" and launch oneself "to where distance fails to follow" (386–87). The enclosing cycles argue for the potential for at-homeness among the things of this world, but that argument is qualified beyond any chance of repair by the desires of the subtext that finally, in these last pages, comes fully into its own. In the last words of the text, Thoreau speaks of fastening the boat "to the wild apple-tree, whose stem still bore the mark which its chain had worn in the chafing of the spring freshets" (393); but all that the subtext had just revealed of the impulse to break open another sort of chain, "the fetters of astronomical orbits," shows that cycles like this can offer a certain mode of at-homeness, but it is the kind that ties and binds and will not let us loose to say all that remains to be said.

• I •

A Week said so cogently so much of what had to be said—and did so at the appropriate point, the beginning of Thoreau's major productivity—that it served as a place of alignment as well as a jumping-off place, that is, as a locus of reference for the developments that were to follow. What *A Week* prepares us to see is the consistency of Thoreau's concerns, the obsessiveness of his interest in questions of home places, his proto-Heideggerean recognition of the relations of being, dwelling, and location and what these have to do with being at home in the world.

Still, that consistency should not lead us into simple identification of, say, *A Week* and *Walden*, or, to take the opposing tack, simple treatment of them as contraries. Where *A Week* begins with an assertion about bifurcation, a splitting of mind and body—an assertion that loses its grip almost as soon as it is made—*Walden* works out an attempt to *combine* the forces of mind and body and to focus those forces on a single, stubborn issue—the problem of shaping a place for every aspect of himself in a cabin beside *that* pond. Another attempt to set up opposition appears in the relations of place, gesture, and task in each of these texts. What happened on the rivers was a journey through space, a climbing toward the source. What happened at Walden Pond was a journey in place, a digging toward the source. Both experiences are quests for the same elemental principle, but their modes of questing are designed to be precisely opposed. Each seeks to be the other's mirror image, but those modes will surely not stay so comfortably contrary as Thoreau's designs would make them. Once again we return to what *A Week* had predicted, the consistency of Thoreau's concerns, the continuing interplay of being, dwelling, and location. From this consistency we can guess that *Walden* will turn out to be far closer to *A Week* than the patent attempt to distinguish them would lead us to expect.

Yet with all these alignments we make for the sake of accuracy, journeys through space and in place cannot be precisely the same, cannot fuse each with the other. That is, we cannot accept still another putative binary structure, simple identification or precise opposition. Our problem—and we have had it all along—is not in Thoreau but in ourselves, in our need to learn how to read what seems so comfortably neat, but is nothing of the kind, nothing kind.[4]

What, for example, shall we do with the matter of housing in *Walden*, an act of home making so aggressive that it has to be taken as more than a gesture about economics? That this act is an answer to the ambiguities of home making in *A Week* seems to be one aspect of its character. It is not too strong to call the cabin building blatant, a firm and urgent response saying, Yes, I *can* do it here—reacting against the opening up with which *A Week* had ended, continuing the Goethean assertion that "here or nowhere is our Heaven." But why is there so much urgency, why the blatant and aggressive building, why the need to make this point so fervently here in Concord? Part of the urgency comes from Thoreau's profound understanding of the nature of his dwelling and, what must follow, of the act of dwelling as such.

To gather what is at stake, we have to keep in mind that *dwelling* would be, for Thoreau, both gerund and noun, the latter necessarily preceding the former. Heidegger's point that "we attain to dwelling, it seems, only by means of building" would have meant a great deal to Thoreau, as can be shown by the nature of some of the earliest acts in *Walden*, the borrowing of the ax, the beginning of the making of shelter.[5] This is not, however, to say that Thoreau would accept all that follows in Heidegger's comments on building and dwelling, for Heidegger goes on to characterize dwelling and being as essentially the same gesture. He comes to that result by playing on the old meaning of *bauen* as "to dwell," as well as on its relation to certain versions of *bin*. "Man *is*," Heidegger concludes, "insofar as he *dwells*"; or, in another way, "building as dwelling" means "being on the earth" (147). That Heidegger gives us some useful tools with which to understand the matter of housing in *Walden* seems clear enough; whether Thoreau would fully accept what Heidegger himself builds with them is certainly much less clear.

Consider the possibility that *Walden* continues *A Week* in terms of putting our Heaven here, and does so in part through that act of making a home which is central to the later text. How odd a continuation it is, the oddity beginning with Thoreau's first speculations on the nature of his dwelling; on, in effect, the act of dwelling. At the beginning of his meditations on houses, Thoreau argues that houses are shelters before they are anything else, before they take in "the warmth of the affections" (27–28). To the degree that the house is a shelter it need not, for most of the year, do more than hardly exist. We prefer it that way because insofar as it has walls, it is to that degree confining, an obstruction. It prevents us from living where we would most desire to live, in the open air: "Man was not made so large limbed and robust but that he must seek to narrow his world, and wall in a space such as fitted him" (27). The preferred mode of being in the world offers an absolute continuity between oneself and the surrounding air: "It would be well perhaps if we were to spend more of our days and nights without any obstruction between us and the celestial bodies, if the poet did not speak so much from under a roof, or the saint dwell there so long. Birds do not sing in caves, nor do doves cherish their innocence in dovecots" (28). Such continuity implies that utmost completion, a fractureless, seamless joining. Thus, closing oneself in a house is far less desirable than the fullest opening out. Such severing is not, finally, the best we can do for ourselves. Consider, further, some later comments. Arguing that, for the sake of renewal, we must strip not only our walls but our lives, Thoreau goes on to contend that the best sort of living comes when there is no house: "a taste for the beautiful is most cultivated out of doors, where there is no house and no housekeeper" (38). And when he finally got something like a house underway, it was, in its earliest state, merely "a defense against the rain" (84), a "frame, so slightly clad" that it was only "a sort of crystallization around me," in effect, "a picture in outlines" (85).[6] Even that was, however, only the slightest concession, for "it was not so much within doors as behind a door where I sat, even in the rainiest weather." If this is beginning to sound like a subterranean echo of the play of closure and opening that ends *A Week*, then we are coming to see continuities in a most unexpected place, the central activity of *Walden*.

The conclusion can hardly be avoided. We are less at home in the world to the degree that we build a house. Insofar as we shelter our-selves (and we inevitably must do so), we cut into that continuity with the surrounding air that is the most desirable state, cut into our best, fullest at-homeness. Home making and house making seem to be contradictory acts. Dwelling in the largest sense of being at home in the world cannot be fully compatible with the building of a dwelling.[7] All that *Walden* is later to show about houses and our dwelling within them has to be seriously qualified by the cautionary comments that are the first ones in *Walden* on the matter of housing. Whatever fol-lows in the text cannot get out from under the cool light thrown by those introductory lines on our acts of housing in the world.

Though we have to accomplish those acts, they cannot get out from under the burden of secondariness. We saw that condition earlier in the questions of language and writing, where written speech is shown to be secondary to the spoken and the spoken secondary to silence, the mode that speaks most of all (see, e.g., *W*, 174). The fashioning of houses goes along with these other fashionings: incising words and digging cellars come down to the same thing. These acts of inscribing are essential modes of home making but are second-best nonetheless. Thoreau could not be more open in his establishing of that point: why else say all that he said about the secondariness of language, why else put his remarks about housing as second-best precisely at the be-ginning of *Walden*'s comments on housing? We ought to be equally open in our receptivity to his remarks. We ought, that is, to remind ourselves of Stanley Cavell's comment that Thoreau wants his words to mean all that they can say.

Heidegger can help us here as well. In "Building Dwelling Think-ing," he speaks of two distinct acts as lesser modes of building, that is, of dwelling in the world: the first is construction, the second culti-vation (151). Whatever the disagreements Thoreau would have had with Heidegger he is, in fact, no mean proto-Heideggerean. The building of a dwelling and the cultivation of the earth are the most prominent acts in *Walden*. He mentions cultivation as early as the first chapter, putting it, in importance, just after building a dwelling. So far, so Heideggerean, and there are also predictable, only slightly ironic comments about himself as "the home-staying, laborious native of the soil," as well as a remark about the "homestead" at which he labors (157). But this is Thoreau's reading of these gestures, and it should come as no surprise that he associates cultivating, a literal incising of the soil, with another sort of incising, the act of writing. First he had suggested his likeness to a sculptor, "dabbling like a plastic artist in the dewy and crumbling sand" (156). Then he shifts arts, turning the turf into a text, "making the yellow soil express its summer thought . . . making the earth say beans instead of grass" (157). Witty but ultimately solemn, this is a gentle yoking of ideas that are not, at bottom, at all heterogeneous; and as house building and writing are secondary gestures, so too is this cultivating, that other act of incising that Thoreau, like Heidegger, sees as an aspect of dwelling.

We have plenty of evidence that making a homestead is not, finally, to be as fully at home as we can imagine ourselves to be. Put in another way: making a homestead in this world may be the fullest way we have of being at home within it; but we can guess at modes of at-homeness that are unavailable now but would, it seems certain, offer the fullness we lack. The sounds of the fable, once again in a quasi-idealist phase, appear to be floating back to the surface.

Still, if making a homestead may be the fullest way we have now, there is another not nearly so full—it is, in fact, predicated upon absence—but that has its own particular (also quasi-idealist) satisfactions because of the aspect of absence. That way has its ancestry in poems like "*Tintern Abbey*," which turn, in part, on a change of being and location that nature can be made to go through, that is, on the transforming of nature into consciousness:

> These beauteous forms,
> Through a long absence, have not been to me
> As is a landscape to a blind man's eye:
> But oft, in lonely rooms, and 'mid the din
> Of towns and cities, I have owed to them
> In hours of weariness, sensations sweet,
> Felt in the blood, and felt along the heart;
> And passing even into my purer mind,
> With tranquil restoration.

And in that purer site this transformation also places "feelings too / Of unremembered pleasure," which may have influenced what is best in our lives, our "little, nameless, unremembered, acts / Of kindness and of love."[8] That Thoreau used such beauteous forms for sweet sensations can be demonstrated anywhere in his work. (Whether those forms could have been developed into unremembered acts of kindness and of love would need more speculation.) Turning nature into consciousness, the ultimate act of Romantic humanism, came instinctively to Thoreau, and the act took many forms. One of the most useful for his purposes was a special version of the process, a kind of home owning in the mind in which a homestead managed to have two owners at once, himself and the "lawful" one, the latter wholly unaware of this surreptitious sharing in which each of them had it all.

"A man is rich," Thoreau said, "in proportion to the number of things which he can afford to let alone" (*W*, 82). That is not only a classic Thoreauvian paradox of the sort that so annoyed Emerson but, coming closer to radical Thoreau, a version of the play of presence and absence, of positive acts of negation, that he was perpetually seeking out. He goes on to give an instance: "My imagination carried me so far that I even had the refusal of several farms,—the refusal was all I wanted,—but I never got my fingers burned by actual possession" (82). And he then tells of the time he came closest to such possession, of how he actually arranged to buy the Hollowell place but that, before he got the deed, the owner's wife changed her mind. Thoreau got the deal and got himself out of it, both so close together that they were almost simultaneous; but in fact he never lost what he never legally had, for "I retained the landscape, and I have since annually carried off what it yielded without a wheel-barrow" (82). Yet, in terms of the Wordsworthian base, the story is even more complex. It seems that the real attraction of the Hollowell farm was "the recollection I had of it from my earliest voyages up the river, when the house was concealed behind a dense grove of red maples, through which I heard the house-dog bark"—as clear an example of Wordsworthian transformation into sensations as Thoreau ever offered (83).

The homestead had long ago been turned into consciousness, and Thoreau sought, this once, to reverse the process, transmuting the internal into the external, absence into presence (or, in another reading, one kind of presence into another that asks much more). Only the farmer's wife saved him from back sliding into such presence, from undoing a quite pleasantly positive act of negation.

But what kind of home making is this, finally? Openly and delightedly negative, it can be no more than a kind of play, an evasion of the central task of getting to be at home in this world that we taste and see, the source of the sweet sensations. Thoreau transforms elements of Romantic tradition into his situation at Concord, but it will do for him and us in only a limited way, and certainly not for long. The central act in *Walden* is the construction of a palpable homestead, not the owning of one in the mind. For one thing, such construction has a good deal to say about many other matters, and even more to say about matters of absence and presence. For another, what about winter?

That "what about" has to do with the nature of the shelter he had built in the summer, and also what "shelter" points to, how the stages of the edifice respond to the stages of his experience. One way to conceive of this interplay is in terms of directions, a whirl of centrifugal and centripetal moves; another is in terms of spaces and what fills them, the qualities of condensation and density. The final stages of the interplay begin early in "House-Warming" and, particularly, with the essential winter gesture as performed by an army of wasps who, after visiting him for a while, "gradually disappeared, into what crevices I do not know" (240). He introduces his own part in the wintering sequence with a final sitting in the sun at the northeast side of the pond, holding as long as he can to the communion without walls until he has to go within them.

That turn within is a diametrical reversal, from a seamless spreading out with no foreseeable limits to a focusing on a single element, not just the cabin but its central point, the fireplace, "the most vital part of the house" (241). Thoreau makes much of the late-summer making of the chimney, bragging over his use of secondhand bricks, pointing out the relative independence of the chimney that "stand[s] on the ground and link[s] us to the heavens" (241–42), the structure sometimes remaining even after the house has burned down. That linking of ground and heaven is his wintry substitute for the communion with the warm air of the summer and the warmish autumn sun. The chimney keeps him in touch with the far poles of experience even as his way of being in the world shifts from the centrifugal to the centripetal, from the borderless to a precisely focused detail, from the immediate to the mediated. (The chimney is a mediating instrument that points upward to the location of a warmth we do not make but which we gladly receive when it is ready to come to us. Here Thoreau shares understanding with figures as different as Hölderlin and Casper David Friedrich). Further, the business of the chimney as survivor of the house that is no longer there puts the chimney precisely in line with all we saw of cellar-holes, especially their status as modes of inscribing. That goes far toward explaining Thoreau's stiffly comic remark about not reading the name of Nebuchadnezzar on the secondhand bricks he used for his chimney. The remark echoes his frequent searches for names and dates inscribed into old chimneys, a passion he often evinces when he hears that an old house has been destroyed.[9] Looking for the owner's name on the hearth at the heart of the house, and particularly the date when the chimney was put into place, becomes still another version of Thoreau's hunt for the indexical, with all that it implies of continuity and fragmentation, presence and absence, modes of at-homeness at once stubborn and incomplete.

Part of the reason Thoreau lights on fireplaces, chimneys, and hearths as indexical locations has to do with all that they mean in terms of warming centers. He lit on them early in his work and continued until the end, one of the earliest lightings occurring in "The Landlord," an underappreciated essay of 1843. The essay has Thoreau playing at being Charles Lamb with a certain degree of success, especially in passages like the following: "And why should we have any serious disgust at kitchens? Perhaps they are the holiest recess of the house. There is the hearth, after all,—and the settle, and the fagots, and the kettle, and the crickets. . . . They are the heart, the left ventricle, the very vital part of the house" (*Excursions*, 101). At the central point stands the locus and source of heat, "vital" and, therefore, arguably, the site of the core of life. (The phrase "vital heat" appears often in Thoreau, even referring to the heart of trains [*W*, 117].) This instance in "The Landlord" has to do with hospitality, making others comfortably at home. Versions of that gesture turn up in all manner of places and in other lines of work that extend the meaning of "hospitality." For example, one of the defining instances of the image of the hearth, extending into the acts by which we make a human world, appears at the end of "Chesuncook." The logger and pioneer, late versions of John the Baptist, precede the poet in places like the Maine woods. They have "eaten the wild honey, it may be, but the locusts also; banished decaying wood and the spongy mosses which feed on it, and built hearths and humanized Nature for him" (*MW*, 156). Makers of warm centers set up the world for makers of words. Hearths are at the center of what it is to be human in this world. As for the hearth at the heart of "House-Warming," it was made by a maker of words who found a source of vital heat in making, for himself, his own site of central warmth.

The play on "hearth" and "heart" came naturally and stuck, but the play does far more than tickle his punning funny bone. For one thing, it reinforces the centering that stands as contrast to the communion Thoreau got through spreading out. For another, the persistent emphasis on the need for central warmth (which gets far more play than the joys of spreading out) shows as tellingly as any of Thoreau's more tenacious points that this world is radically wintry and the search for a warm core is therefore one of our basic acts. What the play on "hearth" and "heart" can do for that search appears as early as "The Landlord" and so often in the canon that it points to a practice that has to be central in Thoreau, a confrontation of cores.

Take, for example, a passage in the *Journal* for August 15, 1851, in which he pleaded for the sustaining of his own vital heat: "May I never let the vestal fire go out in my recesses" (*J* 2:390). Three months later he exulted over that heat, in the fact that, mosquitoes and insects gone, "crickets gone into winter quarters" and his friends into their own, "you [are] left to walk on frozen ground, with your hands in your pockets. Ah, but is not this a glorious time for your deep inward fires?" (*J* 3:111). It is, of course, yet there is far more to this passage, which prefigures Stevens's "The Snow Man" and, through no coincidence, suggests some of the complexities of *Walden*'s "House-Warming." This is a time of absolute nothing, "nothing but the echo of your steps over the frozen ground," nothing, that is, except potential danger to the best of himself: "All fields lie fallow. Shall not your mind?" It shall not because of those "deep inward fires." Objectified into thoughts, those fires become, through an extraordinary metonymy, branches of white oak or scrub oak or evergreen, the fuel that lights the fires. Nearly seven years later, he put the point on inner warmth more plainly and sentimentally when, complaining of October coolness, he exulted that "so much the more I have a hearth and heart within me" (*J* 11:246). These examples show something more than a play of correspondences, a terrestrial version of "as there, so here." Given the part it plays in the search for a warm core, this likening goes deep into all that we are and have, here and now, all that we can and must do in this radically wintry world. The likening of centers offers a needed boost in the deadest Stevensian winter, but it carries implications that, taken to their limits, query the matter of at-homeness and illuminate it in a way that reveals our acts of homing to be tentative gestures at best.

Walden, as we would expect, lays these matters out at their densest. In its initial ponderings on the necessaries of life, the text tells how "by proper Shelter and Clothing we legitimately retain our own internal heat" (12); but then, quoting Liebig's assertion that "man's body is a stove," it goes on quickly to caution that "of course the vital heat is not to be confounded with fire" (13). Since no reader of Thoreau seems likely to be that literal, we have to conclude that Thoreau is saying something quite different, telling us to let the analogy speak all it wants to speak, even the unexpectedly grim, like the "Snow Man" passage from the *Journal*. We ought not, then, to take his point reductively when he says that "the grand necessity . . . for our bodies, is to keep warm, to keep the vital heat within us," for "how can a man be a philosopher and not maintain his vital heat by better methods than other men?" (13, 15). One way a man can do that is to so work at his metaphors that he can spread their implications to others of their like and thus expand what they all can say. "The Village," for example, has Thoreau returning from town late on a dark and tempestuous night, wandering like a ship setting sail "from some bright village parlor or lecture room . . . for my snug harbor in the woods" (169). That the image of the ship echoes the metaphorical work of *A Week*, including not only the vessel but the acts of bifurcation, comes through in the way he left "only my outer man at the helm." In fact, several strains of metaphor, taking in both *A Week* and *Walden*, come together in his centering play: "I had many a genial thought by the cabin fire 'as I sailed.' " The passage goes on to become a dense meditation on the question of bifurcation, now inextricably tied to the image of central warmth, both now part and parcel of the basic business of homing. Thus, to reveal its fullest sense, the making of the fireplace in "House-Warming" draws on not only the intertextual life of the canon but all the prefigurations that *Walden* prepared within itself. Saying that the fireplace is "the most vital part of the house" draws on a great deal, all that goes on within "vital." Saying "I withdrew yet farther into my shell, and endeavored to keep a bright fire both within my house and within my breast" (249) puts us and our hearths into the densest of relations, implying that the relation involves much more than a punning play at likeness.

Yet to say these is not to say that we and our hearths or houses are in any sense ultimately the same. From the point in "Economy" when he begins to discuss houses, Thoreau's metaphors encompass the subtlest gradations of difference. He sees houses as enclosures, sometimes figured as boxes, sometimes as shells, sometimes as the firmer equivalent of the clothes we put around us. Houses are sur*round*ings, not so much wraparounds as build-arounds, since the wraparound implies a certain snugness of fit that no house ought ever to have. There must be spaces between us and the walls, spaces that permit our freedom of movement within the enclosure and therefore emphasize the distinction between the surrounded and the surrounding, that which is enclosed and that which not only encloses but is the part that faces the world. A house is a continuation of our thick outer garments, for it is, finally, "this outside garment of all" (30). Still, Thoreau does not reject every sort of continuity between within and without. In a brilliantly conceived passage that achieves, at once, likeness and difference, continuity and distinction, he speculates on architectural ornaments. Rejecting the superficial, he wants to know "how the inhabitant, the indweller, might build truly within and without," the repeated stress on *in* making the spatial point precisely (46–47). He wants to know that what he sees is organic, that it "has gradually grown from within outward, out of the necessities and character of the indweller, who is the only builder" (47). He admires the houses of the poor, for they show "the life of the inhabitants whose shells they are, and not any peculiarity in their surfaces merely."

All that we saw in the first paragraph of *Walden* about us and our texts comes into play again. Houses are texts in which we inscribe ourselves, yet they are not the same as ourselves. Another way to put this is to say that, to the degree that we inscribe ourselves in our houses (and Thoreau believes that we ought to and that we usually do so), we turn our houses into texts, scenes of inscribing, locations of an index which points to the inscriber. But we have to keep in mind that indexical instruments are by nature incomplete, pointers that have to be metonyms and not the entire story that the metonym stands there to finger. This means, in the case of the house as well as the cellar-hole that survives it, that the object of the index, the inscriber to whom it points, can never be exactly identified with the index. What Thoreau says in the first chapter of *Walden* about houses and their ornamentation and the inscribing of the indweller; what he shows of the spaces that have to exist between indweller and outer surface; these together give us additional understanding of Thoreau's reading of the index and of what he can expect when he stands in cellar-holes or meditates on stand-alone chimneys. Again we see the persistency of elements in his thinking as well as the profound relations among elements that appear to be far apart.

This takes us back to the radical analogy of hearth and heart and to the comment in "House-Warming" that bears repeating at this point: "I withdrew yet farther into my shell, and endeavored to keep a bright fire both within my house and within my breast" (249). Hearth and heart are parallel instances, answering images but not identical ones. Continuity is not identity. Likeness is not twinning. Conclusions of that sort profoundly affect—disturb, undo, correct, incite—Thoreau's understanding of at-homeness in this world.

This troubling also grounds and determines the tone of Thoreau's description of the ideal house, a passage that embodies many of the ideals worked out in *Walden*. Singular, primitive, bare, "standing in a golden age, of enduring materials," this house is vast but not grand, its upper parts so dark that "you must reach up a torch upon a pole to see the roof" (243). Such spaces permit the inhabitants to live anywhere within the house, at one or another end of the hall or up on the rafter with the spiders. No inhabitant, it seems, is in the way of any of the others, though all are under the same roof ("a sort of lower heaven over one's head" [243]) of what is clearly the House of Man. It holds all the necessary treasures though no more than those, so that all can be taken in within a single glance. "One view" parallels "one room" to support not only oneness in the sense of unity but also in the senses of singularity and simplicity (Thoreau's equation of "single" and "simple" was instinctive but by no means peculiar to him). We are separate yet together, our goods sufficient but uncluttered. The house is therefore "as open and manifest as a bird's nest," with just enough people in it, each at a respectable (respectful, respected) distance, so that "you cannot go in at the front door and out at the back without seeing some of its inhabitants" (244). How different, Thoreau points out, from our usual experience of hospitality, where we are given a corner of a house and kept at the greatest distance, on the "premises" but not in the "house." How different also from the distances we actually live in, the parlor far from the kitchen and workshop, our lives passing at remoteness from their symbols, our metaphors and tropes "necessarily so far fetched . . . as if only the savage dwelt near enough to Nature and Truth to borrow a trope from them" (244–54). The finest sort of at-homeness would so order our words and spaces that nearness and distance, forever oxymoronic, come into fruitful relation, echoing and supporting the play of singularity and community that is basic to the ideal house and to *Walden* as well.

In the spaces of the ideal house, our language will be fetched as far as Nature and Truth will permit. Given their inevitable perfection, the words of that language will necessarily derive from the word of words, the syntax of that language ordering the great, serene sentence. Now we know something more about the ultimate language, the way it holds off (but not too much), the way it encompasses (without smothering), permitting the objects of which it speaks to be entirely themselves and yet members of a hospitable community. That language, like the ideal house, makes everything it contains "as open and manifest as a bird's nest" (244). Further, the houses of the fable, like the houses we make in the world, are texts that speak of us without quite being us; but since that ultimate language holds all that can be said and says it effortlessly and always, its confrere, the ultimate house, will no longer be only an index because all that we can become will be there within that house, just as it is in the ultimate language. Only then can building and saying be absolutely complete and, in a way we can now understand, essentially the same project. In terms of another of Thoreau's gestures, one would no longer seek to own a house only in the mind, for in the ultimate times we no more own a house than we own the language we speak.

But the context makes clear that those are other times than now, and in fact what this description does to the now and here puts our current acts of housing into their proper place. As though to emphasize the subversiveness of the passage on the ideal house, Thoreau ends the chapter on "House-Warming" with a devastating reminder of how fragile our current state is, how the at-homeness we now make is not only secondary and second-best but tenuous and tentative, threatened with the deepest chill of all, the ultimate unhousing: "But the most luxuriously housed has little to boast of in this respect, nor need we trouble ourselves to speculate how the human race may be at last destroyed. It would be easy to cut their threads any time with a little sharper blast from the north. We go on dating from Cold Fridays and Great Snows; but a little colder Friday, or greater snow, would put a period to man's existence on the globe" (254). The last words of the chapter sound out of a wretched poem by a Mrs. Hooper. Our current state beside the hearth, it says, is one of stasis, the middle way of the survivor glad for what he has, "where nothing cheers nor saddens, but a fire / Warms feet and hands—nor does to more aspire" (255). At best the fire offers a "utilitarian heap," a phrasing that rises out of the doggerel to pinpoint Thoreau's reading of all that houses and hearths can do for us here and now.

No wonder, then, that the final chapter begins with the image of a hunt and with the game clearly in mind, this image alternating with that of a voyage designed to explore "a thousand regions in your mind / yet undiscovered . . . home-cosmography" (320). After all the elaborate business of building a shell around ourselves, the direction of endeavor reverses and looks for home-places within. And where there are spaces inside the house that are between us and the walls, the spaces envisioned inside us are contained by our physical being, the counterpart of those walls. Directions and frames and spaces alternate and echo each other, one set of frames and spaces contained within the other as often as we ensconce ourselves within the walls of a house. Consider, further, the implicit structure of opposing cones, their small ends put together, their large ends at opposite sides, the internal one pointing outside to the entire physical world, the external one pointing inside to the Africa within us, so much of which remains essentially unexplored. Though Thoreau implies the images of outer skins rather than cones, the latter brings out more clearly the mirror-image setup of locales within and without, alternative cosmographies that spread out from where we are. He reveals opposing cosmographies that meet at the point where we meet the world—a point that is usually defined as home: "The other side of the globe is but the home of our correspondent" (320). To miss their opposing symmetries is to miss not only their relation but their difference. (It is characteristic of Thoreau to stress the aspect of difference in metaphorical systems, of which this is one of his densest.) To miss that symmetry and its oxymoronic elements is to miss the fullest import of the placement of this material. Set squarely and aggressively at the beginning of the final chapter, it comes immediately after the words that ended the previous chapter by stressing the conclusion of the natural cycle: "Thus was my first year's life in the woods completed" (319). At the end of that cycle (which stands for the shape of the entire sojourn) he faces the results of his dwelling and cultivating. He found that the quest implicit in his sojourn did not turn up what he wanted, that there were other cosmographies to explore. His proto-Heideggerean acts of dwelling and cultivation did not fully, finally satisfy. Of course we knew from the beginning of the text that they could not finally suffice, that house making was essentially a secondary act, and thus the beginning of "Conclusion" cannot come as an entire surprise. Neither can we be surprised by Thoreau's suggestion that if we learn to know ourselves we would be "naturalized in all climes," that is, natives everywhere (322), for it seems an inevitable point in speaking of home cosmography; yet that too is not enough, for we have seen that to be such natives is to point to insufficiency. Every time Thoreau speaks of our being at home everywhere, he also defines us as travelers, precisely as he does on this page ("if you would travel farther than all travellers"), and insofar as we are travelers, we are not yet where we are going. Thus, exploring home cosmography, though surely closer to where we want to be than making a house can bring us, is still an interim practice, a stop along the way. Wherever we go in Thoreau, we hear the sounds of the fable. The best he can do in this world is never, it seems, enough.

No wonder, too, that *Walden* ends just as *A Week* had done, with a refusal to accept the closure of natural cycles.[10] Given all that *Walden* says about the making of houses, the text could end in no other way. However overarching the circular shape of the seasons, *Walden* ends with an origin that evades conclusive shapes. The "strong and beautiful bug" that gnaws its way out of the old apple-tree table gnaws open the closure that seeks to impose itself on the text. The hearth by which we huddle in our compulsive centripetal impulse (our necessary reaction to the course of the natural cycle) gives way, at the end, to another source of heat: "the sun is but a morning star" (333).

We end with the beginning of an ultimate constellation so grand that we cannot envision more than this point of beginning. The threat of a bleak unhousing with which "House-Warming" had ended concedes to a new unhousing, this time no threat but an open-ended suggestion that there is a summer out there to be seen. Our different discourses, it is clear, deal with different sorts of housing, and therefore different readings of the potential of unhousing. For the remainder of this chapter we shall examine other readings, counterpart speculations on discourses and houses and that matter of at-homeness that seemed to get ever grimmer as Thoreau wandered the landscapes where homes could be made.[11]

• II •

Of course this is not to say that there was nothing but grimness, or that there was an unswerving move toward a deeper, more widespread unhousing. Two sets of examples from the later *Journal* can stand as synecdoches for other sets of examples that point in other directions.

On October 26, 1857, he records a fitting and fitted that meshes exactly with the work of the Wordsworth of *The Recluse*. The phenomena of the season, he said, are "simply and plainly phenomena or phases of my life" (*J* 10:127). Nothing can be added or subtracted; his moods are periodical, just as Nature's are. The result is "the perfect correspondence of Nature to man, so that he is at home in her."[12] That correspondence had appeared in elements of Emerson's *Nature*, and it remained a central issue in most versions of Transcendentalism, including Thoreau's own. So it was on that date, in that entry.[13] Slightly less than a month later, on November 20, the question of at-homeness took a form that turns up regularly in Thoreau: "In books . . . what comes home to the most cherished private experience of the greatest number" is the book of him "who has lived the deepest and been most at home" (*J* 10:190). A reporter should be permanently planted, "not a mere passer-by." Putting the issue another way, we are worth most to others and ourselves where we are most ourselves, "most contented and at home." Richest and strongest on our native soil, we threaten ourselves with excommunication when we think it better to be somewhere else. This echoes not only the beginning of *Walden* ("I have travelled a great deal in Concord") but so much else in his writing that we can call it classic Thoreau, textbook Thoreau. Yet the following, written four days later, is also classic Thoreau (though hardly textbook Thoreau), as we have seen so often in this study: in youth, ideals are "exhibited to us distinctly which all our lives after we may aim at but not attain" (*J* 10:202). As the fable would lead us to expect, the move toward the attainment of this impossible goal is figured in terms of the traveling we ought to be doing: "It would be vain for us to be looking ever into promised lands toward which in the meanwhile we were not steadily and earnestly travelling." And as we would also expect, domiciliation is held out as an image of being in place in that envisioned world: "We are shown fair scenes in order that we may be tempted to inhabit them, and not simply tell what we have seen." So much, then, for the themes of four days earlier and the dreamer who excommunicates himself by "thinking that it is better to be somewhere else" (191). If the earlier passage says that a man is worth more to others where he is most at home, the later passage adds that such at-homeness cannot be found in the place remarked on earlier, for that is only the place through which we happen now to be traveling. This too should be textbook Thoreau.

A year after the entries recorded in these passages, Thoreau looked out over another November evening, one that seemed, at once, "a familiar thing come round again" and yet so strange that he was uncertain whether he had known it or divined it (*J* 11:273). Contradicting absolutely the Transcendental union he had argued for a year earlier, he argues now that the richest relations are possible only when we distance ourselves from our object, for it is only then that we *see*: "We are independent on all that we see. The hangman whom I have *seen* cannot hang me. The earth which I have *seen* cannot bury me. Such doubleness and distance does sight prove. . . . You cannot see anything until you are clear of it" (*J* 11:273). As the passage goes on, he settles into acknowledging the comforting familiarity of the scene ("Nature gets thumbed like an old spelling-book"), and the result is an effective compromise. Halfway through the passage he arrives at a balance of nearness and distance that joins his earlier and current statements in a tense but viable harmony. He accomplishes that balance in a curiously incomplete sentence: "sure to keep just so far apart in our orbits still, in obedience to the laws of attraction and repulsion, affording each other only steady but indispensable starlight" (274). As the sentence stands in the text, it is syntactically incomplete, its subject never stated. In fact, in the passage as a whole, its reference is clearly imprecise, and that, it seems, is exactly what Thoreau wants. In one aspect it refers to his relations with other persons ("I was no nearer, methinks, nor further off from my friends"), a classic Thoreauvian stance; but in another it refers to his preferred relations with Nature, that nearness *and* distancing he had just so memorably described. The sentence helps him get at the compromise of space that seems, for him in his world, the aptest positioning.

Another sort of compromise comes out of these carefully balanced groupings. If there is radical, dependable stability in the November that one looks out at, there is also an area of change, but it appears in the seeing subject, and only there: "The utmost possible novelty would be the difference between me and myself a year ago." Expressed in its entirety, that package of stasis and movement looks, in Thoreau's words, like this: "Give me the old familiar walk, post-office and all, with this ever new self, with this infinite expectation and faith, which does not know when it is beaten"; and the Goethean phrasing that had echoed through Thoreau's work for decades comes in to cap it off: "Here I am at home." (*J* 11:274–75). There "here" includes all that we see from this proximate distance—Nature, town, friends.

That was on November 1, 1858. On November 3, he continues the meditation on nearness and distance but this time in another key, taking off from what seems to have been a disappointing encounter with friends. Finding them distant and other ("I cannot conceive of persons more strange to me than they actually are"), he goes on to admit that when he gets away from his friends his thoughts return to them: "That is the way I *can* visit them" (282). But he can do this with his friends only by dematerializing them: "I forget the actual person and remember only my ideal. Then I have a friend again." His next move is inevitable: he is, he says, "not so ready to perceive the illusion that is in Nature"; there, at least, he feels like a welcome guest. Still, that welcome can go only so far: "Yet, strictly speaking, the same must be true of nature and of man; our ideal is the only real. It is not the finite and temporal that satisfies or concerns us in either case." (Recall the analogies of nature and person set out in the entry of November 1.) Once again he is on the road, this home place only the place that he happens to be passing through.

What follows in Thoreau's writings has a great deal to do with houses and homes and their making in strange places (strange to a Concordian who claims to find all the world just around him at home); and what follows focuses plainly on the precariousness of it all, especially in the collections called *The Maine Woods* and *Cape Cod*. With these texts, the matter of dating has to be kept carefully in mind. Published in 1864, two years after Thoreau's death, *The Maine Woods* collects essays about trips made in 1846 (while Thoreau was living at the pond and writing *A Week*), 1853 (the year before *Walden*'s publication), and 1857. Also published in 1864, *Cape Cod* records excursions to the Cape in 1849, 1850, and 1855 (an excursion of 1857 made it into the *Journal* but not into the book). While he was working intently at the earlier part of his canon and all that those texts say about home making in the world, Thoreau was going through related experiences that showed with uncanny vividness how difficult it was to make any sort of home, how uncertain and open-ended and always to be worked at the process had to be. Some suggestions of that sort (suggestions far more than subtextual) in *A Week* and especially in

Walden surely got into those texts through the fact that the writing and excursions were going on at the same time. On the other hand, it is clear from texts like "The Landlord" that such suggestions had been around from the beginning of his writing, that what Thoreau went through in Maine and at the Cape *reinforced* what was already there, adding substance but above all some very dramatic instances of all it had always meant to make a home in this world.

I have dealt with *The Maine Woods* sufficiently in this study and elsewhere and need to recall only a few scenes, such as the section where Thoreau's friend gets lost and Thoreau (in a rarely recorded emotion) panics. We saw then how writing has this time to be taken as primary, since it gives not only a human definition to a place but a human claim to a place in the eerie untracked. Much the same has to be said for houses, whose import in this context exceeds even that of writing. That is why so much of the early pages of "Ktaadn" has to do with Thoreau's comments on the cabins in the woods, how from clusters they become sparser and then farther apart until—even the often-empty logger's huts gone past—they finally stop (35–56). Thoreau puts the point as plainly as possible toward the end of the last essay, as though leaving us with a last word about the last of such excursions. Speaking generally of the making of camps and the processes thereof—collecting wood, getting supper, pitching a tent—he speaks also of the closed-in thickness from which they have carved a clearing for their camp: "In some of those dense fir and spruce woods there is hardly room for the smoke to go up. The trees are a *standing* night" (275); and everywhere in these woods you have to refrain from exploring the sights beyond the camp because "at a hundred rods you might be lost past recovery." Such is the precariousness into which the last houses reach, in which the passing camps are made. The end of the *The Maine Woods* looks back to its beginning in "Ktaadn," the beginning and end framing and defining the place of our homes in this place that is never, finally, our own.

Cape Cod makes its appropriate versions of such points, its relation to *The Maine Woods* almost certainly designed to establish a mirror-image symmetry. *Cape Cod* sets up an opposite that is never entirely different because it ends by saying the same things about matters common to both. The sense of one's alien status (alien to *this* place) that runs through the essays on Maine—beginning early in "Ktaadn" and culminating in the scene at the mountaintop, continuing through to the very end, to the material we just inspected—appears, carefully laid out, in the first paragraph of *Cape Cod*: "My readers must expect only so much saltness as the land breeze acquires from blowing over an arm of the sea, or is tasted on the windows and the bark of trees twenty miles inland, after September gales" (3). His will be an outsider's way of writing, never entirely of the flavor that a homegrown way would have, inevitably deficient because inevitably distanced. And though he goes right on to say that he can "make a book on Cape Cod, as well as my neighbor on 'Human Culture.' It is but another name for the same thing, and hardly a sandier phase of it," there will be spaces in that writing that never can be crossed over, no matter where the traveler goes. Sometimes his alien status appears in lack of knowingness: "All an inlander's notions of growth and fertility will be confounded by a visit to these parts, and he will not be able, for some time afterward, to distinguish soil from sand" (36). Or it may have to do, amusingly, with the capacity to conceal oneself, the difficulty in doing so a sure sign of the stranger: "The Cape is so long and narrow, and so bare withal, that it is well-nigh impossible for a stranger to visit it without the knowledge of its inhabitants, generally, unless he is wrecked on to it in the night" (177). More tellingly, most unnervingly, his alienness appears in the questioning of ontology, the inability to fix not only where but what: "to an inlander, the Cape landscape is a constant mirage" (41).

Recall Thoreau's bragging about our ability to be at home wherever we choose to travel. Were he to work that here, it would fall as flat as the Cape landscape, even more than it would in Maine. In Maine there was a clearly defined sense of pushing out into the wilderness; and, though the houses and camps were strung out to a patent end, there would surely come a time when much of those woods would be open to human habitation. Thoreau reads that landscape in terms of lines reaching into the darkness, of clearings and centers where the rare house opens a space. He reads the Cape landscape in a very different way, partly in terms of a bleak narrowness, partly in terms of height. Where the Maine woods threaten because of their broad and unending lushness, that density which enfolds us in a "*standing* night" so soon as we leave the barely beaten paths, the Cape threatens because it is narrow and barren and easily traversed. There are places on the Cape where the land is so slimly put that one can see both coasts at once, but that is hardly the thrill it might seem. Such vantage points make clear that the tallest elements on the Cape are not what Nature has put there. They are, rather, our own steeples and windmills: "Being on elevated ground, and high in themselves, they serve as landmarks,—for there are no tall trees, or other objects commonly, which can be seen at a distance in the horizon" (34–35). Precisely because Thoreau reads this landscape in terms of short and slim scarcity, the Cape is so inhospitable that anything which holds on has to do so with permanent alertness. Cabins put down in Maine are most likely there to stay, beads along a string that will someday string out centers. Houses put down on the Cape have little hope to be more than what they start out to be, and that may be hard to manage. One cannot claim to be at home in every sort of place when one can encounter places whose saltiness is not our own and where the local makers of homes are threatened with excess of local salt.

Still, the landscape of Cape Cod sometimes got through to Thoreau in conditions and places that put him in a rare Wordsworthian mood, a visionary dreariness that touches on the mode of *The Prelude's* spots of time as well as, in one instance, tonalities perceptible in "Resolution and Independence." The text begins in a grisly scene of shipwreck, a mode of realism almost unique in Thoreau and a major determinant of the tonalities of *Cape Cod.* Yet we are not quite prepared for all of Thoreau's reactions to the scenes around the shore. Speaking of how a white spot in the water turned out to be the body of a woman "risen in an upright position," her white cap blown back, he goes on: "I saw that the beauty of the shore itself was wrecked for many a lonely walker there, until he could perceive, at last, how its beauty was enhanced by wrecks like this, and it acquired thus a rarer and sublimer beauty still" (12). It was not Thoreau's way to worry about offending with what might seem an unfeeling statement: witness his comments on charity in *Walden.* And that appears to be what happens with this statement. Thoreau goes on to speak of our bodies with scorn ("they really have no friends but the worms and fishes"), to speak of Spirit as resistant to the strongest wind, to say how "a just man's purpose" cannot be hurt by rocks but will "split rocks till it succeeds" (13). This is obviously designed to account for Thoreau's argument for "a rarer and sublimer beauty" in these scenes of desolation, in a sense to justify the argument. If that accounting succeeds somewhat in its immediate context (though even there the justification is not fully persuasive), a subsequent comment sheds the wrappings of that context and tells a good deal more about the nature and qualities of this visionary dreariness.

The third chapter takes the travelers over the plains of Nauset, a bleak and barren land, the houses few and far between, small and rusty though kept in good repair (32). Those houses hold tight to their sandy but firm anchoring, stubbornly grounded in their world, at home in its limitations: "To whom it was merely *terra firma* and *cognita*, not yet *fertilis* and *jucunda*." This comment is basic Thoreau, radically revelatory of how he reads the world. It puts quite plainly an extreme but accurate version of what he sees as our general condition, saying the same as the softer assertions but saying it about a very bleak situation. We are dealing it seems, with a spectrum, a unified continuum and not a series of separate events. Yet Thoreau does not acknowledge the special qualities of this scene but instead seeks to argue that the way the houses position themselves in this place of paucity affects him far less than the qualities of the place itself. Dropping the point about the houses as though it were a passing remark, he goes on to state that "every landscape which is dreary enough has a certain beauty to my eyes, and in this instance its permanent qualities were enhanced by the weather." Where before he had posited beauty and then justified his reaction, he now posits a cleanly contoured, full but minimal act of home making and then, without reaction, goes on to argue that this place has the beauty that every dreary landscape has. After that, he offers a long disquisition on stunted apple trees.

These passages are closely, subliminally related and at some level deal with essentially the same issues, but they have trouble within themselves and further trouble fitting together. To dismiss them as aestheticizing is easy and not quite accurate. They struggle to express a reaction that is at once moral and aesthetic, a struggle Thoreau must have known he was making, a struggle he loses. The comments on bodies and Spirit never quite jibe with his remarks on visionary dreariness and end by seeming forced and irrelevant at best. The comments on the houses happy with mere terra firma give way with no sense of juncture to the comments on beautiful dreariness, this time with no attempt to pull the moral and aesthetic together, in fact, with the patent impression that they have nothing to do with each other. We can see their insufficiency more clearly by looking at a similar passage, a muted response to the dunes around Provincetown: "Notwithstanding the universal barrenness, and the contiguity of the desert, I never saw an autumnal landscape so beautifully painted as this was" (193). This time barrenness and beauty come together with full conviction, conviction on Thoreau's part and therefore on ours, the richness held not only in the marvelous plainness of syntax and in the rhythm and balance of ideas but in what "notwithstanding" says about the difficulties of coming to terms with these conditions.

These passages show that Thoreau cannot handle the Cape as fluently as he would like, that the mastery which, by now, had come to be second nature might have to give way to bleakness that he cannot bring into his sphere. The bodies and the beauty and the land hugging and the beauty ought somehow to fit together, to make mutual sense, but he has not found a way to make that sense happen. Seeking to clarify issues as basic as any in his world, finding those issues here in this place where he found himself a stranger, distanced just enough so that he could never be fully at home, he sought to grasp what he saw in terms of endemic beauty; but the shock of the Cape won out, its effect only rarely was controlled. Thoreau handles the shock perfectly in the brief comments about Provincetown. He handles it in another way, with another sort of Wordsworthian success, in the scene that echoes "Resolution and Independence."

Thoreau's old man, like Wordsworth's, haunted a stretch of water, though his was the sea, not a pond, and he hunted for driftwood, not leeches. To call him a mere scavenger would not be to the point, since what he finds, even if only "fragments of wrecked vessels . . . is a godsend to the inhabitants" (58–59). Thus does the ocean take and give back, in a parody of the law that nothing is ever destroyed but only transformed. Of such ironic harmonies is the life on the Cape made, and of similar sounding harmonies is the old driftwood gatherer made. His face was bleached and weather-beaten but curiously anonymous; "within whose wrinkles I could distinguish no particular feature." It is not that the old man is stripped of personality but that Thoreau plays down distinguishing features that would separate him from the place where he made his home. Everything about the old man moves toward (equivocal) reconciliation. That is why Thoreau piles on a series of images drawn from the old man's surroundings. Each one links him to another local element, the whole knitting the old man into a context that could never be said to welcome him, that does not *seek* to destroy him but destroys him as it does its business. Each image puts him more fully at home in his world, yet that world has no more place for him than any other piece of driftwood, and he holds as the houses hold, precariously, tenaciously.

As the series of images links him to the beach they do as their counterparts in Wordsworth's poem do, move him up the Great Chain of Being. Wordsworth's old man begins as a huge stone that "seems a thing endued with sense," and then that elemental thing comes to seem "like a sea-beast crawled forth," the whole an extraordinary telescoping of images. Thoreau's old man comes out of a more rapid heaping up, the first images defining him as "an old sail endowed with life,—a hanging-cliff of weather-beaten flesh,—like one of the clay boulders which occurred in that sand-bank." (Those boulders echo closely the stone and rock in Wordsworth.) With the old man established in his world as part of its purely material element, the part not endowed with life, the passage works through echoes of Joseph's coat of many colors until it brings on the next simile, that one, at last, likening him to a living creature, an oddly anthropomorphic clam: "as indifferent as a clam,—like a sea-clam with hat on and legs, that was out walking the strand." The comedy is as grave as Wordsworth's, the raising of the old man up the hierarchy of being a small but sufficient boost, enough to put him in motion. And that is what Thoreau does next, shows him searching, cutting, carrying until the description ends with the old man now seen to be "the true monarch of the beach . . . as much identified with it as a beach-bird" (60). That bird is as high on the chain as the similes will take the old man but, combined with the man's role as monarch, it puts him at home in every place. At-homeness so earned can never be taken for granted and, in fact, has to be earned whenever it is put to the test; which is, on this beach, always. The landscape of "Resolution and Independence" is an inlander's landscape, like that of *Walden* and most of Thoreau's essays. The landscape of *Cape Cod* holds little more than the permanent threat of failure, the failure of driftwood to wash up, of houses to hold. Thoreau's passage on the driftwood gatherer offers a masterly blend of threat and linkage, uncertainty and odd bonding, putting the old man squarely within the Great Chain of Being, putting our home making on that chain into the profoundest precariousness. It is one of several passages in *Cape Cod* that puts those points so plainly. Few put them so richly, with such resonant effect.

Another of those that does turns up at the end of chapter 4, the passage on the "charity house" or "Humane house" (74–78). The passage holds more ironies than the ironic comments on charity with which Thoreau concludes it. Such houses are minimal but, if properly built, sufficient, their purpose to offer emergency shelter for shipwrecked sailors. This sentence sets their tone precisely: "Far away in some desolate hollow by the seaside, just within the bank, stands a lonely building on piles driven into the sand, with a slight nail put through the staple, which a freezing man can bend, with some straw, perchance, on the floor on which he may lie, or which he may burn in the fireplace to keep him alive" (74). Like those Cape houses happy with little more than the terra firma, this shelter is bare bones; but unlike those houses, which, though "not yet *fertilis* and *jucunda*," can envision that possibility, the charity houses speak only of "the tragedy of the winter evening spent by human beings around their hearths." No one else would willingly occupy their grim context, which "appeared but a stage to the grave." Thoreau seems (or chooses) to miss the point about these houses, which are designed precisely to put off the last stages to the grave, and he chides their volunteer keepers for forgetting matches and straw; yet it is clear that his interests are elsewhere. Singling out such a house in this bleak and barren context, emphasizing its condition during the worst of wintry storms (compare this passage to "House-warming"), Thoreau sees the charity house as synecdoche and symbol, one of the kinds of houses on the

Cape, the one that speaks most cogently of the edge of disaster and therefore shows most clearly the nature of the permanent threat. It projects those extreme cases that are, finally, *only* extreme, outlandish but clearly no more than the furthest instance of the experience we all share. Though the houses may be stupidly built—one was built with a chimney and in a spot with no beach grass, so that the sand undermined the house and the weight of the chimney brought it down—that stupidity comes to mean something more than misplaced charity, as Thoreau's description of their encounter with one of the houses makes eminently clear. Thoreau and his companion, curious about the shelter, chose not to remove the nail put through the staple but, instead, peeked through a knothole in the door. That is, they keep themselves as distant from the scene within as Thoreau describes himself to be on the first page of the text, the outsider looking in, the inlander inspecting life on the beach. Inevitably he plays with the possibilities of vision, his tone mocking himself and his companion more than anything they see: "knowing that, though to him that knocketh it may not always be opened, yet to him that looketh long enough through a knot-hole the inside shall be visible" (77). Keeping one eye covered, "putting the outward world behind us," they manage finally to see within: "we obtain the long wished for insight." The passage on charity houses turns out to be an allegory of life at the Cape, but the description of the house they come upon adds much more to the context. That it is also an allegory of seeing, dealing in particular with the strain of looking within; that house and self are often, in Thoreau, surrogates for each other; that what he sees within is not only as bleak but as barren as the Cape itself—no matches, straw, or hay; these say all that needs to be said about a basic part of his reading of the condition of man at the Cape. Set so sullenly, precariously, at the edge of the inhumane, in a true Blakean manner we become like what we face: "how cold is charity! how inhumane humanity!" (78). Once again, our housing betrays us.

And so does our inscribing, that other major act through which we put ourselves into our world. On that crucial first page in which Thoreau laid out his distance from what he saw (the surveyor always concerned with the precise demarcation of space), he also lays out that question of demarcation, which has as much importance in the exploring of Cape Cod as it does in the Maine woods. To demarcate a piece of the world is, in an important sense, to possess it. To demarcate is to inscribe some representative of ourselves upon the world, a surrogate that speaks for us in the world (these signposts show that someone owns this land) and to us about the world (these are the kinds of territorial relations that exist in this place). This means that

all maps are texts, so that when we say we "read" a map, we are reading the lines and colors as we read any other text. To demarcate,
then, is to make reading possible. Thus, we should give our fullest
attention to such matters as landmarks, keeping in mind all that we
saw about "marks" in the Maine woods, about Thoreau's obsession
with the word and with all the varieties of inscribing it signified in
Maine. Certain of those varieties appear in *Cape Cod* as well.

In "The Plain of Nauset," he points out that "the most foreign and
picturesque structures on the Cape, to an inlander, not excepting the
salt-works, are the windmills" (34). Putting it that way puts him into
the windmills' territory but backed away from it as well—precisely the
paradoxical positioning he sought to establish on the first page when
he spoke of the degree of "saltness" we could expect from his writing. It is perfectly consistent, then, for him to be concerned with
marks, in terms of his writing, and spaces, in terms of his self-place-
ment. That makes his next big point inevitable: "Being on elevated
ground, and high in themselves, they serve as landmarks."[14] Insofar
as we have such marks, we have a purchase on the world of the Cape.
Our windmill inscribes our mark just as the logger's camp does, just
as the ringbolt in the Maine rock locates so much of what we can
mean.

And as though to confirm all this by a dramatically negative instance, Thoreau speaks, a few pages later, about what happens without such marks. Setting out for Nauset Lights, they leave the road
and strike out across the country. At once they lose their bearings;
most guiding elements are gone, the few scattered marks not enough
to give these strangers a purchase on the place:

> We found ourselves at once on an apparently boundless plain, without a
> tree or a fence or, with one or two exceptions, a house in sight. . . . As there
> were no hills, but only here and there a dry hollow in the midst of the
> waste, and the distant horizon was concealed by mist, we did not know
> whether it was high or low. . . . Men and boys would have appeared alike
> at a little distance, there being no object by which to measure them. In-
> deed, to an inlander, the Cape landscape is a constant mirage. (41)

Mirages cannot be the subject of marking (what the marking is about)
or subject to marking (capable of demarcation). They cannot be tex-
tualized, inscribed, which means that the inlander cannot "write up"
with reasonable accuracy all that he thinks he sees. And yet they seem
to hold the only (though fallacious) substance in this markless landscape, where we are so far without purchase that we cannot tell high
from low. At one point in *Cape Cod*, Thoreau brings out his old argument about the distinctions between representations and their ob-

jects, the insufficiency of our markings in the face of the things out there: "there I found it all out of doors, huge and real, Cape Cod! as it cannot be represented on a map, color it as you will; the thing itself, than which there is nothing more like it, no truer picture or account" (65). But what these other "markless" passages show with deep, unsettling plainness is that much of the Cape landscape may well be beyond textualization, that it may not be a question of the insufficiency of representation but of its impossibility in these places for us as inlanders. That turned out to be as true in the township of Truro as it was at Nauset Lights. Through a sly play of simile, Thoreau takes his reader into the landscape around Truro but turns that landscape into the sea, questioning even the nature of the places where we stand: "To walk over it makes on a stranger such as impression as being at sea, and he finds it impossible to estimate distances in any weather" (134). If we cannot estimate distances, we cannot demarcate, inscribe, textualize, represent, so little salted are we; we are, in effect, at sea but not of it.

That "we" comes finally to include not only inlanders or inhabitants of cleared spaces in the woods but everyone who lives on the Cape or in Maine, for those books speak ultimately of all modes of home making in the world. If the inhabitants of the Cape are more at home in their places than any inlander can be, we have seen enough of the nature of that at-homeness to register its awareness of the precariousness of things. And the deeper Thoreau goes into the density of the Maine woods, the truer the registering becomes about that place as well. Thoreau's posthumous volumes of travel speak in the same voice. We ourselves can conclude only that these final commentaries tell not only of extremes but of a basic human condition, shifting in degree as we change where we live but never shifting in kind. To see Thoreau whole, we have to take him from beginning to end and not treat the middle, as brilliant as it may be, as most of what he says. If we have to let each of his words say all that it can say, the writings as a whole deserve the same respect.

Chapter Seven

A SENSE OF HIERARCHY

ARLIER in this study, I argued for the significance of a kind of natural writing, such as the way rocks inscribe themselves in a riverbed. Barbara Novak and others have shown that one can frame such inscribing in terms of geologic time, a built-in natural history that lends itself comfortably to all sorts of self-locating. That kind of time figures in Joan Burbick's *Thoreau's Alternative History*, which argues persuasively for Thoreau's attempts to write a different reading of American history, different from the sort that argues for God's involvement in the establishment of the nation or for the inevitability of secular civilized progress.[1] Texts like *A Week* show that Thoreau saw civilization as only a particular stage within a much larger movement (larger not only because it is longer but because it takes in much more than what we call "civilization"). To counter our tendency to narrow our framework, he proposed what Burbick calls an "uncivil" history "that both challenged the stories of civilization and accepted the implications of geologic time."[2] The uncivil historian focuses on personal observation rather than on written documentation, on specificity rather than on generality. He seeks a redeeming of time and the spirit through the immediacies of a broader experience than the civil historian recognizes.

Burbick's study is a discourse on method that enlarges our understanding of Thoreau's ways of reading his world. It sets us to pondering those meanings of "uncivil" that put it in contrast with all that "civility" suggests about modes of behavior that speak of modes of being in the world. Burbick's reading ties in with classic readings of Thoreau that identify the civil with the decorous stiffness of the town as well as the town's incomprehension of what Thoreau was about, specifically all that he meant by "wildness." Still, civility has to do with much more than history writing or even with a certain decorum that always made Thoreau uncomfortable. Consider, for example, what we saw in the previous chapter about the meaning of hospitality in "The Landlord" and other texts, especially hospitality considered as a kind of making-at-home. If civility can be thought of in terms of getting to be at home in the world—and its connection with hospitality, one of the basic aspects of civility, shows clearly that it can—then Thoreau's understanding of civility is a much more complex business than we usually take it to be. If we can profit from Burbick's reading of Thoreau as uncivil historian, we can also profit from remembering that it is unusual for Thoreau to be on only one side of an issue. In fact, he rarely conceives of issues in terms of sides but, rather, of categories that tend to flow together and therefore make it difficult to treat subjects like civility in an unqualified way.

It is not quite as odd as it seems to connect these issues with Thoreau's ascent of Saddleback, not only because its import dominates so much of Thoreau's writing but because so much of that import comes about through a play of difference, all that Saddleback does in relation to what its counterparts do. One of these, we saw, was the ascent up Agiocochook. But as I also pointed out earlier, there are two mountain ascents in the "Tuesday" chapter of *A Week*, and among the many purposes of the second is its function as Saddleback's complement and contrary. Introduced, as Saddleback was, as a purported "fill-in" story, the second ascent has to do not with fogs but with civility, though like many other passages in Thoreau, it accomplishes much more than its preamble promises.

With an irony that it takes the entire episode to uncover, Thoreau came prepared—or prepared himself as he went along—for a meeting with the fabulous, as though the very fact of ascending opened up such expectations. Following along a stream, he advanced into the mountains that hemmed in "the course of the river, so that at last I could not see where it came from, and was at liberty to imagine the most wonderful meanderings and descents" (202). If in one sense there is obstruction, in another there is license, their ratio direct. Closing off opens up, one kind of seeing gives way to another, the whole produces a scene at once familiar and fabulous. The towns he passes through have names he had seen on teamsters' wagons "that had come from far up country," and he now walks through those once-imagined towns "musing, and enchanted by rows of sugar maples."[3] In fact, there are two related movements going on at once, for as Thoreau goes up the mountain, he also goes back into literary history: "enchanted" is no casual term but exactly the right one to establish what is going to be the tonality of the Romance. Confirmation of that mode comes with another closing off: "The hills approached nearer and nearer to the stream, until at last they closed behind me, and I found myself just before night-fall, in a romantic and retired valley" (202-03). This is the secluded, enclosed, enchanted valley that turns up at all stages of the Romance, from *The Fairie Queene* through *Rasselas* to *Lost Horizon* and beyond. Another valley opens, "concealing the former, and of the same character with it," and then we hear of the last and highest valley, which turns out, as he gets there, to be the darkest and most solitary of all. By now the text has established not only a mode but a scene, the final, ironic fillip of the quotation from *The Fairie Queene* acting partly as punctuation (here the scene setting concludes), partly as a touch of literary history to put the Romance making into perspective.

What happens next deepens and complicates that perspective. Thoreau's announced intent in introducing the story was to take up the matters of incivility and hospitality as one meets them in the mountains; yet the result has as much to do with ways of being in the world as with questions of nature and culture. Though Thoreau had been warned that Rice, the owner of the home in that last and highest valley, was "a rather rude and uncivil man," his apprehension was immediately eased by the cattle around the place, the signs of the making of maple sugar, the sounds of children. Pondering what he sees, Thoreau concludes that Rice "was not so rude as [he] had anticipated" (204). Yet the corrected anticipation comes quickly uncorrected again, confirmed as it is by Rice's gruff greeting as well as by the "sullen invitation" implied by the owner's name on the outside. If there was no rudeness in immediate nature but signs of the redeeming of "a wild and rugged country" (205), there was an elemental rudeness (in several senses of the term) in the man who had done the redeeming. Given the anticipations fostered not only by the warnings of other people but by the tonality of the Romance, this play with degrees of the civil could have brought forth a Polyphemus or even a Green Knight, for the Other in the Romance is often a paragon of uncivility; instead, the play sets out a sequence that comes closest to prefiguring the early chapters of *Wuthering Heights*.

What Thoreau cannot quite square, despite his "pardoning this incivility to the wildness of the scenery" (204), is the contrast between the man and what he has done to this place, as though there *had* to be a parity between the differing modes of the civil, the redeeming of a segment of this wild and rugged country and the redeeming of the roughness of the man who had cleared these lands. In his prefatory remarks, Thoreau had argued that the one necessarily fosters the other: "They need only to extend their clearings, and let in more sunlight, to seek out the southern slopes of the hills, from which they may look down on the civil plain or ocean, and temper their diet with the cereal fruits, consuming less wild meat and acorns, to become like the inhabitants of cities" (201). But the encounter with Rice undoes such sentimentality, whatever the glimmers of graciousness he evinces as he eases up. Thoreau was once amused and discomfited, aware that he has become his own ultimate victim. He slides out of the dilemma gracefully by grounding a radical paradox: he who has tamed nature is himself implacably nature, as though preserving within himself all that he conquers outside: "I suffered him to pass for what he was, for why should I quarrel with nature?" (206). After stating that he "would not question nature" and "would rather have him as he was," Thoreau turns Rice into that which this pioneer works upon: "He was earthy enough, but yet there was good soil in him" (207). Still, to be nature in this way is to be elementally unthinking, low on the scale of awareness, impervious to the understanding of even one's own awkward instincts. As Rice lit the lamp, Thoreau "detected a gleam of true hospitality and ancient civility, a beam of pure and even gentle humanity from his bleared and moist eyes"; yet this look "was more significant than any Rice of those parts could even comprehend, and long anticipated the man's culture." Rice and his gleam were at different civil stages, just as Rice and his domicile were. Thoreau's point about parity could not hold out in such a context.

In one sense, then, Thoreau is surely defeated, but in another he gains much more than he has lost: the encounter clarified some deeply troubling issues that were to help him identify some of the relations between being and doing. Set off in the upper end of a series of enclosed, secluded valleys, Rice's place had within it all that he needed to have. In fact, part of the purpose of those echoes of Romance landscape must have been to prepare the way for understanding Rice's autonomy: in the forms of islands or valleys, such enclosures have always signaled sovereign self-sufficiency, and the signaling in literary forms from the mid-eighteenth century on was as dense, detailed, and pertinent as at any time in their history.[4] Though Rice knows nothing of such matters, he knows something of what they mean. Touchy and defensive about Thoreau's admiring comments on the wildness of the landscape, Rice properly calls attention to all that he has made. Like the enclaves Thoreau came across deep in the Maine woods, this place is an image of enclosed completeness, a model of home making in the world. There is, therefore, no ultimate difference in *kind* among McCauslin's place in Maine, Rice's in western Massachusetts, and Thoreau's cabin at Walden. Each is a sufficient metonym in the same encompassing whole. McCauslin's place finds a context in its echoes of similar places in the same general location, Rice's its context in the echoes of Romance. Thoreau's place found its own in the way his reading and his experience confirmed his intuition about the most basic thing he could do.

For one so obsessed with home making in the world that he turned that gesture into the central act of his life, this encounter with Rice could hardly be a trivial affair. That makes it all the more significant that what concerns Thoreau most is less the completeness of the place than the completer's personality, especially his inability to understand his own "gleam of true hospitality and ancient civility." Though Rice is a master of home making in the world, he is little more than a child when it comes to a certain alertness that Thoreau obviously treasures. To put it in terms of one of the best Romances we have, Rice plays the part of a skillful but unredeemed Caliban, and Thoreau a part somewhere between Prospero and the Duke, his brother. That raises a number of questions that Thoreau was to work at answering whenever the chance came up. To put several of them succinctly: What kind of person can get to be most at home in the world? Do self-sufficient enclosures come inevitably from self-sufficient personalities (this is the parity question again)? If the answer to the latter is yes, does their personal self-sufficiency meet Thoreau's demands for an alertness to all that is best within ourselves? Putting the question in terms of the fable, is it possible even for someone with all the alertness Thoreau requires to make what *for Thoreau* would be a sufficient home in this world? There is a very important sense in which that is the basic question Thoreau had been asking from the beginning of his work, the single and central query that determined the thrust of his life. (It is surely the basic question this study has asked from its own beginning.) What we have seen in the sequence on Rice shows that the issue is hierarchical, that there are kinds and degrees of sufficiency, that sufficiency at one point in the hierarchical system is not necessarily (not at all likely to be) sufficiency at another. If there is no essential difference in kind among the edifices built by McCauslin, Rice, and Thoreau, there is a great deal of difference among the makers of those edifices, that is, among what such making was able to mean to each.

The result is more material supporting that sense of open-endedness we have by now seen often in Thoreau. When he reported on his meeting with Rice, Thoreau set out the conditions for a kind of irresolution, an ultimate unparity that he was never able to resolve. Consider the success of the two ascents in the "Tuesday" chapter of *A Week*. The first one fails and has the ascender returning to the gloomy place below the clouds; the second turns up an accomplished terrestrial at-homeness but with the home maker too far down the ladder of alertness to understand fully all that is possible in his place. Though the text sets out these ascents in broad and deliberate contrast, they do not work through a clear pattern of valorization, an unmistakable preference or rejection. One can hardly favor a pattern that leaves us under dark clouds and among those who thought that such clouds made up the entire day. And though Rice may be dense, he has at least the minimal gleam, while the story of the rude old man that immediately follows the one on Rice shows even that minimum lacking. The "Tuesday" chapter concludes with no clear choice at hand, a situation that has appeared at several other points in this study. In fact, that condition characterizes the tenor of Thoreau's writing as much as anything else our criticism has taught us to see within it.

It characterizes our view not only of Rice himself but of several similar figures elsewhere in the canon, figures in whom these matters of civility and the civil come to be central, defining. One can approach that definition by drawing, as I did above, on the image of Caliban: after all, Thoreau identifies Rice with the earth he has turned to profit ("He was earthy enough, but yet there was good soil in him"), and when Prospero first calls to Caliban, he addresses him as "thou earth." It is hardly stretching the point to see in Thoreau's text an implicit equation of Caliban and Rice, given Thoreau's reading of Rice as so much the natural man that he cannot be affected by his own civilizing gestures. We can come closer to the import of Thoreau's complicated reading by looking at a later reading of Caliban in America, that of D. H. Lawrence. In the introductory chapter of *Studies in Classic American Literature*, Lawrence explains the spirit of American place as one of "rebellion against the old parenthood of Europe."[5] In fact, given the "hordes from eastern Europe" the country might well be considered "a vast republic of escaped slaves," a comment Lawrence flavors with a misquotation from *The Tempest*, a snippet of Caliban's drunken song celebrating his release from servitude to Prospero: "Ca ca Caliban / Get a new master, be a new man."[6] Lawrence puts the whole of America into the paradigm of Caliban, Prospero's deformed and treacherous slave, spawn of a devil and an uncommonly difficult witch; yet Caliban's corrupt lineage is clearly not in Lawrence's mind. He takes from Shakespeare's brute only a single, subsidiary aspect, seen in that moment when Caliban sings of his (illusory) release, and he makes that aspect of Caliban an image for all the inhabitants of America, Puritans to Eastern Europeans. It is not a happy choice, either for Caliban or for us, and in fact it reduces him considerably: Shakespeare's figure functions as more than a slave who wants to be freed. Caliban images all that is elementally natural—Prospero calls him "thou tortoise" as well as "thou earth"— and much in him speaks of the radically earthy and fierce, all that is pushed by compulsive forces just barely under control. Those elements put Caliban in the ancient line of the wild men, natural man in an especially bestial phase. We can rescue Lawrence's paradigm by relating the figure of Caliban not only to much in Lawrence's own work (for example, his later comments on New Mexico) but also, and especially, to the imagery of America populated by wild, natural men, imagery that preceded Shakespeare and stayed on for centuries in European awareness of America. That particular view of the spirit of American place ties Caliban to much of what America had come to mean.

Yet there is more to Caliban even than this, that more having to do with another aspect of place. Frank Kermode thinks of Caliban as natural man in a pastoral landscape, carrying the role that the shepherd plays in traditional pastoral, functioning as a "type of Nature . . . against whom civility and the Art which improves Nature may be measured," usually to the detriment of the nobles involved.[7] Though Kermode's point is important for the function of Caliban as paradigm, it has to be heavily qualified: calling Caliban "an inverted pastoral hero"[8] gives none of the requisite weight to his brutishness, his radical vileness, and no pastoral hero, inverted or straight up, shares those attributes with him; nor does the analogy of Caliban and the pastoral swain do any kind of justice to the relations of either figure to the contexts that surround them. We can touch up Kermode's point by handling the matter temporally, by thinking of pastoral at its place in time. Pastoral is both a state, a way of being in the world, and a stage, a mark in the movement of civilization. Pastoral nature is nurtured nature, something more amenable to man than it was in its original state. It is the aptest home for the pastoral hero, who is surely no inverted wild man (he would have to be so if Caliban were "an inverted pastoral hero") but is at the stage beyond that. Caliban images the nature that precedes pastoral nature, that is, its raw and original state. If he is natural man in a pastoral landscape, his kind of naturalness stands out as oddly anachronistic. That tells us a great deal not only about Caliban but about the place he lives in and the others he lives with, those who are more in tune with the place, less indexical than he is about the conditions of origin.

It also tells us much about the effectiveness of Caliban as paradigm. Take the Canadian woodchopper in the "Visitors" chapter of *Walden*, an acquaintance whose name Thoreau refuses to print because it will seem that he made it up, it is "so suitable and poetic" (144). Whatever its French antecedents, "Alex Therien" was suitable and poetic because Thoreau heard in it the Greek θηρίον, a generic word for animal. It was suitable because "in him the animal man chiefly was developed," and Thoreau plays out that point by elaborately linking the woodchopper with woodchucks: Therien eats the animals cold; his dog catches one on the way to the woods, and the woodchopper wonders for half an hour whether he should sink the corpse into the pond; woodchucks are among the sources of meat Therien could live on should he decide to become a hunter.[9] Then, slyly linking this momentum to some elemental practices of civility, Thoreau argues that "no introduction would serve to introduce him, more than if you introduced a woodchuck to your neighbor" (147). Therien has more innocence than this string of analogies has. Some seventy pages later, Thoreau was to tell how the sight of the woodchuck raised in him not only "a thrill of savage delight" but also the temptation to devour the animal for the sake of "that wildness which he represented" (210). Insofar as Therien is "animal man"—and we have to talk of him in terms of that entire phrase and not just of either component—to touch at his context is to touch by analogy at all that Thoreau saw in woodchucks; tempered, as the full phrase implies, by the other half of the description. ("Animal" and "man" not only qualify each other but are each qualified by "chiefly." Thoreau insists on the fullest attention, precisely the sort of alertness he could not expect from Rice.) Yet there are times when the woodchopper seems to be even more elemental, his place on the Chain of Being as slippery as that of Wordsworth's leech gatherer, and in precisely the same way: "In physical endurance and contentment he was cousin to the pine and the rock" (146–47). At this point the earthiness of Rice, and Caliban's status as "thou earth," seem just a step ahead, the next stage on the Great Chain after Therien's pine and rock.

Still, there is more to Therien than animal or earth. Shifting his analogies from archetypal to cultural discourse, Thoreau speaks of the woodchopper as a model of "simple and natural man." As man, Therien can think, and as exemplary natural man, he is surely closer to origin, which means that he can think about civil institutions such as money in a way that indicates why they began. In a set of puns that point the woodchopper toward beginnings, Thoreau tells how Therien's "positive originality . . . amounted to the re-origination of many institutions of society" (150). In being *and* in thought he is therefore a man of origins, as close to a unity of self as any character in the canon, certainly more than Thoreau himself is; and it is precisely that unity that conspires to keep Therien from being more than a beginning. "His thinking was so primitive and immersed in his animal life" that they could never be pried apart, mind and animality linked in him so intimately that his thoughts could never rise from the embrace of their animal frame.

It follows that Therien is, like Rice, fully at home in his world, though still without enough money to buy a farm within it. In fact, Thoreau finds Therien so very much at home that he can impersonate Young Man Winter in "A Winter Walk," a figure as upbeat as the

rest of the essay and perfectly consonant with the archetypal resonance of the reading of the woodchopper in *Walden*: "Though winter
is represented in the almanac as an old man, facing the wind and
sleet, and drawing his cloak about him, we rather think of him as a
merry wood-chopper, and warm-blooded youth, as blithe as summer" (*Excursions*, 132). Put in our recent terms, Therien is, like Caliban, natural man in a pastoral landscape, an image of an earlier state
in a largely pastoral book.[10] Yet he is very different from Caliban, in
part because the latter, forever grim and grumpy, seeks only to undo
all that is civil and orderly, while Therien not only stands in thorough
harmony with every season but stands out as an image of every season's natural joy. Good humor overflows at his eyes; his mirth is pure
and barely suppressed by his "exuberance of animal spirits" (146).
Thoreau said in the "Solitude" chapter that "nothing can compel a
simple and brave man to a vulgar sadness," a man who would hear
no sorrow in nature because he has "a healthy and innocent ear"
(131). Therien is innocent to that degree (he is compared to a child
nearly as often as he is to a woodchuck), but it is the sort of untutored
innocence seen in Blake's pastoral children; and if there is nothing in
Thoreau about the exploitation of such innocence, there is, just as in
Blake, everything about what it costs to be that way. Still, the comparison with Blake has important limitations: for one thing, Blake's children are only seemingly at home, the world of guile well practiced at
gobbling them up; for another, a little learning has managed to stick
onto Therien—nurture onto nature—so that he is several steps into
that aspect of the civil. Able to read both French and English, he
knows enough about Homer to sound out some Greek, though he
has to ask Thoreau for a translation of the *Iliad*. Yet the little that he
has serves mainly to clarify all he can never have. He has been educated to "the degree of trust and reverence" but not to "the degree
of consciousness," not to the level of "the intellectual and what is
called the spiritual man" (147). At once woodchuck and child, thoroughly at home in the forest world he has hewn for himself, he is far
less at home in the pastoral world Thoreau made at the lake and in
his book. Protected by that coherence of being that makes him both
happy and impervious to change, Therien is in many ways like Schiller's naive poet, who is as thoroughly self-sufficient as animals and
children, as fully at home in his world as they are in their own; but
Thoreau is less ambivalent than Schiller turned out to be. Thoreau,
unlike Schiller, had no problem with nostalgia, at least not at this
point. Where Schiller saw a set of counterpart possibilities, Thoreau
saw mainly a ladder of alertness; yet the result is much the same, for
high on that ladder there is a place for the sentimental poet, whose

unsatisfied longings are finally less for origin than for that which the sentimental can guess at but cannot have. The absolute enclosedness of the naive/woodchuck world stands as the precise contrary of sentimental unclosure; which means, at the very least, that Schiller would have understood the thrust of Thoreau's fable.[11]

We are now coming to see that the fable has much to do with a sense of hierarchy in the world. Certain "natural" figures focus those issues for Thoreau, though this should not be taken to mean that we always ascend the ladder of alertness when we focus on figures closer to an openly pastoral condition. In fact, the more we probe these issues, the more we see that alertness and civility and at-homeness in the world are so intimately connected that a deficit in any one is sure to weaken at least òne of the others.

One of the subtlest, canniest readings of precisely this interconnection turns up in the "Baker Farm" chapter of Walden. After describing a nature so lush that it seems almost sexually threatening (though sexuality would, in itself, be a more-than-sufficient threat for Thoreau), he turns to describing a time when he stood in "the very abutment of a rainbow's arch" and then to describing the way he sometimes wondered at "the halo of light around [his] shadow" that led him to fancy himself "one of the elect" (202). That stroke is one of the sliest in a chapter full of such moves, tying in several modes of discourse and a series of patterns of culture and possibilities in the world. That it also erects a hierarchy and begins to sketch out a history of this American place makes the stroke at least as political as it is sociocultural. Further, it is a comment on what some, the happy few to whom Thoreau ultimately speaks, are able to do. This interplay of history, culture, hierarchy, and possibilities of being continues in the following sentence, another of Thoreau's occasional cracks at Irish immigrants: "One who visited me declared that the shadows of some Irishmen before him had no halo about them, that it was only natives that were so distinguished." Together these sentences link some two hundred years of this place's experience, Puritans at one end and Irishmen at the other, a linking that also separates and distinguishes.

The purpose of all this is to illuminate the ladder of alertness, a point that comes out with pristine clarity at the conclusion of the passage. After reporting on a section of Cellini's memoirs that describes a similar halo effect, Thoreau seems to edge toward dismissing the whole affair by speaking of Cellini's "excitable imagination"; but what he actually does is no more than acknowledge the possibility of dismissing it. Such refinement of gesture leaves in an even stronger position those who are higher on the ladder of alertness: "But are they not indeed distinguished who are conscious that they are regarded at

all?" (203). The elect, it turns out, are distinguished by their attentiveness, their alertness to their place in their context. This brings
into the picture all that we have seen about Rice and Therien, and
that has a major influence on what Thoreau goes on to say.

Six weeks after he moved to Walden, Thoreau walked over to
Baker Farm, where he had once thought of living before he decided
on Walden, and the rest of the chapter describes what he found on
that day. There he met an Irishman, John Field, and his ragged family. A laborer and therefore a swain in the oldest sense of the term,
Field participates in the pastoralism of Thoreau's world because, like
Thoreau, he works at the soil, turning up a meadow with a bog hoe.
He thus partakes of that middle state between the wild and the civil
that is the essence of Thoreauvian pastoral. Thoreau takes on Field
as a test case, trying to play Prospero with the immigrant swain, giving him a short lesson in Thoreauvian economy. His attempt to teach
Field how to live simply and with little effort was not, however, the
same as that testing of fundamental ideas that he tried out with Therien. With Therien, Thoreau acted not only as Prospero but as Soc-
rates with Meno, probing radical intellect, proving it even in this local
instance of natural man. His work with Field, on the other hand, had
something in it of his working with the soil, seeking to bring to it the
finest of pastoral cultivation, seeking, as he put it in "The Bean-
Field," to make it say beans instead of grass. That linking of modes
of labor not only turns up in the imagery he uses for Field but comes
to be the outlet for his quickly found frustration: "the culture of an
Irishman is an enterprise to be undertaken with a sort of moral bog
hoe" (205–6). Cultivating this field was fruitless. The Irishman ends
by going off fishing with his guest.

Still, there is more to these matters than the nurture of fields or
Field. First there is the fact that Thoreau had thought of living there
before he decided on Walden. Then there is the house, which "had
long been uninhabited" and which, according to Ellery Channing's
poem "Baker Farm," had a curious history:

And here a poet builded,
    In the completed years,
For behold a trivial cabin
    That to destruction steers.

(204)

By linking himself to Baker Farm, and then linking "a poet" to this
ramshackle hut, Thoreau sets up a pattern of mirrors that results in
a series of ironies.

As the vignette goes on, they turn on every visible target, himself perhaps most of all. He runs to the hut for shelter (one of Thoreau's associated meanings of housing-in-the-world) and quickly finds a startling likeness between the place and the family it houses: each is equally shabby within and without, in surface and substance. To phrase the likeness differently, John Field's thinking leaks as much as the hut that houses him. These parallels find their aptest reinforcement from Thoreau himself (who is nothing if not condescending) as he goes on to describe not only the house he had built at Walden but all that it can mean for a way of being in the world: "I too, who came a-fishing here, and looked like a loafer, was getting my living like himself; . . . I lived in a tight light and clean house, which hardly cost more than the annual rent of such a ruin as his commonly amounts to; . . . if he chose, he might in a month or two build himself a place of his own" (205). And he ends his report of what he said to Field with "a man will not need to study history to find out what is best for his own culture," a comment that pulls in the play with "cultivation" and its cognates that *Walden* works with throughout and that also links Field back to Rice and Therien as well as to Thoreau himself.

Thoreau sets himself up as a parallel with Field, at once mentor and ironic mirror, though markedly better in the latter. In fact, he goes so far as to lay claim to a kind of priority with the hut, emphasizing not only Field's immigrant status but his own linkage to the place: "I had sat there many times of old before the ship was built that floated this family to America" (204). There is much more here than Thoreau's (the nation's) habitual chauvinism or even his scorn for the Irish laborers who came in droves to build those railroads that Thoreau (and some of the nation) could take only with ambivalence. If that ramshackle hut stayed leaky because the swain knew so little that he could not plug up the holes, if the parity of hut and inhabitants was as patent as the equivalent parity of the cabin at Walden and its sole occupant, Thoreau's blunt assertion of priority underscores the import of all that might have been. This could, in fact, have been the site from which Thoreau began his remaking of America, the center of his own free working, one of its results a book that might have been called *Baker Farm*. The subtext of this vignette holds a stereoscopic vision, focusing on the hut that is and also on the one it could have become, focusing on Field himself as well as the occupant who never was; and if it also focuses, in a counterpart stereoscopy, on this hut and the cabin at Walden, that additional blend of vision only complicates a scene whose intricacies reach into every level of the book as well as to the center of Thoreau's enterprise.

Field cannot adapt to the needs of hut repairing, any more than he can adapt old-world ways of fishing to the new, any more than he can turn his feckless pastoralism into the kind that is a refashioning of one's ways of being in the world. Though he has, as Thoreau puts it, "a horizon of his own," Field also has "boggy ways." He does have a sense of hospitality that he exercises as he can, its centrality to the vignette appearing in the emphasis Thoreau puts upon it:

> When I had got without I asked for a drink, hoping to get a sight of the well bottom, to complete my survey of the premises; but there, alas! are shallows and quicksands, and rope broken withal, and bucket irrecoverable. Meanwhile the right culinary vessel was selected, water was seemingly distilled, and after consultation and long delay passed out to the thirsty one,—not suffered to cool, not yet to settle. Such gruel sustains life here, I thought; so, shutting my eyes, and excluding the motes by a skilfully directed under-current, I drank to genuine hospitality the heartiest draught I could. I am not squeamish in such cases when manners are concerned. (206–7)

Field's civility is more open than that of Rice, higher on the scale, more than a gleam in a primitive eye; and yet it is as hapless as Field himself, whose minimal understanding of all that the civil means floats helplessly in the sea of his vast unawareness. As for Thoreau, the fact that he reveals himself as nosy *and* civil shows that he shares his host's respect for the civilly needful but that he is capable of being ironic about his own condescension. It is precisely such multidimensioning that none of the models he studies seems capable of bringing off. What the scene with Field adds to these issues is an especially intricate reading of how home making in the world stands as a kind of metadiscourse that comments on all the others and seems finally to hold them together.

We can watch it commenting on classic pastoral discourse in a passage from *A Week*, one that has strong subtextual ties to the vignette on John Field as well as to the story of the meeting with Rice that had appeared a few pages before. In fact, the passage plays with elements of a rhetoric we now know to be endemic to Thoreau. Remarking in the "Wednesday" chapter on the houses along the river, Thoreau singles out the lock-men's houses, "particularly well placed, retired, and high," like Rice's house up on the mountain (241), but he shifts the pattern of rhetoric from the one he had just used on Rice, speaking instead of "these humble dwellings, homely and sincere, in which a hearth was still the essential part." That hearth brings in Thoreau's rhetoric of centrality (and, with the hearth's chimney as trace, the rhetoric of indexicality as well), the language through which he reads houses and homes at so many points in his work; but here he does more than that, tying his private speech into a traditional pattern of rhetoric that enfolds an ancient fantasy about home making in the world. Speculating on his reception in one of these "barracks of repose," he imagines his quiet welcome by a "Yankee-Hindoo woman," his entrance into her bright, scoured house, his sight of her sailor brother, "their representative man," even the dogs, the kitten, and the clean water in the well. To give the picture point, Thoreau taps into the language of traditional pastoral (part of it echoed from Keats), with all its attendant paraphernalia: "there are no more quiet Tempes, or more poetic and Arcadian lives, than may be lived in these New England dwellings. We thought that the employment of their inhabitants by day would be to tend the flowers and herds, and at night, like the shepherds of old, to cluster and give names to the stars from the river banks" (243). He makes the same distinction Wordsworth makes in *Home at Grasmere*, between old and fabulous modes and the tangible realities of more immediate and local experience.[12] In Thoreau's terms, "I have not read of any Arcadian life which surpasses the actual luxury and serenity of these New England dwellings" (242). That is chauvinistic, of course, but it is also an important instance of the reification of pastoral (itself another aspect of the naturalizing of the fabulous) that appears in every version of Romanticism. Once again, this is pastoral as state and stage, a quality of being as well as a time of it; and if it is also a time of still-viable ancient rhetoric, that serves largely to demonstrate the lineage of the "Yankee-Hindoo" woman, her place in more systems of discourse than she can possibly understand. In fact, that "Hindoo" business makes the rhetoric syncretic, for we hear also of "Oriental dreamers" and "Oriental fantasies," vague but effective echoes of still another rhetoric with its own archaic figments.

This passage gains its fullest import only when allied with its successor and contrary, the well-known scene in the "Sounds" chapter of *Walden* that shows the train flying past, carrying away the old pastoral life. It is as if, Thoreau says in that passage, "a pastoral valley were going by," though what is going by is more than just significant turf but the old pastoral ways, "your pastoral life whirled past and away" (121–22). Here, as in *A Week*, Thoreau leans heavily on the defining paraphernalia, envisioning on the train "the cattle of a thousand hills, sheepcots, stables, and cowyards in the air, drovers with their stocks, and shepherd boys in the midst of their flocks." But now they signify only that which no longer has a vocation in a world that is moving even farther away from origin, down to the terminus in the city. States and stages shift, as do qualities and modes of being. The Arcadia above the Merrimack seemed to have settled into a comfortable stasis of state, stage, and language; yet the stability of the language was as illusory as the stability of the conditions it describes. Now the old speech can be used only as Thoreau uses it here, mixing the ironic and the poignant. Every kind of rhetoric is a way of defining and framing, and therefore of capturing and possessing, yet the language in the *Walden* passage is a language of *dis*possession, signifying a loss not only of a language but of its involvement in a way of being. Dispossession has an old history in pastoral, taking in not only Genesis but Virgil's first eclogue and later texts like *The Tempest*.[13] Though every one of these instances involves the dispossession of a home, none of them also implies the dispossession of a mode of discourse. That this double dispossession turns up in Thoreau—and in Blake and Wordsworth and most pastoralists of their time—shows that he and his contemporaries had come to understand how their languages function as modes of being in the world, of home making in the world. It also shows the tenuousness not only of language and mode but, through connections Thoreau had long ago learned to make, the uncertainty of all our practiced modes of inscribing. Putting the passages from *A Week* and *Walden* together in the same frame brings forth their radical import, that frame enfolding a synecdoche of a deep and essential condition.

The mode of home possessing least subject to dispossession is surely the one where Thoreau speaks of owning a place in the mind (*W*, 82–84). That he also seems to have owned an Arcadia in the mind appears some pages before the comments on that special owning of homes: "To what end, pray, is so much stone hammered? In Arcadia, when I was there, I did not see any hammering stone" (57). There was nothing so palpable as stone in that Arcadia, no more than there is in the farms that are possessed in poetic modes and thus within the margins of the mind: "Why, the owner does not know it for many years when a poet has put his farm in rhyme, the most admirable kind of invisible fence" (82–83). The farm in the mind has all the positive values of the Arcadia in the mind: in the former, he "never got [his] fingers burned by actual possession"; in the latter, one need only recall the elegiac context of Poussin's *Et in Arcadia Ego* (the old phrase echoes in Thoreau's comment on Arcadian stones) to gather that such Arcadias are best kept in the mind.[14] Only there can one be certain to be "unmolested in [one's] possession of" the best sort of home (83). Only in such possession can one have language and home and freedom in all the fullness they can realize in the world where they find themselves.

And it is precisely in that relation of freedom and fullness that Lawrence's comparison of Americans to Calibans takes its most curious turn. Our Calibans, Lawrence argues, left Europe to escape the old hierarchies, the church, the "true aristocracy," all that he calls "fatherhood."[15] It was just that kind of hierarchy that characterized the old pastoral, which, as much as it privileged sheep, took its impetus from the urbane audience for which it was written, that of Theocritus in Alexandria, that of Virgil in Rome, that of Marlowe and Raleigh among the educated classes who knew the history out of which contemporary modes came forth. No other mode we have had takes in so many meanings of cultivation, none is so subtly hierarchical or makes of matters of hierarchy so much of its subtextual life. Freedom of the sort that Thoreau and Lawrence spoke of (the freedom Thoreau elaborated on in his lesson to John Field) was freedom *from* hierarchy as well as freedom to seek out a re-originating of home. Yet Thoreau's own experiences with Rice, Therien and Field revealed another species of hierarchy, one that takes its origin from Thoreau's attempts to establish a contemporary pastoral, a kind that is possible, he often argues, to anyone who understands what is involved in taking it up. Such understanding is the problem, and that problem is the ultimate source of this part of his sense of hierarchy. Thoreau's new kind of pastoral brought in a new kind of hierarchy in which figures like Therien and Field, however genial and eager, were irrecoverably stuck at the bottom of the scale. Though Therien was as free as anyone Thoreau ever knew, as fully at home in his world as it was possible for him to be, his freedom and success were bound by his profound limitations of awareness. Though Field has "a horizon of his own" to work with, and far more freedom to work toward it than Ireland would ever have granted, he lacked all that he needed to adapt Thoreau's model of home making. And if Rice was also a model of a sort of home making in the world, he lacked so much that was central that, with all his civil accomplishments, the fittest analogy for him was in Shakespeare's Caliban.

Thoreauvian pastoral works in an area midway between the wild and the civil, the woods and Concord, a point made plain in the "Bean-Field" chapter of *Walden*. It therefore stresses middles rather than origins and ends, its language the language of middles and thus inaccessible to Therien, whose likeness of thought and being kept him close to the condition of origin. That language was also closed off to John Field, who had reached a middling state of awareness and had shown that it was not nearly enough. The surly mountain settler, the natural man as woodchuck, the boggy immigrant swain, and the lady rendered in a language she could never understand could go only so far. Thoreau's own kind of pastoral is as hierarchical as the old, substituting for the strata of society an elaborate ladder of alertness.

At this point, the inevitable question insinuates itself quietly but with stubborn and compelling insistence: Is it only a Rice or a Therien who can be fully at home in this world? Put another way, is it only a Rice or a Therien who can be satisfied with such at-homeness as is achievable in this world? Thoreau answers through a pattern that appears at every point in his work, an uneasiness with closure, a compulsion to open out. At his deepest reaches of awareness, there is a kind of claustrophobia that affects (and effects) not only the shapes of his major books but that of his fable as well. We shall see several versions of it in the material of the next chapter.

Chapter Eight

ORIGINS AND ENDS

THE "SUNDAY" chapter of *A Week* begins with their first morning out on the river, and it establishes conditions and suggestions that were to characterize the beginnings of most of the subsequent chapters. "Covered with a dense fog, through which the smoke of [their] fire curled up like a still subtiler mist," the area seems self-enclosed, as though the world were beginning again and this were all there was so far (43). The tonality of this Sunday intensified the effect, making it seem as though those conditions dated from "earlier than the fall of man" and were still pristine enough to possess "a heathenish integrity." We should take integrity in its fullest possible sense, seeing it as signifying the first (and only?) wholeness. A poem follows and elaborates, turning the morning into

> An early uncoverted Saint,
> Free from noontide or evening taint,
> Heathen without reproach,
> That did upon the civil day encroach,
> And ever since its birth
> Had trod the outskirts of the earth.

Whole, pure, and (in a special sense) uncivil, this state lasts only until the sun disperses the fog, slipping so far out of mind that "not even the most 'persevering mortal' can preserve the memory of its freshness to mid-day" (43–44). One kind of mist replaces another as, trailing echoes of Wordsworth's *Immortality* ode, we edge our way into the light of civil day.

The beginning of the subsequent chapter elaborates on these points and patterns, confirming that the conditions of this Sunday morning were not idiosyncratic. The headnotes begin with a quotation from Gower about "the world which neweth every daie," and the text takes originating even further by going back to the scene "when the first light dawned on the earth." Yet this emphasis on earliness (and all that the image shows of what earliness holds of saintliness) does much more for the text. For one thing, it clearly privileges priority. For another—given what "Sunday" shows of the integrity of earliness, its wholeness *and* freedom from taint—the emphasis establishes a moral priority as well. Still, these passages hold more than matters of purity. If they institute the patterns through which most of the subsequent chapters figure a fascination with origin, they also disclose the fogginess that surrounds origin as well as the fact that the memory of its freshness cannot be preserved until midday. The "Sunday" and "Monday" chapters establish for the rest of the book that the beginnings of days and chapters have their ground and echo in the very beginning of things. In so doing, they affirm how murk and mist envelop the origin of the day and, therefore, our view of the veritable introduction of the world.

They also affect our reading of the mountain ascents in *A Week*. The Saddleback section builds not only on the introductory material to the "Tuesday" chapter (it is because of the dense fog that he pauses to tell the Saddleback story) but that of the two previous chapters as well; and though his story has him climbing above their climatic conditions, it also confirms their statements about primal beginning. When he wakes up on Saddleback, he finds below him another morning of fog, "an ocean of mist [that] shut out every vestige of the earth" (188). Yet that is by no means undesirable, because it puts all the focus on where he wants to go, "the region of eternal day," the site of that ultimate origin which is also the final goal. Up above the fog he finds extraordinary clarity, giving him ease to see in the direction where he would go; but nothing in his experience is quite as upsetting as that ease, for the place of ultimate origin remains as inaccessible as though it were blocked by the densest fog. That clarity is nagging, ironic, and cruel, eternity's tease upon time. So too is the clarity that greets him on Agiocochook. If Saddleback has to do with transcendent origin, then the source of the stream on which they had been traveling, the point of terrestrial origin, ought, one thinks, to get its own share of awe. It is, after all, the goal of the counterpart quest, and one could hardly ask for more clarity than can be found in this mirroring journey; yet the moment of getting there is given extremely short shrift. In Thoreau's valorization, this is an ultimately trivial affair. If the interplay of Saddleback and Agiocochook puts the privileging precisely, it also defines the pains with pinprick precision.

Our reading of these ascents through the question of the clarity of origin establishes other valorizations that have a profound and unsettling effect upon the rest of the text. Obsessed with all manner of cycles and therefore with various returns to origin, *A Week* finds clarity and a kind of rest (if not a final satisfaction) in all the returns it shows: for example, in the travelers' arrival, at the end, at "the wild apple-tree, whose stem still bore the mark which [their boat's] chain had worn in the chafing of the spring freshets" (393). The structures of season, day, and trip coincide at this point; yet the shadow of the brightness above Saddleback—the clarity that veils the most painful inaccessibility—looms over these multiple returns, whose achievement is clearly lesser simply because it is possible now.

A Week is by no means the only text where Thoreau focuses on origin. The subject haunted him all his life and appears, in one form or another, in every major published text as well as in the entries in the *Journal*, where it emerges in different guises throughout the history of those entries. The subject turns up persistently in his reading of Therien, our version of "animal man," who had "a certain positive originality," whose ideas "amounted to the re-origination of many of the institutions of society" (*W*, 146, 150). Yet Therien not only re-originates institutions but, by predating pastoral, gets as close to origin as any with whom Thoreau can carry on meaningful conversation. In *Cape Cod*, Thoreau speaks often about the sea, the site of our creaturely origin, which threatens always to take us back. The challenge is made so dramatically in the introductory chapter that it affects the rest of the text, not only through the violence of storms but the more subtle undoing through which the sea eats at the land. Perhaps the most insidious version comes from the sand the sea creates, the grit that becomes the surrogate of its maker, undoing our edifices in those places the sea cannot reach. Questions of origin climax "Ktaadn" and, through it, much of *The Maine Woods*, as Thoreau stands on top of the mountain and speculates on such sites as "among the unfinished parts of the globe" (65). These are the spaces of radical Matter, the earliest Earth, "made out of Chaos and Old Night," unhandseled and therefore virgin, before all inauguration (70). No site in Thoreau's writing is as threatening as this, with the single exception of the sea in *Cape Cod*. That threat offers one more reason why the place of terrestrial origin is passed over so quickly on Agiocochook: *The Maine Woods* and *Cape Cod* show that the locus of such origin may be deadly and terrifying, threatening in Maine the loss of what we see in ourselves as the basis of human being, threatening in the sea the ultimate loss of life. Still, we may choose to argue otherwise, to say as we previously did that Agiocochook was simply not significant enough to merit more than it got. This would mean that the terror (by no means too strong a word) that Thoreau would sometimes associate with places of earthly origin grew in him as he grew older and took other trips.

Yet even these events do not tell the entire story, because the canon contains versions of earthly origin that are not as disappointing as Therien or as menacing as the mountain and the sea. Somewhere within us, Thoreau argues in "Walking," there lives a wild savage, and that may be the place where we store our savage name, the signifier of what we radically, originally are (*Excursions*, 200–201). This sense of origin as underneath, Thoreau's archeologism, appears throughout "Walking" and sometimes in *Walden* as well; for example, this comment from "Walking": "The civilized nations—Greece, Rome, England—have been sustained by the primitive forests which anciently rotted where they stood" (*Excursions*, 191). Such instances point to one of the broader and more persistent versions of Thoreau's quest for origins, his passionate craving for wildness, which he treats always as the condition wherein one starts, whether one is a person, a nation, or a culture. He had said in *A Week* that "there is in [his] nature, methinks, a singular yearning toward all wildness" (54). In fact, it is toward more than wildness, for that yearning addresses origin, the field of which wildness is his most prominent metonym.

All those differing tonalities that will never comfortably mesh show that his attitude toward origin can never be single or simple, that it can be characterized only by a profound and pervasive ambivalence. We can clarify that ambivalence by inspecting several examples of the reason why it happens, examples whose conflicts are more than sufficient to cause such a condition. Some of our finest readers of Thoreau, figures like Sherman Paul and Stanley Cavell, have shown the importance in Thoreau of the idea of self-renewal, a refashioning of oneself that—Thoreau offering himself as an instance—ought finally to effect a comparable redoing of society.[1] Given what we have seen of Thoreau's passion for origins, his impetus toward self-remaking can be seen in other terms, like self-re-originating. His canon contains occasional moments of such finding, as well as other moments that are urgings toward re-origination rather than instances of it. One pristine example of success from "Walking": "When I would recreate myself, I seek the darkest wood, the thickest and most interminable, and, to the citizen, most dismal swamp. I enter a swamp as a sacred place,—a *sanctum sanctorum*. There is the strength, the marrow of Nature" (*Excursions*, 190). To get down to the marrow is to get to the central place, here a locale of wildness, uncultivated lands. The counterpart of this action is the digging toward origin that we have seen in other contexts, and in fact, the subsequent sentence brings that relationship out: "The wild-wood covers the virgin mould,—and the same soil is good for men and for trees."[2] It is the compulsion to re-originate that drives Thoreau's excursions into versions of the wild. That he can re-originate successfully—that we could all do so, following his knowledge and his model—comes through clearly in this passage, one of many that could be cited. The grandest of those, of course, is the return of spring in *Walden*, that renewal of earth which is also proffered as a potential renewal of ourselves. (One may, however, question the ultimate efficacy *for us* of that grand re-origination.)

To these models of successful renewal one ought to add the many exhortatory passages that urge toward self-refashioning, a successful remaking of origin within ourselves. Take, once again, "Walking." Thoreau speaks of friends who were "so blessed as to lose themselves for half an hour in the woods" (164). What happens in the woods is what happens in the swamps, a re-creation of oneself; at one point he specifically identifies such excursions with a quest for the place of beginnings: "If you would get exercise, go in search of the springs of life. Think of a man's swinging dumb-bells for his health, when those springs are bubbling up in far-off pastures unsought by him" (167). Yet even such goading may have its built-in subversion, emergences of a subtext that also prods and exhorts but to contradictory purpose.

In the chapter on "Reading" in *Walden* he speaks of the father tongue, "a reserved and select expression, too significant to be heard by the ear, which we must be born again in order to speak" (101). Several pages later he refers to the reading of books so potent (obviously written in the father tongue) that they might "put a new aspect on the face of things for us. How many a man has dated a new era in his life from the reading of a book" (107, cf. 108). Thoreau's openly hesitant qualifiers—"probably . . . possibly . . . perchance"—ought to be taken in all their pregnant uneasiness. Surely they stem in part from the problems raised when we put these passages together: we must be reborn in order to handle the father tongue, but we must be able to read books written in that tongue in order to be renewed.

In such paradoxes we sense a subliminal uneasiness, enough, surely, to urge the qualifying of reports, such as the ones in "Walking," that do not qualify themselves. The subtext suggests that the sort of being in the world that these passages define may not turn out to be entirely coherent or successful. No single statement seems able to carry the full freight of his feelings. Only when we put a set of such statements together can we begin to get a sense of the thoroughly mottled makeup of his pervasive quest for renewal.

A Week on the Concord and Merrimack Rivers proposes a spectrum on the issue of the tryst with origin, as though setting up possibilities for Thoreau to elaborate upon in his later writings. And elaborate he does, not only in other examples we have seen, early and late in the writings, but sometimes in entire themes, for example, that of the Indian. *The Maine Woods* does for the later writings what *A Week* had done at the beginning.

Thoreau had engaged an Indian to guide his party on the trip to

Ktaadn. The Indian did not, however, show up until much later, mumbling an unbelievable apology, drawing the party's anger and contempt as well as comments by Thoreau on "a remarkable and un-expected resemblance between the degraded savage and the lowest classes in a great city" (78). The narrative then turns to pondering the white man on the edge of the wild, living, as it were, "in the prim-itive age of the world . . . three thousand years deep into time" (79). As Thoreau puts it two pages later, going back into the interior means going back into time, those acts the horizontal counterpart to that digging toward origin that appears in "Walking" and elsewhere. Still, white men on the margin, clearly visible to Thoreau at that three-thousand-year-old edge, have not gone in (or back) as far as it is possible to go:

> Can you well go further back in history than this? Ay! ay!—for there turns up but now into the mouth of Millinocket stream a still more ancient and primitive man, whose history is not brought down even to the former. In a bark vessel sewn with the roots of the spruce, with horn-beam paddles he dips his way along. He is but dim and misty to me, obscured by the aeons that lie between the bark canoe and the batteau. He builds no house of logs, but a wigwam of skins. He eats no hot-bread and sweetcake, but mus-quash and moose-meat and the fat of bears. He glides up the Millinocket and is lost to my sight, as a more distant and misty cloud is seen flitting by behind a nearer, and is lost in space. So he goes about his destiny, the red face of man. (79)

Thoreau, we know, can shift suddenly but rarely as startlingly as the change, within a page, from the remarks about the "degraded sav-age" to what we see in this eloquent passage. Whatever Thoreau's disgust with the individual Indian, the presence of the native in this place of rawness and dark inner spaces opened up areas of meaning that transcended the individual figure (now generic as "the red face of man") and linked him to other ideas about origin that Thoreau had already broached. That linking is particularly clear in this passage because it so patently echoes the day/chapter beginnings that set so much of the tone of *A Week*: "dim and misty to me . . . a more distant and misty cloud," those echoes serving an awesome move that leads backward in time to closer to where time began. Thoreau's intuitions about the murkiness of beginnings had taken some years of medita-tion to reach this elaborate state, coming finally to coalesce with his experience of Indians. But the echoes express more than intertextual continuity, for they complicate the issue by distinguishing two con-trary conditions: the first shows the oldest times to be effortlessly ac-cessible to a kind of Caliban; the second is figured in a place at the

edge of the wild, the seat on which sit most of Thoreau's kind. These
Indian Calibans own the mindless access to origin that Therien had
owned. It may be that only mindlessness makes accessibility possible.
If so, that offers still another reason why Thoreau, in particular, will
always stay at the edge. The mists have long since settled into permanent place, no longer dispersible because no light that he knows
can reach into the world of these dim and misty figures.

All that we saw earlier about an often vexatious play of presence and
absence—nearness and distance, proximity and aloofness—has a
place in these passages on the Indian. Though sitting next to the Indian in the canoe, or walking beside him on the treks through the
woods, Thoreau seems always to stand at a kind of porous glass wall
through which he can see and communicate but never penetrate.
What he speaks of in "The Allegash and East Branch" as "that
strange remoteness in which the Indian ever dwells to the white man"
(158) must be qualified (though it can never be overcome or even
subordinated) by that proximity he generally finds easy to obtain for
hire. Like his counterparts in Maine who have edged up to the point
where they are three thousand years back, he stands at a margin he
can never go beyond, knowing the direction that leads back to the
times of origin but knowing also that the way will always be blocked
because he is what he is. The analogy to the experience on Saddleback—halfway up but never more than that, kept back by all that he
has within himself—is patent, potent, and unnerving. Saddleback was
not unique nor were the mornings on the river. This scene at the
edge of dim depths contains elements from the earlier scenes, linking
them to these figures who function as indexes of that which *can* be
reached but never by those who understand the meaning of the figures.

The play of achievable proximity and irrevocable distance comes
out in still another area that exercises Thoreau. In "Chesuncook," he
describes an evening when they were lying near a campfire, listening
to their Indian guide, Joe Aitteon, speaking with a St. Francis Indian
who was one of a group they had encountered. Thoreau makes much
of the point that these two were the only pure Indians in the group
(132), and he wants that point stressed, because he goes on to describe what it was like to hear them speaking together in their native
language. Through what we now know to be no coincidence, what he
hears confirms the geography of origin, their accessibility to it, his
ineradicable distance: "There can be no more startling evidence of
their being a distinct and comparatively aboriginal race, than to hear
this unaltered Indian language, which the white man cannot speak
nor understand" (136). Since, as Thoreau says, we have no need to

suspect deterioration in their language, these figures too can stand as indexes of the oldest times. All the ironies of Thoreau's proximity come out at the end of the passage: "I felt that I stood, or rather lay, as near to the primitive man of America, that night, as any of its discoverers ever did" (137). That "near" can only be sardonic. Nearness of that sort, the best that he can get, is not really what counts. Proximity and distance combine in a piercing oxymoron that enters the deepest reaches of what had always moved Thoreau.

That piercing does not end with the essays in *The Maine Woods*. In a passage of the later *Journal* (March 5, 1858; *J* 10: 294–95), Thoreau speaks of scientific language, how words like "arbor-vitae" do not offer a "tree of life." Indian language, however, implying "a more practical and vital science," has twenty different words for the tree and its parts. That, in turn, implies not only more supple and fluent relations but a greater intimacy; and Thoreau succeeds that point with a barrage of terms laying out a temporal/spatial geography that privileges Indians: "nearer . . . receded . . . distance . . . a rumor has come down to us." An early settler might have heard a lion roar, but the Indian slept on its skin.

Most important, though, is how the commentary ends. After saying how Indian language reveals a life adjacent to but outside our own (a variant phrasing of the nearness-distance oxymoron), Thoreau concludes this way: "The Indian's earthly life was as far off from us as heaven is." Saddleback and the Indian come together once again. The trips to Maine had linked them into an ironic relationship that the rest of a lifetime of pondering was never able to shake.

• I •

The play of nearness and distance has to do with much more than Indians and origin, because the play may well turn up in some very different contexts—for example, in Thoreau's most ecstatic moments, when he seems most at home in the world. We see the play in so many places, because that oxymoron reveals a deep subtextual urging that seems always to find a way of bringing its mutterings to the surface. Take, for example, the comments from the *Journal* of August 17, 1851, written while *Walden*, with its announcements of cyclical redemption, was still being worked upon (*J* 2; 390–93). Remarking on the coolness of the morning, Thoreau hopes that such weather will do him good, fostering a "fertile sadness" that would keep his life from being trivial. Sensitized, thus, to the sounds working around him, he recovers his spirits, wishing that his moods would always match Nature's in this way; that is (echoing, once again, Wordsworth's *Immortality* ode), in the way of "natural piety." Still, the pensiveness cannot quite shake its overtones of sadness. After all this communal rejoicing (much more than is offered in the Wordsworth poem), Thoreau speaks of his own inadequacies, drawing phrases from old discourses to define his current state: "I am impure and worthless, and yet the world is gilded for my delight and holidays are prepared for me, and my path is strewn with flowers" (392). Such self-denigrating comments were commonplace in the literature of saints and in related writings. His comments call upon a long and elaborate history, largely through his echoes of old phrases and attitudes: "I thank you, God, I do not deserve anything. I am unworthy of the least regard; and yet I am made to rejoice" (392). Still, there is much more involved here than establishing a lineage or setting the tones of saintly existence in the context of New England's Nature. Readers of Thoreau know how matters of purity obsess him, most potently in places like the top of Saddleback Mountain, where his further travel is frustrated by some stain within himself. Linking questions of purity with an allegorical journey was routine in the discourse on which Thoreau draws, and he echoes the practice not only in the Saddleback material but in this ecstasy on a cool August morning. By anchoring its uneasiness in ancient modes of speaking, the subtext draws not only on the prestige of that discourse but on its credibility as well.

Echoes from that discourse sound through the rest of the passage as the allegorical journey comes to be more explicit. Thoreau goes on to argue that he himself is so rarely fully composed that, projecting from his own experience, he cannot always be certain who his audience precisely is: "And why should I speak to my friends? for how rarely is it that I am I; and are they, then, they?" Such puzzles of identity are promised solution in the next sentence, which brings the implicit journey up to the surface of the text: "We will meet, then, far away" (392). Now clearly defined as a spiritual traveler, he can relish the beauties of Nature as he passes through Nature's place, then personalize the classic image by bringing in sounds from his own fable. Once again echoing a favorite passage in *As You Like It* (speaking of the "sybilline sentences" of the brook), he defines what the local stream cannot do for him: "The rill I stopped to drink at I drink in more than I expected. I satisfy and still provoke the thirst of thirsts" (392–93). To satisfy and provoke at once is not finally to satiate. It is clear that the "thirst of thirsts" can be quenched only at that place where he finds the "word of words" and its "great and serene sentence." Uttering and slaking will then be simultaneous acts, perhaps

the same act seen from differing perspectives. (The structural identity of the phrases on thirst and word supports this suggestion of
their radical sameness.) Yet we are not through with the mapping
such moves quietly accomplish. Given the broadest of hints, we may
now choose to suspect that the place of the word of words has the
directest sort of link with the place where it all began, the origin of
the rill: "It is not in vain that I have drunk. I have drunk an arrowhead. It flows from where all fountains rise." That point confirms and
completes the implicit allegory, the excursion that underlies not only
the ancient discourse but his own quite active fable. Of course he is
at home among these natural marvels, the gilded world and its holidays, the paths strewn with flowers, but the glorious at-homeness he
experiences in this place can be experienced only in passing, however
long and pleasurable the time he spends there. The thirst of thirsts
will always keep him on his way.

One way of handling what happens in this and similar passages is
to see them as saying, "yes, of course . . . but then . . ." Thoreau had
spent so much of his life defining what could happen in Concord
that, even toward the end of his life and whatever the contrary provocation, the establishing of at-homeness in this local universal was always a primary goal; but all that we have seen from the beginning of
this study shows that it was not an exclusive one. It is not that Thoreau *wants* to have it several ways at once but that he so often finds
himself pulled by contradictory impulses, sometimes simultaneously
(as in the passage we just inspected) or in immediate succession (as in
the next we shall look at). It would have been easier for him were he
able to say, "yes, and . . . ," promising that concord he often punned
on; but it was more often to be "yes, but . . . ," and that is perhaps the
most encompassing way to contain all the versions of his endemic ambivalence. That encompassing would also include our latest oxymoron, the one that wants, at once, both nearness and distance, the one
that has him spending the evening around a campfire chatting with
an Indian but astonished another day, to hear that same Indian
speaking cozily, caressingly, to a musquash. Thoreau, we ought never
to forget, was a professional surveyor. One way of handling this oxymoron is to think of it as figuring a kind of spiritual geography, the
point of which is to tell us who we are by showing us where we are
and where we can never be—or, as often in Thoreau, where we cannot be right now.

It is only with "yes, but . . ." that we can finally explain a concate-
nation of passages (one of which we looked at earlier for other purposes) in the *Journal* for November, 1858. "Nature," he said in the
first passage, "gets thumbed like an old spelling-book" (*J* 11:274), yet

there is always change in us and therefore in the way we spend our time with Nature: "give me the old familiar walk . . . with this ever new self." We need no "Europe or another world," since this oxymoronic combination of the recurring and the novel will very comfortably do. No wonder, then, that he speaks so happily of a series of repetitions ("another walk to the Cliff, another row on the river, another skate on the meadow" [274]). He knows that these will bring him perfect satisfaction, for "here I am at home" (275). That the echo of Goethe hangs on after so many busy years shows how deeply it resounded in the most elemental Thoreau.

That happened on November 1, what we might call the day of the "yes." The walk that he took on the afternoon of November 3 had other points to make. Complaining that the friends who were so satisfying just two days before are now so many strangers, he finds that he can get along with them only when he withdraws from them. It is not, he says, the same with his relations with Nature, yet he surrounds that saying with other remarks that call his saying openly into question. After making an odd statement about being "not so ready to perceive the illusion that is in Nature" (282), he goes on to state that he communes with her every day, "*as I think*" (Thoreau's emphasis); but he then goes on to argue that, finally, "our ideal is the only real. It is not the finite and temporal that satisfies or concerns us in either case." If November 1 was the day of "yes" on the matter of at-homeness in Nature, the third is the day of "but"; yet it is also the day that carries within itself the whole "yes, but . . ." Though the passage does not reject the Goethean assertion, it complicates it so much that it cannot be the same, taking an additional import as we see it in a larger context. Once we begin to sense the movement of the fable's implicit journey, that assertion comes to be seen as no more than a single element in a paradoxical scheme.

By now it should be clear that "yes, but . . ." can occur even within the echoes of Goethe. Some of them expand on the original quotation, as in Thoreau's account of a day on the river in August 1852. He feels as though he had embarked with all his belongings, home, and furniture, for he experiences a greater sense of completeness than any walk can give (*J* 4:325). Two things result, linked and in succession. He begins a train of ideas by saying "I find myself *at home* in new scenery" (327; Thoreau's italics), the emphasis not only affirming his special relation to this new place but also recalling all the meaning of that phrase in his work. After that affirmation, he speaks of an unusual plethora of being, confirming what, in this case, it means to be so much at home: "I carry more of myself with me; I am more entirely abroad, as when a man takes his children into the fields with him. I carry so many me's with [me]" (327–28). Differing modes of travel get to be differently connected with at-homeness in the world and therefore with ourselves as beings-in-the-world. His ordinary excursions tend to be somewhat scantier that this one ("it seems a more complete adventure than a walk"), and what turns out to be scantier is the amount of himself involved. Thus, the more of himself there is, the more at-homeness there is.

Now that we have that equation, we can clarify other comments as well. If we have heard Thoreau say that he can be at home everywhere, we now can understand a contradictory remark that he made sometime between 1842 and 1844: he said then that "all travelling grows out of a wish to return home and stay at home—if the traveller can find it" (*J 2:73). At-homeness and fullness of being imply and implicate each other. To the degree that he finds the one, to that degree will he find the other. It would seem, then, that traveling is a search for the utmost fullness of being, a point that expands our understanding of the journey that guides Thoreau's fable.

That there are even more complex degrees in this intricate, critical relationship appears in a *Journal* entry for June 16, 1857 (*J* 9:428), describing an excursion on Cape Cod. After bragging that, with his chart and compass, he usually finds a shorter way than any of the locals knows, he says that when his travels take him through villages, his legs "ache at the prospect of the hard gravelled walk." At such times he feels as strange as though he were traveling through "a town in China." But that feeling lasts only briefly, and the Goethean assertion returns, this time, as often, triumphant: "but soon I am at home in the wide world again, and my feet rebound from the yielding turf." Even on a walk, it seems, there are degrees of at-homeness. The ratios at issue in this passage—less in the town, more in the country—progress, some four months later, to the extremest possible degree, the fullest possible at-homeness resulting from the purest solipsism:

> These regular phenomena of the seasons get at last to be—they were *at first* of course—simply and plainly phenomena or phases of my life. The seasons and all their changes are in me. I see not a dead eel or floating snake, or a gull, but it rounds my life and is like a line or accent in its poem. Almost I believe the Concord would not rise and overflow its banks again, were I not here. After a while I learn what my moods and seasons are. I would have nothing subtracted. I can imagine nothing added. My moods are thus periodical, not two days in my year alike. The perfect correspondence of Nature to man, so that he is at home in her! (October 25, 1857; *J* 10:127)

One could ask for no greater quantification than this, either of himself or of at-homeness. One cannot be more at home in Nature than when one *is* Nature.

Yet we can go back several years and find quite the opposite occurring, confirming, once again, the need to take in *all* that Thoreau says in order to find out *what* he says. In the *Journal* for October 31, 1850 (*J* 2:76), Thoreau remarks that this was "such a day as I think Italy never sees" (that he has Goethe's Italy in mind comes through later in the passage). After an odd comment that rings subterranean echoes of his occasional solipsism ("Why was this beautiful day made and no man to improve it?"), Thoreau speaks of a sight that always fascinated him, the rays of the western sun. That this sight would bring to mind the move toward final things becomes apparent in, for example, the last pages of "Walking." It does so here as well, and in a way that turns his Goetheanism completely upside down: "Looking through a stately pine grove, I saw the western sun falling in golden streams through its aisles. Its west side, opposite to me, was all lit up with golden light; but what was I to it? Such sights remind me of houses which we never inhabit,—that commonly I am not at home in the world. I see somewhat fairer than I enjoy or possess" (*J* 2:76). From everywhere at home to commonly not at home is a very big leap indeed, and he takes it again and again. Some ten months later, complaining of what he needs to carry when he goes on an extensive walk, he argues that "man does not travel as easily as the birds migrate. He is not everywhere at home, like flies" (*J* 2:402). And the remark we looked at above about all traveling being, finally, a wish to return home, can mean only that this obsessive traveler has not yet gotten there. The lifelong echoes of Goethean at-homeness are not one thing *or* another but themselves prey to the ironies of the oxymoronic "yes, but . . ."

The reasons for that are clear. Since the extraordinary passage from Goethe is a central one for Thoreau, it necessarily partakes in the ambivalence that dogs his profoundest urgings and speculations. His acts of at-homeness could no more settle into completion than Thoreau himself could, whatever the efficacies of swamps, whatever the special success of the cabin by the pond or those shelters in the Maine woods. Clearly one does not need occasional passages of extreme despair to elucidate this point, passages like his paean to disease on September 3, 1851. Thoreau argued then that "disease is not the accident of the individual, nor even of the generation, but of life itself" (*J* 2:449). In a phrasing that echoes the sad and bitter sounds of *Walden's* chapter on "Higher Laws," he tells how "man begins by quarrelling with the animal in him" and that "the diseases of the body answer to the troubles and defeats of the spirit." These are occasional tones in Thoreau, products of an attitude impelled by his running sense (more precisely, by the sense that ran after him) that our physical beings were born degraded and went downhill after that. Such instances are, however, elements in a larger picture, one most accurately delineated by the simultaneous presence of both his lifelong desire for at-homeness in the world and also the equally long-standing recognition that such at-homeness would never happen in a way to satisfy him fully. More definitive and more typical than the extravagant passage on disease is this comment, at the beginning of "The Landlord," from 1843, thus very early in his published writings: "nowhere on the earth stands the entire and perfect house" (*Excursions*, 97). We have heard of the word of words and the spring of springs, and know where they are to be found. Now we know that in that place we shall find the landlord's "entire and perfect house," that is, the house of houses. As for the present, our home making will be just as our language is, incomplete, imperfect, open-ended, unresolved.

• II •

We are beginning to sense indefiniteness at either end of the temporal spectrum. A passage in the later *Journal* that has counterparts all over the canon helps us to see not only this point but, what supports and gives the point substance, the close alliance of elements that appear quite disparate. Looking westward over Walden Pond at evening, through "a bewitching stillness," Thoreau singles out two sounds, "the strokes of a lingering woodchopper . . . and the melodious hooting of an owl" (December 1856; *J* 9:172). The bird sounds speak of a mystery, for few have seen the owl, whether hooting or sitting "silent on his perch." Thoreau himself saw the owl only once in a decade, though he hears the bird's voice every week. Yet this creature, Thoreau notes, is as stubborn as it is mysterious. However much the chopper works at making the woods disappear, "still [the bird's] aboriginal voice is heard indefinitely far and sweet." Pristine, primordial sounds continue to resonate *just* beyond our sight while our civil lives go forward, while the woods go rapidly down so that farms and homesteads can grow. By this point, the circumstances have come to seem familiar, the geography one that we know. When we stand on mountaintops or watch Indians in Maine paddling their way upstream, we see fogs and mists that blanket the origin we know is beyond. Listening in the woods to the sounds of an unseen owl who utters primeval cries has precisely the same effect: the distance, however short, between us and the invisible bird functions just as the fog does to mask original scenes, to hide from sight's desire what our instincts know to be there. Origin and invisibility seem inevitably paired for Thoreau. Still, there are complications here that we have not seen before, for in this case we are working our way toward America's *future*, spreading the civil around in what most would call progress. The dimness of perception that plays around earliest things seems to have settled in over future things as well. Perhaps we can never cut away the voice of origin. That, surely, is one level of what Thoreau says, but the passage takes in more: first, that fogginess can cover the future; second, that such fogginess may be akin to the sort we associate with origin. Take the whole one step further: what the woodchopper does is, obviously, a major preparatory act for home making in the world. That such acts cannot dispel the now-familiar fogginess says a great deal about not only our current condition and the ways we go about home making, but also about what remains for us to do about them.

Given the facts of the fable, it is little less than inevitable that a narrative should be implied in this linking of terminuses. Origin is hazy and largely inaccessible. Home making in this world can occupy most of our natural lives, but the chances are that it will satisfy little more than those lives. One turns quite understandably to futurity and finds that futurity looks as foggy as what we saw in the other direction, a point that ought to be disconcerting yet seems never to bother Thoreau. That surely comes in part because the fog over futurity seems far easier to live with: its openness confines us less than the shape of origin does. (Origin is mysterious but not vague: what we are came out of it, and we know too well what we are.) That Thoreau should make his words not only tell us of all this but act it out as well should itself be as inevitable as the rigorous temporality that works within the landscape of this foggy geography. Consider once again the first paragraph of "Sounds."

That study of hierarchies of language ended like this: "Will you be a reader, a student merely, or a seer? Read your fate, see what is before you, and walk on into futurity" (111). The progression implied in the last sentence ("read . . . see . . . walk") is in part hierarchial, beginning with the mereness of a reader, in part a narrative of what we will be doing when we are doing the best for ourselves. The best sort of reading will show what writing can show of what has been settled for us ("read your fate"). Seeing (it is always good, so there is no "best" sort) will show us not only what fronts us in the world but what, with such activities, can be expected from futurity. Reading and seeing should then set us in motion, walking with all the richness of the act seen in the essay of that name. The paragraph ends with a favorite Romantic and Thoreauvian gesture, an opening out in which we look at or walk into an expansiveness so immense that it holds promises for every aspect of ourselves. Keats opens out this way at the end of the sonnet on Chapman's Homer and also at the end of "When I have Fears." Thoreau opens out at the end of, among others, *A Week, Walden* and, in a limited version, "Civil Disobedience." *A Week* takes us out beyond what astronomy knows; *Walden* takes us toward the vastest sort of westering.[3] "Civil Disobedience" draws us toward its ending by wondering what our democracy would look like from the highest point of view and then ends with a remark Thoreau makes often, that he can make up in his head what he has never yet fronted in the world: "A State which bore this kind of fruit, and suffered it to drop off as fast as it ripened, would prepare the way for a still more perfect and glorious State, which also I have imagined, but not yet anywhere seen" (*RP*, 90). Tentative in its assessment of possibilities, that ending is a more enclosed instance of the openness in the other texts and at the end of the paragraph from "Sounds."

The latter ends with "futurity," a prodigious word denoting the address in time but fixing nothing further about more specific qualities. And indeed, no currently available words could do that satisfactorily. Since we will be walking into futurity with the fullest sort of attentiveness, and since in futurity there is the potential for everything, no words more precise than the most general will do. Every word leaves out some possibilities, but the biggest leave out less. At the end of this paragraph that meditates on language, Thoreau shows that he believes what he has been saying throughout it. Our current words can point to where we ought to go but they cannot take us there. Mother and father get us going, the mother in the body, the father in the spirit, but they cannot go all the way with us. One way to put that is broached in Matt. 10:37: "He that loveth father or mother more than me is not worthy of me." That is a good way to put it, but it is, like all the others, a limiting one, and we are now at the point where we will no longer tolerate limits to where we can walk. "Futurity" acknowledges that intolerance and acquiesces to it, at the same time doing all that is asked of it in this demanding context. Given both the hierarchy and the narrative emergent in the final sentence, the word is not only fitting in what it denotes but in what it is and can do. The last word in the paragraph tells us at least as much about words as it does about the future. What it is like and is capable of performing are as much a part of its meaning as the openness to which it points. Within its limits, "futurity" is as self-reflexive as the text in which it takes part and the inscriber who wrote it in.

Yet, however open-ended futurity might be, there are suggestions about its content scattered throughout Thoreau's writings, as well as in many comments about what we should be and do in relation to it. Consider the passage we looked at in the "Sunday" Chapter of *A Week* about the cry of an owl "as from a nature behind the common, unexplored by science or by literature" (56). (That cry, we recall, figures an origin that seems always ahead of us, indestructible, inaccessible.) The passage goes on to speak of the "red Election-bird," the full colors of which could be seen only "in proportion as I advanced further into the darkness and solitude of the forest," a gesture accomplished, he says, only in fancy (the relation to Keats and his nightingale is exact and possibly ominous). For our present purpose, the point is that there is "a nature behind the common," the place of Keats's nightingale, of the owl Thoreau hears, and of that state of the Election-bird he has never managed to see. That is the place of a nature more fully itself than the one we commonly know, a nature that cannot be more than envisioned but can be at least surmised.

This passage is by no means unique in *A Week*. What had seemed, early in the text, to be a hunch about a realized nature is echoed and affirmed in a series of passages in the final chapter that show the business on owls and Election-birds to be a very good guess. This time, however, there is no accessible place to which we could go if we so wished but only the sense that a place is there and that our lives are an opening out to that which is just beyond:

> We are sensible that behind the rustling leaves, and the stacks of grain, and the bare clusters of the grape, there is the field of a wholly new life, which no man has lived; that even this earth was made for more mysterious and nobler inhabitants than men and women. In the hues of October sunsets, we see the portals to other mansions than those which we occupy, not far off geographically.—
>
>> "There is a place beyond that flaming hill,
>>   From whence the stars their thin appearance shed,
>> A place beyond all place, where never ill,
>>   Nor impure thought was ever harbored. . . ."
>
> (377–78)

Thoreau is thinking not of an extraterrestrial existence but of a transformed earth (he says two pages later that "here or nowhere is our heaven" [380]). Yet the locale he envisions is "a place beyond all place," which is another way of saying that it is the place of places. That phrasing turns out to be the best name we have found for the locale that houses not only the word of words but the subjects of all the other genetival phrases.

Several pages later—determined to lay out and emphasize this gesture that obsesses him—Thoreau reinforces the point:

> These things imply, perchance, that we live on the verge of another and purer realm, from which these odors and sounds are wafted over to us. The borders of our plot are set with flowers, whose seeds were blown from more Elysian fields adjacent. They are the pot-herbs of the gods. Some fairer fruits and sweeter fragrances wafted over to us, betray another realm's vicinity. (381)

The geography is the same we have seen in both origin and end. End is, we gather—guessing through the haze—*just* beyond where we are but inaccessible for now. Two pages later, the place of places is acknowledged to be the nature beyond nature: "there is only necessary a moment's sanity and sound senses, to teach us that there is a nature behind the ordinary, in which we have only some vague preëmption right and western reserve as yet" (383).

Sometimes—rarely—we get a glimpse of what is beyond, perhaps even a scent. In the *Journal* for May 17, 1853, Thoreau speaks of perceiving, at Potter's fence, "the first whiff of that ineffable fragrance from the Wheeler meadow" (*J* 5:164). It is an odor of promise, suggesting strawberries and pineapples, one that prefigures ("foreruns") summer and autumn. But it foreruns more than such temporal structures, for "the odors of no garden are to be named with it. It is wafted from the garden of gardens." This garden is clearly planted in the "place beyond all place," the home, it turns out, of still another genetive that signifies the existence of still another paragon.

Obviously absent from these passages is any sense of frustration, any acknowledgment that the nature behind the ordinary, just beyond our reach, may be teasing us beyond endurance. In a passage from the *Journal* for February 21, 1842 (**J* 1:365), such tonalities begin to show through: "I was always conscious of sounds in nature which my ears could never hear—that I caught but the prelude to a strain—She always retreats as I advance—Away behind and behind is she and her meaning—Will not this faith and expectation make to itself ears at length." Aspects of nature perpetually defer themselves, whatever the stretch of our gestures. We live in a state of continuing open-endedness, of a closure that, for now, can be only envisioned— that envisioning itself a part of the tantalizing condition this nature has drawn us into. Only when we get to the place of nature's fullest meaning can there be satisfactory closure. Only there can there be the truest sort of at-homeness. Since we are now surrounded by fogs at either end of the narrative, our home making can suffice only for the moment in which we do it, in this place tied up in place.

This means that we can speak of several homes at once, as Thoreau occasionally does, always with the same import. One of those occasions turns up in *The Maine Woods*, where the issue of open-endedness makes many sorts of sense. For one thing, the essays focus on home making in this world as intensely as do any of Thoreau's writings. For another, these texts are shot through with claustrophobic passages, hemmings-in among the density of the overhanging trees, the texts punctuated occasionally by moments of relief as the travelers emerge into clearings that Thoreau will often identify with the civil. That he felt these issues early in his experience in those woods comes out clearly in the appearance, near the beginning of the first essay, of an open-ended geography that focuses on home. Looking up the Aroostook road, he sees a man riding upon it in a rude, original wagon: "He offered to carry a message for us to anybody in that country, cheerfully. I suspect, that if you should go to the end of the world, you would find somebody there going further, as if just starting for home at sundown, and having a last word before he drove off" (13). At the end of the world, there is a starting out whose goal is something like a home. Nothing is defined more precisely than "as if," though the long history of similar fabulous journeys makes "home" a plausible image for the goals those journeys envision. Yet that plausibility has to do with more than intertextual life, for Thoreau makes the remark in a context where the act of home making is especially urgent and compelling, and where the act can be associated with the opening up of spaces. Putting *this* image in *this* place sets up reverberations that go on long after Thoreau turns the text to other issues.

He gets somewhat more specific in a passage from the *Journal* for May 23, 1853 (*J* 5:187). Thoreau had been noting how bird sounds change as the day cools, and he wondered whether that had to do with the way the air seems to strain impurities, or with the counterpart way in which the mind—undergoing its own shedding of impurities—becomes "cooler, more clarified and precise": "A certain lateness in the sound, pleasing to hear, which released me from the obligation to return in any particular season. I have passed the Rubicon of staying out. I have said to myself, that way is not homeward; I will wander further from what I have called my home—to the home which is forever inviting me." Since the beckoning goes on unceasingly, the invitation is open-ended. It is unaccepted, surely, not because he refuses but because he cannot yet accept. More clearly than the comparable passage in *The Maine Woods*, this one speaks of two sorts of home, "my home," the one he has dug out in the turf/text of this world, and also the one forever inviting, the one located in what has to be the "place beyond all place." That means that the home forever beckoning him is the home of homes.

Thoreau made that point as clearly as he could on several other occasions, and on some of those he linked the invitation to questions of writing. In the first chapter, we looked at a passage that has Thoreau bemoaning the inadequacy of any writer to show him all that there is in the woods. He can find no author, he says, who will "sail as far forward into the bay of nature as my thought—they stay at home—I would go home" (*J* I, 375). The thin leaves of their books are too dessicated to hold the nature he can imagine. "Nature lies far and fair behind them all," he says, surveying the familiar foggy geography. Given the relationships we have seen, it is perfectly understandable that the entry immediately following should be the one that begins by telling of "the great and serene sentence—which does not reveal itself."

And what of our relation to the condition of opening out? In the face of the open-endedness that stands so invitingly before us, we have to keep in place a counterpart condition, an indefiniteness in front. For us to be otherwise would cause a bad fit, an encounter of incompatibles. Thoreau's consistency on this point is remarkable, for he broached it first in the *Journal* for March 13, 1841 (*J* 1:288), and it stuck with him to emerge in one of the canon's most eloquent sections, the conclusion of *Walden*. In that first, inchoate attempt, he touches on the sense of the seashore that Keats had come across when he was seeking to make the same point in "When I Have Fears." Thoreau remarks on the necessary aloneness of our lives, how "we dwell on the sea-shore and none between us and the sea." Whatever our relations to others, "this is the one bare side of every man—There is no fence—it is clear before him to the bounds of space" (*J* 1:288). Thoreau says nothing about the way we should comport ourselves. There is only the condition of bareness, which refers as much to ourselves as to the world at which we gaze, that world for which the empty sea seems the most appropriate image. It is as though Thoreau were seeking to understand a state of things before he could then go on to work out how we must *be* in that state.

A year or so later he had clarified the point, coming to the understanding that we must be like what we see. To put it in Blakean terms but in tones more positive than Blake's, he became what he beheld. Sometime in 1842, Thoreau transcribed the following passage into the *Journal*: "In view of the possible and future—we should live quite laxly—and be more straightened behind than before. If there were a true and natural development we should all be undefined in front our outlines dim and shadowy on that side—as the crown of a rising flower shows newly from day to day—and from hour to hour" (*J 1:429). To be most natural in the face of possibility, we should steer away from straightness (straitness), the undeviating *and* the narrow, leaving ourselves with foggy contours and thus available for anything. That new recognition causes a subtle shift in tone, as Thoreau puts by the talk of being "exposed to the fates" or to an unfenced bareness. This time there is talk not only of possibility but of ourselves as rising flowers, daily and hourly renewed as we stand over against what we see. We are not, it seems, so bare after all, but can develop ways of being that show us how to stand.

Still, however advanced, this must have seemed sentimental to Thoreau, for in the passage's final version, he keeps the openness to possibility but without using the floral device: "In view of the future or possible, we should live quite laxly and undefined in front, our outlines dim and misty on that side; as our shadows reveal an insensible perspiration toward the sun" (*W,* 324–25). Exhortative and ironic at once, this version condenses the import but adds a blunt, canny reminder that the requisite indefiniteness is anything but sentimental, that it demands an effort of the body that acknowledges the body's doings, that plays down but never forgets its materiality. The barely perceptible perspiration on a shadow: that is all, finally, that we should take our bodies to mean. And that meaning is precisely analogous to what we get from our best words, as Thoreau makes clear in the sentences immediately following: "The volatile truth of our words should continually betray the inadequacy of the residual statement. Their truth is instantly *translated*: its literal monument alone remains." In a remarkably precise parallelism, the shadowy residue of our bodies is seen to be the counterpart to the residue of words. This means, further, that as the best part of our words is "*translated,*" so, surely, will be the best part of ourselves. His logic firmly consistent, Thoreau goes on to tell more about those words: "The words which express our faith and piety are not definite; yet they are significant and fragrant like frankincense to superior natures." Our best words—words like "futurity" as he uses it in "Sounds"—are as we ourselves ought to be, open to possibility; as he said a few sentences before, "undefined in front." Our best words are in the world as we ought to be in the world, indefinite yet significant, shadowy yet pointing. When he puts himself into this condition of ultimate stance, Thoreau reconciles himself with language, at least with the best words that our language can currently offer.

And that brings us to a final point about Thoreau's fable, one of the most curious points about it. That the fable is a version of the classic Quest Romance has been clear to us for some time.[4] It is, however, a peculiarly shifty version, one that has Thoreau shifting the direction of his feelings from backward to forward, from origin to end, from insufficient inscribings to sentences not yet encountered that will be able to say it all. The fact that the fable treats (indexes) materials it can only suggest shows that the fable, too, has to be open-ended. Its quest is not yet complete and cannot yet be so, given what we are and what this place of our home making is. This also comes to mean that, given the nature of the material with which the fable deals, it cannot be complete until it reaches the home of that which is capable of completing it.

Put it another way: the fable involves not only a quest but a search for the finest of methods with which to perform the quest. Those methods include not only the endemic, stubborn subtext with its cranky, upsetting mutterings but that oxymoronic bent—something more than the paradoxes Emerson saw as endemic to Thoreau—that makes it possible for him to think in terms of contraries that have somehow learned to make plausible sense together.[5] Thoreau developed those methods along the way and put them to elaborate use, but they were clearly not sufficient to lay the fable out in its perfect, completest form, the form that it would take when spelled out in the serene sentence. That means that he will not have the equipment with which to complete the fable until he takes the fable to where it is finally going—surely the ultimate paradox that holds the others together.

The fable as we know it cannot say all that it envisions, all that it knows will be possible to be said. It says—and is sensitive to the fact that it is limited to saying—only what can and needs to be said now. The fable is, therefore, about the conditions of its own utterance, especially the difficulties thereof. And though it is, in great part, an allegory of the quest of its own perfect saying, we see now that it cannot be perfectly said until it is finally over. There is a very important sense in which getting to be at home in the world meant, for Thoreau, learning to live with that situation. All in all, he seems to have done it remarkably well.

NOTES

CHAPTER ONE
WORDS, INSTITUTIONS, HIERARCHIES

1. Sharon Cameron, *Writing Nature: Henry Thoreau's* Journal (New York: Oxford University Press, 1985); Stanley Cavell, *The Senses of* Walden (San Francisco: North Point Press, 1981); John Hildebidle, *Thoreau: A Naturalist's Liberty* (Cambridge, Mass.: Harvard University Press, 1983); William Howarth, *The Book of Concord: Thoreau's Life as a Writer* (New York: Penguin Books, 1982).

2. Cavell, *Senses of* Walden, p. xiii.

3. Ibid., pp. 16, 34–35, 92, 80.

4. For related material by Cavell, see "In Quest of the Ordinary: Texts of Recovery," in *Romanticism and Contemporary Criticism*, ed. Morris Eaves and Michael Fischer (Ithaca, N.Y.: Cornell University Press, 1986), pp. 183–239; and *"Walden* & The Fantastic," *American Poetry Review* 15 (1986): 45–47.

5. Cameron, *Writing Nature*, p. 160.

6. Ibid., pp. 16, 84, 140.

7. Cavell, *Senses of* Walden, p. 62.

8. For a study of the relation of Thoreau to some theorists of language, see Michael West, "Thoreau and the Language Theories of the French Enlightenment," *ELH* 51 (1984): 747–70. See also note 11, below, for another essay by West. The subject of Thoreau and language has hardly been explored, and it deserves a separate book that deals not only with historical influences but also with the very complex question of his attitudes toward language. There is important material in David Suchoff's " 'A More Conscious Silence': Friendship and Language in Thoreau's *Week*," *ELH* 49 (1982): 673–88. Suchoff's description of Thoreau's uneasiness with language in *A Week* is carefully put, amply supported, and fully convincing. For a view of Thoreau on language that shows him as far more confident, see the chapter on Thoreau in Philip Gura, *The Wisdom of Words: Language, Theology and Literature in the New England Renaissance* (Middletown, Conn.: Wesleyan University Press, 1981). Leonard Neufeldt describes Thoreau's use of the discourse of republicanism in "Henry David Thoreau's Political Economy," *New England Quarterly* 57 (1984): 359–82. There is a useful collection of essays on language and the English romanticists in *Romanticism & Language*, ed. Arden Reed (Ithaca, N.Y.: Cornell University Press, 1984).

9. For a differing but significantly related view, see some of the comments on language in "Walking," where Thoreau argues for our need of a poet who has "nailed words to their primitive senses [and] derived his words as often as he used them" (*Excursions*, p. 154). In this passage Thoreau goes in a direction contrary to the one laid out in the *Journal* passage, that is, he wants to go back into history, to go against the push of its current and return to origins. An important, large-scale version of the same directional interplay

(not nearly as binary as it sounds in its simple form) will turn up later in my remarks on *A Week* and related texts.

10. To get the most accurate picture of the complexities of this business one has to be aware of Thoreau's frequent use of the rhetoric of self-correction. He wrote the passage we are inspecting on February 2, 1841. The next day he adjusted his comments so as to take up immediacy in a much more positive way: "The present seems never to get its due—it is the least obvious—neither before, nor behind, but within us. All the past plays into this moment, and we are what we are. My aspiration is one thing, my reflection another, but over all myself and condition—is and does" (*J* 1:244–45). This new comment does not negate his previous feelings about language and aspiration but puts them in a different perspective, in which the emphases are distributed differently. He does not redo the map but shades its elements in another way.

11. For more on Thoreau and similar material, see Michael West, "Scatology and Eschatology: The Heroic Dimensions of Thoreau's Wordplay," *PMLA* 89 (1974): 1043–64.

12. See the important study by John T. Irwin, *American Hieroglyphics: The Symbol of the Egyptian Hieroglyphics in the American Renaissance* (Baltimore, Md.: Johns Hopkins University Press, 1983). Thoreau's attitude toward hieroglyphics is various. Note, for example, the *Journal* entry for April 21, 1853 (*J* 5:113), where he exults in objects like dandelions: "How surprising this bright-yellow disk! Why study other hieroglyphs?"

13. The Wordsworth lines are from "The Excursion," "Preface to the Edition of 1814," in *The Poetical Works of William Wordsworth*, Vol. 5, ed. E. de Selincourt and Helen Darbishire (Oxford: Clarendon Press, 1949), lines 63–68. The Blake quotation is from *The Complete Poetry and Prose of William Blake*, ed. David Erdman (Garden City, N.Y.: Doubleday, 1982), pp. 666–67.

14. On page 26 of *The Senses of* Walden, Cavell comments briefly on this material in "Sounds" but does not discuss its implications for Thoreau's view of language. He does quote, appropriately, a passage from the chapter on "Reading" that, like the rest of that chapter, exalts written language, but he quotes none of the many contrary passages elsewhere in Thoreau's writings.

15. Ralph Waldo Emerson, *Essays and Lectures*, ed. Joel Porte (New York: Library of America, 1983), p. 8.

CHAPTER TWO
WRITING, SUBTEXT, SCENE

1. Keats put it this way: "if Poetry comes not as naturally as the Leaves to a tree it had better not come at all." See *Selected Poems and Letters*, ed. Douglas Bush (Boston: Houghton Mifflin, 1959), p. 267, the letter to John Taylor of February 27, 1818.

2. See my comments on Schiller in *The Autonomy of the Self from Richardson to Huysmans* (Princeton: Princeton University Press, 1982), especially pp. 124–29.

3. Thoreau's essay on "Homer, Ossian, Chaucer," printed in *EEM*, 154–73, was distributed throughout the text of *A Week*.

4. See Walter Harding, *The Days of Henry Thoreau* (Princeton: Princeton University Press, 1982), p. 112.

5. See Barbara Novak, *Nature and Culture: American Landscape and Painting, 1825–1875* (New York: Oxford University Press, 1980), chap. 2.

6. Ibid., p. 49.

7. See Meyer Abrams, *Natural Supernaturalism: Tradition and Revolution in Romantic Literature* (New York: Norton, 1971), p. 32.

CHAPTER THREE
INSCRIBING

1. Richard Bridgman, *Dark Thoreau* (Lincoln: University of Nebraska Press, 1982). Such readings were long ago persuasively contradicted by studies like Joseph Wood Krutch's *Henry David Thoreau* (New York: William Morrow, 1974), still one of the most perceptive analyses available.

2. Bridgman, *Dark Thoreau*, p. xiv.

3. See **J* 2:91, for several significant comments about systems composed of "elements which lead to human solutions—methods to a method—but never to a ray of absolute or divine knowledge."

4. See *MW*, 173–74, where Thoreau notes, with apparent surprise, that Polis is actually quite well off and, in fact, prefers to hire white men to do his work because they are steadier at it. One of the more intricate patterns in *The Maine Woods* has to do with the figure of Polis and with Thoreau's attitude toward him; in particular, Polis as property owner, worth some six thousand dollars, and Polis as Thoreau's chosen native informant. The interplay of institutions, of commerce and the civil, with Thoreau's sense of the savage (itself the product of a complex cultural history involving, among others, Montaigne and Rousseau and a number of travel books) works as effectively in the figure of Polis as in any other aspect of the text. Thoreau does not quite know what to do with Polis. Consider, as one aspect, the way Thoreau calls Polis "the Indian," his usual name for their guide, the depersonalization playing ironically against Polis's densely developed personality (he is drawn more elaborately than any other figure in Thoreau's work). One can speak of this as still another instance of Thoreauvian ambiguity and its attendant suspension; but it is more accurate in this case to distinguish the Thoreau who calls Polis "the Indian" from the Thoreau who makes the text, the former as much a character within it as Polis himself. That is the only reading that gives full acknowledgment to the intricacies of the context and aligns Thoreau's attitude here with the shrewdness he shows at most points in his work.

For an important study of Thoreau and Indian matters, see Robert F. Sayre, *Thoreau and the American Indian* (Princeton: Princeton University Press, 1977).

5. I have commented extensively on this matter of uneasiness in *Thoreau's*

Redemptive Imagination (New York: New York University Press, 1977), especially pp. 75–93.

6. See Blake's *Vision of the Last Judgment*: "I question not my Corporeal or Vegetative Eye any more than I would Question a Window concerning a Sight I look thro it and not with it," *Poetry and Prose of William Blake*, p. 555. Emerson's concept of the "transparent eye-ball" is also clearly relevant, for the transparency has to do with a lack of impediments within him, especially the sort of obstruction caused by the concerns of self. Once "all mean egotism vanishes . . . the currents of the Universal Being" can circulate through him. See *Nature*, in Emerson, *Essays and Lectures*, p. 10.

CHAPTER FOUR
AUTOGRAPHICAL ACTS

1. Stephen Greenblatt, *Renaissance Self-Fashioning: From More to Shakespeare* (Chicago: University of Chicago Press, 1980), p. 1.

2. Georges Poulet, *Les Métamorphoses du Cercle* (Paris: Plon, 1961), pp. 78–82.

3. Ibid., p. 80.

4. Georges Poulet, "Phenomenology of Reading," *New Literary History* 1 (1969): 58.

5. Greenblatt, *Renaissance Self-Fashioning*, pp. 13, 31 (two quotes), 120.

6. Ibid., p.156. For a complex presentation of this play, see summary on pp. 157–61.

7. Ibid., p. 256.

8. Sacvan Bercovitch, *The Puritan Origins of the American Self* (New Haven: Yale University Press, 1975).

9. Ibid., pp. 11, 13, 19, 28, 31, 136.

10. It is instructive to compare the mode of sociohistorical study in Quentin Anderson's *The Imperial Self: An Essay in American Literary and Cultural History* (New York: Random House, 1971) with the traditional scholarship of Bercovitch and the New Historicism of Greenblatt. Whereas the latter two speak of the imprinting of cultural modes upon the self, Anderson claims for Emerson (and sometimes for Emerson's generation, though he is inconsistent on this point) "the American flight from culture, from the institutions and emotional dispositions of associated life" (3, cf. 29). Bercovitch is far more convincing when he speaks of Emerson's development of Puritan modalities of the self, Greenblatt more persuasive when he sees the imprinting of cultural modes as inescapable and unnerving. Anderson is surely correct in saying that Emerson's more sympathetic contemporaries "saw institutions as passing but necessary shadows of what welled out of the self" (31); though, again, this implies that the self is the maker of what it sees, a mood that is only one among many in Thoreau's spectrum of self-world relations.

11. Bercovitch, *Puritan Origins of the American Self*, p. 161.

12. Ibid., pp. 11–12.

13. See R.W.B. Lewis, *The American Adam: Innocence, Tragedy, and Tradition in the Nineteenth Century* (Chicago: University of Chicago Press, 1955).

14. See Keats's letter to Richard Woodhouse of October 27, 1818, in John Keats, *Selected Poems and Letters*, ed. Douglas Bush (Boston: Houghton Mifflin, 1959), pp. 279–80.

15. See Keats's letter to Benjamin Bailey of November 22, 1817.

16. Ernst Robert Curtius, *European Literature and the Latin Middle Ages*, trans. Willard R. Trask (New York: Pantheon Books, 1953), pp. 313–14.

17. C. S. Peirce, *Philosophical Writings of Peirce*, ed. Justus Buchler (New York: Dover Publications, 1955).

18. Ibid., pp. 108, 109.

19. Ibid., p. 107.

20. Ibid., pp. 108, 105.

21. Meyer Abrams, "Structure and Style in the Greater Romantic Lyric," in *From Sensibility to Romanticism: Essays Presented to Frederick Pottle*, ed. Frederick W. Hilles and Harold Bloom (New York: Oxford University Press, 1965), pp. 527–60.

22. See my study *Self, Text, and Romantic Irony: The Example of Byron* (Princeton: Princeton University Press, 1988).

CHAPTER FIVE
A SPACE FOR SADDLEBACK

1. Henry Seidel Canby, *Thoreau* (Boston: Houghton Mifflin, 1939), p. 272. For comments on the audience, see p. 273.

2. See especially Lawrence Buell, *Literary Transcendentalism: Style and Vision in the American Renaissance* (Ithaca, N.Y.: Cornell University Press, 1973); Sherman Paul, *The Shores of America: Thoreau's Inward Exploration* (Urbana: University of Illinois Press, 1958); William Bysshe Stein, "Thoreau's First Book: A Spoor of Yoga," *Emerson Society Quarterly* 41 (1965): 4–25.

3. Buell, *Literary Transcendentalism*, p. 197.

4. *AW*, 499. Johnson's essay is the best available survey of readings of *A Week*: see "Historical Introduction," *AW*, 433–500.

5. See H. Daniel Peck, " 'Further Down the Stream of Time': Memory and Perspective in Thoreau's *A Week on the Concord and Merrimack Rivers*," *Thoreau Quarterly* 16 (1984): 93–118.

6. For a quick overview of the itinerary, see Richard J. Schneider, *Henry David Thoreau* (Boston: Twayne Publishers, 1987), pp. 26–27. There is a slightly longer sketch in Harding, *Days of Henry Thoreau*, pp. 88–93.

7. Several commentators have read this trip as archetypal. See Paul, *Shores of America*; and Joyce Holland, "Pattern and Meaning in Thoreau's *A Week*," *Emerson Society Quarterly* 50, suppl. 1 (1968): 48–55.

8. Poems by George Herbert are on pp. 48 and 314. On the theory of meditative poetry, see Louis Martz, *The Poetry of Meditation* (New Haven, Conn.: Yale University Press, 1954).

9. Meyer Abrams discusses the establishment of place in such poems in "Structure and Style in the Greater Romantic Lyric," pp. 527–60.

10. See, e.g., *AW*, 377: "here on the stream of the Concord, where we have all the while been bodily."

11. See Blake, *The Complete Poetry and Prose*, p. 34.

12. For examples of these gestures, see my *Thoreau's Redemptive Imagination*, chap. 1.

13. Much of what Thoreau was getting at turns up in Robert Frost's "West-Running Brook," which reads like a late pondering on a number of the anomalies in *A Week*; and yet there are differences so significant that they come to show more clearly what Thoreau is trying to do and what it is possible for him to do. In Frost's poem, the brook that runs west "when all the other country brooks flow east / To reach the ocean" images the flow that is opposed to the expected sweep of natural things (in *The Poetry of Robert Frost*, ed. Edward Connery Lathem [New York: Holt, Rinehart and Winston, 1969], pp. 257–60). But—and here Frost gets at complications similar to Thoreau's, especially Thoreau's uneasiness with binary descriptions—the brook carried its own contrarieties within itself. One of the observers in the poem notices how "the black stream, catching on a sunken rock [is] flung backward on itself in one white wave," the brook, "in that white wave," running "counter to itself." Further, Frost taps into the same archetypal gestures that Thoreau did, seeing in the flowing water "the stream of everything that runs away"; and yet in his reading of that emblem, he takes in possibilities unavailable to even the extremest elements of Thoreauvian discourse. Frost's brook runs away "to fill the abyss's void with emptiness," imaging "the universal cataract of death / That spends to nothingness." It is what Frost can say that Thoreau could never utter that ought to give us caution when we watch Frost doing what Thoreau so often does, seeing in the retrograde motion a figure for all that seems most ourselves:

> It is this backward motion toward the source,
> Against the stream, that most we see ourselves in,
> The tribute of the current to the source.
> It is from this in nature we are from.
> It is most us.

Calling that retrograde motion a "humanizing" one when it moves through Frost's Pascalian spaces would put all sorts of ironies into the term, ironies that Thoreau almost certainly suspected.

14. For details of the trip and the fate of the essay see Harding, *Days of Henry Thoreau*, pp. 132–33.

15. "A Walk to Wachusett" had also begun with indistinctness but says nothing about morning and therefore lacks the tripartite conflation that appears repeatedly in *A Week*. For a comparable passage, see *AW*, 192, which speaks, as "Wachusett" does, of mountains and indistinctness, and connects the sort of seeing that becomes possible in such conditions with the presence of the sublime. But the passage is not at the beginning of a section of the text, and it says nothing about the morning. It is only when all factors are present, as they are in *A Week* and elsewhere, that the full signification comes through. Still, "Wachusett" and this passage ought to alert us to the likelihood that the sublime will be a condition of these scenes of origin. Longinus had seen precisely the same relationship, a point Thoreau surely knew.

16. I deal with further instances in chap. 8, which goes into the question of origins and ends from another, but related, point of view.

17. Compare *W*, 89, which clarifies the poem in "Tuesday": "To him whose elastic and vigorous thought keeps pace with the sun, the day is a perpetual morning."

18. Though there is no figure anything like her elsewhere in Thoreau, we ought to remember that *The Scarlet Letter* was getting underway at about the same time as *A Week*, and there is more than a hint of Hester's sexuality in this young woman of the mountain.

19. It is, I think, possible to argue that the figure of the mountain woman put a nervousness into the passage, and that this bit of bravado was put in to counter it.

20. In an important related passage from the *Journal* of February 12, 1860 (*J* 13:140–42), the reflection of the sky in the ice on the ground persuades Thoreau to think of himself as walking over "a smooth green sea," the heavens happening here on earth (though with earth envisioned as, alternately, either sea or sky): "Here the clouds are these patches of snow or frozen vapor, and the ice is the greenish sky between them." Curiously, though—and quite in line with ambiguities we have seen elsewhere—Thoreau cannot make up his mind about the color that is reflected: "The ice reflects the blue of the sky"; and later, "the shadows are blue, as the sky is forever blue," though the reflections had been green at several points earlier in the passage. Still, whatever the ambiguities of color, there is no question here of stain: "In winter we are purified and translated. The earth does not absorb our thoughts." What he longs for in Saddleback seems to be realized at least this once, though a seasonal purification can hardly be a lasting one.

21. The obvious similarities between the Saddleback ascent and Wordsworth's ascent of Mount Snowdon, recorded in the last book of *The Prelude*, ought not to blot out the patent distinctions. Thoreau's climb has finally to do with a seeking after transcendence and not (one of the major emphases of the Snowdon passage) the way the mind works over the materials of the world. That Wordsworth may have come to accept the Snowdon experience as a kind of second best, since moving beyond Nature seems not, for now, possible, does not cancel out the distinction, though it leagues Thoreau and Wordsworth in all sorts of significant ways. Of equal importance to what we have been developing about Saddleback is the fact that the Snowdon episode took place in 1791, before Wordsworth's distress over the French Revolution, though its placement in *The Prelude* does not make that point clear. See Abrams, *Natural Supernaturalism*, pp. 78 and 493, fn. 16. Several images by Caspar David Friedrich relate to the theme of the "sea of clouds," which was a prevalent one at the time. See, for example, Friedrich's "Traveller Looking Down Over a Sea of Fog."

22. There are actually two mountain ascents in the "Tuesday" chapter, Saddleback at the beginning and, later, that ascent which leads Thoreau to meet a character named Rice. I shall deal extensively with Rice later. Suffice it to say here that Rice comes through as a kind of natural man, a type of the

uncivil, and therefore points back to the ruder days of origin. In that sense, this second ascent speaks of natural origin, much as Agiocochook was to do, and it therefore balances Saddleback within the "Tuesday" chapter. Still, though coherent within its chapter, the second ascent does not tell much of the fuller meaning of Saddleback within *A Week* as a whole. Only the pairing of Saddleback and Agiocochook can bring that fullness out.

23. If I parse this difficult sentence correctly, they did not, in fact, reach the originating *point* of the Merrimack, for they never went on to the "distant source among the mountains" from which their river begins. Should this be an accurate reading, the trip to the natural source is itself not quite complete, an irony of the sort that Thoreau always relished.

24. Here too *A Week* sounds very much like *The Prelude*. Consider, for example, the following from the "Monday" chapter: "The abrupt epochs and chasms are smoothed down in history as the inequalities of the plain are concealed by distance" (125).

25. What Saddleback does to closure affects everything else it does to *A Week* as a whole, including its reading of visionary events. In "The Experience of the Sacred in Thoreau's *Week*" (*ELH* 33 [1966]: 66–91), Jonathan Bishop gives particular attention to the Saddleback ascent and the events at the top of the mountain, figuring the whole, quite correctly, as a type of the experience of the sacred in Thoreau's text. Bishop's awareness of what he calls "some half-recognition of a sacred presence inhabiting the sacred realm" (78) and of a "presence half-discovered in Nature" (83) implies the incompleteness of Thoreau's experience on Saddleback. So too does his comment on the climactic paragraph of the experience, which brings Thoreau "to the verge of an encounter" (74). Yet he tends to take the event as a full-fledged experience of God ("the rising sun [is] an obvious analogue for God" [75]), though Thoreau specifically says that he needs "successive days' journeys" to reach the ultimate place, that however great this point above the clouds, it is only a "platform" (189). But this matter of incompleteness goes further, for Bishop does not give nearly enough emphasis to the aspect of failure, the paradoxical status of Thoreau's return below (an incomplete completion), or the degree of compulsion involved (he says that Thoreau "inhibits himself" on Saddleback [82], though the matter of activity and passivity, the degree of self-reflexiveness of any of the verbs involved, cannot be so easily mastered). Finally, he speaks of "the independence of the story in its context" (73), another phrasing that misses all of that intricate webbing which involves the Saddleback episode in the texture of *A Week*. Saddleback offers far more than Bishop allows: its melancholy sense of inadequacy and its centrality to the text as a whole are inescapable. Still, with all these demurrals granted, Bishop's essay remains one of the key readings of *A Week*.

One ought to complement his essay with Walter Hesford's "'Incessant Tragedies': A Reading of *A Week on the Concord and Merrimack Rivers*," *ELH* 44 (1977): 515–25. The title points the way to Hesford's comments on how, for Thoreau, "history has a fixed tragic motif" and "American progress" is, in the main, "tragic" (520); how there is "a tragic strain that constitutes a constant undercurrent in the book" (523). Hesford properly balances this strain with reference to Thoreau's comments on the traveler's rebirth on the road (518–19) and on the relation of this rebirth to writing (521).

CHAPTER SIX
WRITING HOME

1. See Harding, *Days of Henry Thoreau*, pp. 45–46.

2. The phrasing in Goethe is as follows: "da fühlt man sich doch einmal in der Welt zu Hause and nicht wie geborgt oder im Exil" (*Goethes Werke*, vol. 11, ed. Herbert V. Einem and Erich Trunz [Hamburg: Christian Wegner Verlag, 1964], p. 26). Translation: "Then one feels, for once, at home in the world, and not as though hidden or in exile." Thoreau's later translation of *einmal* ("for once") is clearly more accurate. Goethe would have said *noch einmal* if he meant "once more."

3. A more extended version of what follows in this paragraph appears in my *Thoreau's Redemptive Imagination*, especially pp. 193–98.

4. I place among those too-neat readings my earlier essay on *A Week*, which took that text in a rigidly binary fashion and went on from that taking to set up *A Week* and *Walden* as equally rigid opposites. See "A Space for Saddleback: Thoreau's *A Week on the Concord and Merrimack Rivers*," *Centennial Review* 24 (1980): 322–37.

5. From Martin Heidegger, "Building Dwelling Thinking," in *Poetry, Language, Thought,* trans. Albert Hofstadter (New York: Perennial Library, 1971), p. 145.

6. Compare his speculations on the origin of the roof in *J* 2:74–75.

7. Heidegger comes to a very different conclusion: building a house is the narrower sense of dwelling, but it is fully compatible with the larger sense of the concept, that in which "dwelling is the manner in which mortals are on the earth" ("Building Dwelling Thinking," pp. 151, 148).

8. William Wordsworth, *Selected Poems and Prefaces*, ed. Jack Stillinger (Boston: Houghton Mifflin, 1965), p. 108.

9. Take, as one of many examples, an entry from 1857. In the *Journal* for February 15, Thoreau records that the Lee house, of which he had recently made a plan, had burned down, and only the chimneys and cellar walls were left. Hastening to read a disputed inscription on a chimney, Thoreau makes out a good deal but not all of it, yet he argues for one figure being a "5," "though some took it for a three, but I could *feel* it yet more distinctly" (*J* 9:258). The contact afforded by this tactile immediacy testifies as eloquently as any statement to Thoreau's indexical desires, though there is only a fragment left to be felt, and even that is disputable. But there is touching at both ends: the inscription "appeared to have been made by a finger or a stick, in the mortar when fresh . . . and, where it was too dry and hard, to have been pecked with the point of a trowel." Thoreau touches his finger at marks that might have been made by other fingers. No contact could be more direct than that between his fingers and the old ones he argues for, the fingers of the chimney's maker, which he feels in the inscribed grooves.

For other useful examples, see his remarks, two days later, on the Hunt house (265–66), and also the remarks, two years later, when that house was being pulled down (*J* 12:36–38).

10. I have dealt with this matter at length in the final chapter of *Thoreau's Redemptive Imagination*.

11. In "*Walden*'s False Bottoms" (*Glyph* 1 [1977]: 132–49), Walter Benn Michaels takes up questions that are, properly, part of the matter of at-home-ness, more specifically of home making. Michaels argues that, in one way or another, *Walden* deals with the search for a solid bottom, one that finally turns out to be unlocatable. Nature attracts us as, potentially, a kind of bottom or point d'appui, but Thoreau never finds that point. He wants such a prop because a solid bottom would be "a location for authority, a ground upon which we can make a decision" (147); but no such authority, in Nature or elsewhere, finally comes forth, and the result is a version of undecidability. Michaels seems to me to be incorrect on only one point, when he says that "it is only in *Walden* that the principle of uncertainty is built in" (147). In fact, that principle is endemic in Thoreau, and if he escaped from it at rare moments, there were moments far less rare when he faced squarely his inability to escape. That crucial demurral aside, Michaels's essay remains a classic of modern Thoreau criticism.

12. William Wordsworth's *Home at Grasmere* is part 1, book 1 of *The Recluse*. Compare the following well-known lines from *Home at Grasmere* with Thoreau's remarks:

> How exquisitely the individual Mind
> (And the progressive powers perhaps no less
> Of the whole species) to the external World
> Is fitted; and how exquisitely, too—
> Theme this but little heard of among Men—
> The external Word is fitted to the Mind.
>
> (MS. D, lines 816–21)

See *Home at Grasmere*, ed. Beth Darlington (Ithaca, N.Y.: Cornell University Press, 1977), p. 105.

13. Other aspects of transcendentalism have comparable relations to the matter of homing/housing. Note how Transcendental centrality comes to be focused on the idea of housing in the following passage from the *Journal* of March 16, 1840: "The cabins of the settler are the points whence radiate these rays of green, and yellow and russet over the landscape—out of these go the axes and spades with which the landscape is painted. How much is the Indian summer and the budding of spring related to the cottage? Have not the flight of the crow and the gyrations of the hawk a reference to that roof?" (**J* 1:117).

14. The frontispiece of the AMS edition of *Cape Cod* puts a windmill massively forward, acknowledging, thus, the significance (signification) of this image in the entire text, and its intertwined ramifications.

CHAPTER SEVEN
A SENSE OF HIERARCHY

1. Joan Burbick, *Thoreau's Alternative History,* (Philadelphia: University of Pennsylvania Press, 1987).

2. Ibid., p. 1.

3. The punctuation in the Walden edition—"I walked along, musing and enchanted, by rows of sugar maples"—makes much more sense in the context than the punctuation in the Princeton edition. See *The Writings of Henry David Thoreau* (Boston: Houghton Mifflin, 1906), 1:213.

4. See my study, *Autonomy of the Self,* especially chap. 7, "The Landscape of Desire."

5. D. H. Lawrence, *Studies in Classic American Literature* (Garden City, N.Y.: Doubleday Anchor Books, 1951), p. 15.

6. Ibid., p. 15.

7. See Frank Kermode's edition of Shakespeare's *Tempest* (Cambridge, Mass.: Harvard University Press, 1958), p. xliii.

8. Ibid.

9. Sketching the material on Therien on July 14, 1845, Thoreau added the following, not used later: "The simple man. May the Gods send him many wood chucks" (*J* 2:160).

10. Leo Marx's *The Machine in the Garden: Technology and the Pastoral Ideal in America* (New York: Oxford University Press, 1964) is still the definitive study of Thoreau's pastoralism.

11. In a late entry in the *Journal* (May 29, 1857), Thoreau speaks of various figures who, though not quite natural men, are "more thoroughly naturalized" than ordinary men: "the soil is native to them . . . the thoughts that occupy their brains are different" (*J* 9:384–85). With a bit more elaboration, these figures could take their place in the line of Rice and Therien.

12. See MS. D, 11.800–08, and also 11.104–9 and 625–29 in Darlington, *Home at Grasmere.*

13. For more on this issue, see my essay "Pastoral Spaces," *Texas Studies in Literature and Language* 30 (1988): 431–60.

14. For the history and context of the phrase, see Erwin Panofsky's *"Et in Aracdia Ego*: Poussin and the Elegiac Tradition," in *Meaning in the Visual Arts,* pp. 295-320 (New York: Anchor Books, 1955).

15. Lawrence, *Studies in Classic American Literature,* p. 14.

CHAPTER EIGHT
ORIGINS AND ENDS

1. Paul, *Shores of America*; Cavell, *Senses of Walden.*

2. That such driving toward the center is also a thrust toward origin can be seen in certain Romances and may well be archetypal. For example, in Jules Verne's *Journey to the Center of the Earth* and its various cinematic epigones, one finds at the center a still-surving originary scene with all the attendant flora and fauna.

3. For elaborations of these and other unclosings, see the last chapter of my *Thoreau's Redemptive Imagination*.

4. The most significant study is still Harold Bloom's "The Internalization of Quest Romance," in *The Ringers in the Tower: Studies in the Romantic Tradition* pp. 13–36 (Chicago: The University of Chicago Press, 1971). For a useful general study of Thoreau and myth, see Robert D. Richardson, Jr., *Myth and Literature in the American Renaissance* (Bloomington: Indiana University Press, 1978), pp. 90–137. See also Richardson's *Henry David Thoreau: A Life of the Mind* (Berkeley: University of California Press, 1986), pp. 230–33.

5. Emerson's comments have been frequently reprinted, most conveniently as the prefatory essay to volume 1 of the Walden edition of Thoreau's works, *The Writings of Henry David Thoreau*, 1:ix–xxxiv.

INDEX